JANET PYWELL

Someone Else's Child

A story of friendship, fostering and family.

This book was professionally typeset on Reedsy.
Find out more at reedsy.com

*With grateful thanks to so many people involved in social care
and the volunteers at RNLI and in particular:
Rebecca Askew, Melanie Sacre and Vicky Kypta.*

Foreword

"You can't go back and change the beginning, but you can start where you are and change the ending."

C.S. Lewis.

It's the job of a Social Worker to help individuals, groups, and families prevent and cope with problems in their day-to-day lives and support children who can no longer safely live with their birth families. Clinical Therapists diagnose and treat mental, behavioural, and emotional problems and Social Workers work with Foster Carers and Therapists in the professional teams around children in care.

I have used a wide artistic license and this novel is in no way written to offend or to distract from the incredible professional work done by, and achieved by, thousands of social workers, foster parents and the RNLI (Royal National Lifeboat Institution) volunteers, each day.

Many thanks and happy reading, Janet.

1

Chapter 1

The bedroom door bangs and there's a quick and heavy footfall.

'Where's my football shorts?' Ricky stands on the stairs, his seventeen-year-old chest is pale and bare, and his legs are long in his black school trousers. His hair is naturally dirty blond and his deep blue eyes look worried; so different to Femi's brown skin, dark eyes and braided hair.

She checks her pager and makes herself unavailable on the RNLI app. She couldn't have a shout today, not with Peter coming later.

'Auntie? Are you listening? It's the final today.'

'I know. Are you playing in it?'

'You know I am. Where are they?'

She looks up from her iPhone. 'Did you wash them?'

He shakes his head. 'I left them by the machine.'

'They're probably still there then, Ronaldo.'

'Oh, no, for—' He leaps across the kitchen and darts into the utility room. 'They're not here,' he shouts.

'You'll have to miss the game then.'

'Auntie, for God's sake!'

'Do you think this is a hotel?'

'Come on, Auntie. This is serious. They're my lucky shorts.'

'You said you'd cut the grass.'

'I will.'

'You promised.'

He leans across the table, his blue eyes blazing. 'I've got to have them and if you don't hurry I'm going to be late.'

'Well, you're a very lucky boy, Ronaldo.' She pulls his shorts from a pile of neatly folded washing on the kitchen counter. 'Ta da!' She laughs. 'And here's a clean school shirt.'

He breaks out into a grin. 'Oh, Auntie, you're wonderful.'

'I know. Now we just need to convince Albert of that.' Her tone is playful as she glances at the serious boy, eating breakfast with his elbows on the table.

Ricky grabs the shorts and pulls on his school shirt and then rubs Albert's dark curly hair. 'Alright, Al?'

'Ronaldo hasn't scored in four weeks,' he replies.

'Don't jinx me,' Ricky moans.

'He's rubbish now.' Albert holds his knife and fork properly now and Femi's pleased with his progress. It's only been eighteen months and, for a thirteen-year-old, he's a fast learner. He's fitted in really well and Femi feels he's already 'hers'. He finishes the last of the scrambled eggs on his plate and pats the corner of his mouth with a piece of kitchen roll.

'You're talking rubbish, Al. Do you want to play Minecraft with me later?'

'I want to play Animal Crossing, again.'

'That's so boring.'

'It's not.'

'We'll try and teach Auntie, will we?' Ricky doesn't wait for an answer and he runs from the kitchen and takes the stairs two at a time calling over his shoulder, 'But don't hold your breath, she's not a fast learner.'

'Cheeky!' Femi calls out, pleased the boys have settled in well together.

Albert picks up his plate and mug and places them carefully and silently in the dishwasher. Today is one of his quiet days and she studies him from the corner of her eye as she folds the rest of the washing. His white shirt looks crisp against his black skin, and his striped school tie makes him look like a young man off to work for the first time. He bends to put on his shiny black shoes.

'Have you got your sports bag?'

He hangs it over his shoulder. 'Here.'

'Trainers?'

He taps it.

He's already gone up a size and Femi resists the urge of cautioning him to be careful. It's not his fault the last pair were stolen and besides, she's already spoken to the headmaster about it and the teachers are now aware of the situation. She wasn't going to let anyone bully him. Not after what he's been through. The thought of him getting upset again, upsets her, so instead she smiles brightly.

'Right, where's your blazer, Al? That wind is cold for April, so you'd better wrap up.'

Albert pulls it down from the overloaded hooks behind the kitchen door and Femi's heart swells with pride. If only Albert could understand how loved he was and how Femi felt toward him things might be easier for them all but it was early days yet and Femi knew there were still many challenges ahead.

Ricky reappears pulling his jacket over his school uniform

and he collides with Albert in the utility room.

'Get out of my way, Al. I'm in a hurry.' He shoves him in the back and opens the door.

'Ow! Get off.'

'Good luck, today,' Femi says, pulling Albert aside.

'Yeah, break a leg,' says Albert.

'That only applies in the theatre,' Femi says. 'Certainly not for a football game.'

Ricky pushes past Albert. 'Animal Crossing is for girls,' he whispers.

Albert sticks his foot out but Ricky leaps over it and pauses at the door. 'Missed me.'

'Bet you get sent off.' Albert smiles.

The door bangs behind Ricky and Femi breathes a sigh of relief. As a foster parent, there were days when her life was incredibly tough but there were also days when she thought she had it all, and today fortunately — is one of those days — and, the nagging feeling about Albert's future is momentarily pushed from her mind.

* * *

By the time Femi has done another load of washing, cleaned two bathrooms, vacuumed the house and disinfected the kitchen, dusted countless books on the shelves, she's ready to sit down. She's breathless and tired and, as she sips her hot chocolate and reaches for a biscuit, she's distracted by a van outside the front.

The white van is parked almost across her driveway. A solid looking man with long hair and a hipster beard jumps out and he pulls a key from his pocket. He looks dishevelled, like a aside to let him in.

He has unruly, red hair and big freckles across his nose that Femi would like to join up with a pen. She's curious as to the picture it would make, but she is sure it would be one of kindness and empathy, but also with a splash of humour, just like Peter.

'It's Baltic out there,' he complains, following her into the kitchen and removing a thick, woollen, purple jacket. He hangs it on the hook behind the kitchen door. He's wearing a floral waistcoat and navy shirt with jeans. They're both mid-thirties but he's the size that Femi would like to be; she would love his slim hips. She's not sure that he looks like a social worker but then again, could you guess anyone's profession simply by looking at them?

'Would you like a drink?' she asks.

The mugs, milk and chocolate biscuits are already laid out on the kitchen counter and the kettle has boiled twice.

'No thanks.' Peter looks around the kitchen and his eyes focus on the two brown eyes watching him carefully.

'You've met Peanut before, haven't you?' Femi wishes she wasn't so nervous but the tension is causing heartburn and a pain in her chest.

'Hello, Peanut,' he says, placing his computer bag on the table. Peanut is white and grey and he stretches effortlessly, wags his tail and rolls on his back. His tongue hangs out and he waits patiently but Peter ignores him.

'It's a bit chaotic here,' Femi says, already wishing she didn't sound so apologetic. 'But, you know that.' She laughs nervously and points to the shelves of books, untidy coat rack as she steps over to close the utility door so he can't see the pile of washing.

He smiles. 'You're a hoarder, Femi, but a neat one.'

'That's not what the boys say. Ricky keeps threatening to throw out all my cook books.' She nods at two rows of books above the kitchen window. 'He'd live on burgers if he could.'

'And Albert?'

'So long as he gets scrambled eggs every day, he's happy. Come into the conservatory, Peter. It's warmer in there, the sun came out for an hour.' Femi carries her own coffee mug and she tucks the packet of biscuits into the pocket of her loose-fitting dress.

Peanut follows them, curls up on the floor near the glass doors and stares at a magpie hopping on the lawn while, on the fence, another magpie waits patiently; one for sorrow, two for joy.

Peter has a graceful way of flopping onto the sofa opposite Femi, leaning back and folding his legs and raising his satchel to his knee all in one smooth motion.

'The garden is a mess. Ricky is going to cut the grass and I've still got to sort out the garage one day.' Femi hovers by the window, staring into the garden, wishing she felt more confident. She dreaded these meetings with her social worker. They always made her feel that she was worthless. They hold all the cards. The authorities have parental responsibility and Femi, as a foster parent, has no control over the child's future. With a blink of an eye, the boys could be taken from her — and her life would be ruined. She's simply a carer who looks after the children.

Peter smiles. 'All in good time.' He notices the overhanging twisted willow tree and the ramshackle building at the bottom of the garden with filthy windows. 'You'll clean it up eventually.'

Femi laughs. 'I've only lived here for ten years.'

'It looks like you've a new neighbour moving in.'

'The house has been empty since Mrs Lockley died a year ago, so it will be nice to have other people in there.' She sits down and changes the subject. 'How are things with you, how's everything?'

He sighs. 'I'm exhausted, Femi. There are hundreds of refugees arriving in Dover every day. They all need placements and it's crazy.' He rubs his eyes. 'We're trying to find temporary places before moving them on to other parts of the country but it's not easy. They have nothing, these kids. They've seen their homes destroyed, their country obliterated and, very often, they've witnessed death at first hand. Some of them are still young children yet they've seen their parents or family killed, in front of them.'

'Will they ever get over it?' Femi stares back at Peter.

'They say children are more resilient.' His tone is matter of fact.

'They must be so traumatised — bless them. It's bad enough knowing what Ricky and Albert have been through, and they didn't have to cross the channel like those refugees that you're dealing with.'

'Very true. Right.' Peter clears his throat and straightens the computer on his lap, like a busy man, and he regards Femi thoughtfully. 'Let's go over the courses you've completed and fill in the gaps, and then we can look at your diary and see what's been going on.'

Femi has her notebooks beside her and she checks the details that Peter reads out.

'As well as a trained Paramedic, you've also received bereavement training and you've attended courses at the East

Kent Rape Centre.' He begins tapping on his computer, his fingers moving at an incredible rate. 'Just to confirm you still currently work part-time at the local clinic in Westbay and you're still a volunteer for RNLI, is that correct?'

Femi nods. 'There's rarely a shout at night but if there is, Sandra stays with the boys.'

'Right, I'll email you next week. There's a couple more courses you can do so I'll send you some information about them. Check the dates and then get back to me. Now, we have that all out of the way, how's everything else?'

Femi's mouth feels dry, so she sips her coffee and slides the biscuits from her pocket.

'Albert's father, Delroy, is back on the scene,' she says, biting into a chocolate Hobnob. 'Jamie said Delroy wants to meet Al next weekend.' She pushes the crumbs into the corner of her mouth.

Jamie is Albert's child social worker.

'How do you feel about that?' Peter asks without looking up from the screen.

Femi stares at the top of his head. She wants to scream. She wants to shout at him and complain about the care system but she knows she can't. Instead she replies calmly, 'You know I lost both of my parents by the time I was Albert's age,' Femi pauses, 'and so I do think it's important for him to have the opportunity to meet his father.'

'Delroy lives in London, if I remember correctly.' Peter watches her closely. He has been Femi's social worker for three months and during this time he has grown to admire her and what she's done for her two foster boys. 'It will be an unsupervised visit, then?'

Femi savours the chocolate on her tongue and picks at the

tiny pieces of coconut as they get caught in her teeth before replying, 'Delroy is planning a day trip to Westbay on Saturday and Jamie wants me to drop Albert off to meet him, probably lunch and then they'll go to the beach or something for an hour before Delroy gets the train home.'

'Does that work for you?' Peter looks thoughtful before tapping on his keyboard. He knows from experience how easy it is to be emotionally involved with foster children. A single carer can sometimes be a really positive choice for a child, it's easier for the carer to be focused on the child or children rather than on a partner or in a relationship. He thinks it's one of the reasons why Femi has bonded really well with both of her boys — because she's single.

'Albert's suffered so much domestic abuse in the past. I don't want his PTSD to flare up again, like the last time.'

'It shouldn't do,' Peter says equably. 'How long has Albert been with you now?'

'Eighteen months but we can't let that happen again, Peter.'

'It won't.'

'It happened three months ago, when Delroy promised he would visit and then never turned up. Albert had one of his rages.'

'Speak to Jamie and let him know your feelings. You have to give the family a chance, Femi. Remember we have the PR.'

'I know you have parental responsibility, but I'm just saying that this sort of contact can have a negative effect on Albert.'

'The aim of the social worker is reconciliation with the family — if possible,' Peter insists.

'Even if it isn't always in the child's best interests?' Femi wishes her tone wasn't so insistent.

Peter ignores her and continues, 'I can understand you're

frightened of losing Albert, especially if he gets upset and is unmanageable but, if they *can* reconcile him with his dad, then it's something we all need to encourage. I know you have a strong bond with Albert, and this is hard for you—'

'I've known so many kids who have gone back to their birth families and it hasn't work—'

'I know, Femi, but—'

'And when it doesn't work out, they end up back in care—'

'Yes but—' Peter holds up his hand.

'And not even with the same foster family. They're moved from house to house and sometimes even to a different county—'

'It's what we have to do, Femi, but our prime consideration is the safety of the child.'

Femi stares silently at him. She knows that when it all breaks down these kids really suffer — the expectation, the rejection, the hurt and sadness.

'I hate this system,' she mutters.

'Let me arrange some support for you, a course around supporting positive contact with birth families. Would that help?'

'Yes.'

Peter continues typing and he doesn't look up. 'OK. I'll get that organised. So, it's this Saturday, Delroy is coming?'

'Yes.'

'And you'll take Albert to meet him?'

'Of course, I will. I want him to have a good relationship with his father but I'm worried he'll let him down again,' Femi complains, helping herself to another biscuit. They taste so good and they're reassuring, she'll worry about her diet tonight, she won't eat any potatoes.

Peter looks up. 'Jamie would have explained the risks to Delroy if he lets Albert down again.'

Femi shakes her head. 'Maybe I'm just over protective.'

'You know you can't behave like that. It won't help you.'

'I know.'

'Besides, you said to me before, that you wanted Albert to get to know his father.' Peter has a vague memory of a conversation with Femi a few months ago. 'Look, I know how you feel. You would have loved the opportunity, right?'

Femi stares out of the window. The garden is overgrown and unkempt but there are pretty blue and yellow wild flowers between the dying daffodils, as well as red and purple tulips pushing through the muddled undergrowth. Femi would have to sort out the garage at some stage. It needs a paint. She'd dumped all the boxes when she'd moved here ten years ago. She'd avoided all the memories then; the photographs, diaries, and other memorabilia — she'd left them all boxed up. She didn't have the stomach for it all then and still didn't.

'Femi?'

'My Dad died in a freak boating accident on holiday in Jamaica,' she says.

If Peter had time or bothered to read Femi's file he would know her background; Jamaican father, English mother who died of a drug overdose after her second husband (Femi's father) was killed in a fatal boating accident. She was dual heritage, taken into foster care when she was thirteen. Two older siblings (white) from the mother's first marriage, were fostered together in a different county.

'Does this situation remind you of your father?' he asks gently.

Femi frowns. 'No. Daddy was kind and loving. That's the

irony. I loved him and — he died.'

'Right so we must agree, this is about Albert,' Peter says, checking his watch. 'You must do what's best for him.'

'I don't want him to be hurt.'

'I know.'

'Can the visit be supervised?'

'Albert is thirteen. You wouldn't want people supervising you with your father at that age, would you?'

Femi stares at Peter and eventually she says, 'I don't trust him.'

'Albert?'

'No, Delroy.'

'Why?'

'Well, Jamie says he's clean now and hasn't touched drugs in over a year but—'

'You moved out of London because you wanted a new life by the sea, Femi. You wanted to start again — maybe Delroy feels the same.'

Femi had received a small inheritance from her father's estate on her twenty-first birthday. She'd worked as a paramedic in London and saved money before deciding she'd had enough of city life. Then she'd visited Westbay on a day trip and fallen in love with the town. When she'd got home that night she'd checked her bank account, searched on the website, and realised she had enough money to put down a deposit on this four bedroomed house, only five minutes from the sea and the pretty main street —Harbour Street. She'd even managed to get work as a paramedic in the local medical centre where she had worked full-time for six years but, since Albert came to her —because of his young age — she'd gone part-time. She had no regrets. She wanted desperately to help him. Femi was thirty-six now, and Peter was right. This is a life away from the one in London.

Femi says, 'I understand that many foster relationships with teenagers fall apart as they get older and they get more independent but Ricky is getting top grades at school and if he carries on like this and nothing rocks the boat, he'll probably get into university.'

'I hope he stays focused,' Peter replies. 'You're doing a great job.'

Femi plays with the braids hanging over her shoulder.

He asks, 'Isn't Jenny, Ricky's allocated child social worker?'

Femi's three-and-a-half-year relationship with Ricky has been incredible and she loves him more that she can ever tell anyone. She has worked as a foster parent for six years and she's known a lot of foster families — some stories don't always end well.

'Ricky seems settled at school.' Peter looks up at her. 'At least he's stopped running away.'

She smiles. 'For the time-being.'

'Both Albert and Ricky get on, and they feel at home here.' Peter nods.

Femi takes a deep breath and exhales slowly before she reaches for another biscuit. 'I have a feeling Delroy is going to change all that.'

Peter smiles. He's been through this before many times. They both know that sometimes when one of the birth parents turns up to claim their child the relationship works out, but when it doesn't work out, they both know that it's most likely to leave the child more emotionally vulnerable and with little or no opportunity in life. The social worker pushes to get the best for the child but when the child is eighteen they're often moved into inadequate social housing where the chances of them having a decent quality of life are minimised. They're left to fend for themselves with little or no education, no survival techniques, support or money and surrounded by people who will take advantage of them. Very often they fall into a life of drugs and crime.

'You know how this works, Femi.' Peter slams the lid of his computer closed, his tone is soft and understanding. 'As a foster parent, you have to be prepared for everything and ask for nothing.'

'I know, and that's what scares me, Peter.'

2

Chapter 2

Femi carries the bags from the car, pushes open the back door and flings the carrier bags on the kitchen table letting out a satisfied groan. Peanut runs around enthusiastically, sniffing her ankles and nudging her leg with his nose. She bends down to pet him for a few minutes, giggling at the way he always rolls on his back for a tummy tickle, then she straightens up and with her hand on the banister. 'Albert?' she shouts, 'Come and help me, please?'

She reaches for the kettle. She needs tea. The supermarket was busy and she's tired.

'Albert?' she calls again, but this time she stands at the bottom of the stairs, she doesn't have the energy to climb up three flights.

On the top floor, Albert's bedroom door slams. She nods, satisfied, and returns to the kitchen. She'd called into the supermarket after finishing work but she must get organised and order her shopping online. It would be so much easier that way and save her time.

Albert's feet, unlike her other foster son's, are light on the stairs and, although she doesn't hear him, a few minutes later she senses his presence behind her.

'Hello, Al. Did you finish your homework?' She turns, smiles and hands him the cereal. 'Help me put the shopping away, please.'

Albert nods, takes the box and places it in the cupboard. His big brown eyes are serious and dark. It's unlike him not to rifle though the bags looking for a chocolate bar, but this afternoon he seems distracted, engrossed in his own thoughts. He's in a quiet mood.

When there's only one item left, Femi pulls out his favourite orange chocolate bars playfully from the bag. 'Ta da!' She'd also remembered to replace the biscuits she'd finished off yesterday with Peter but neither seem to be having an effect on Albert. She waves the packet for his attention but Albert doesn't smile. She knows depression is just one of the signs of developmental trauma that she has been trained to look out for and, as a foster mum, it's just one of the courses in the past six years that she's taken. She understands how important it is to take her time with him.

'Let's sit at the table and have some tea,' she suggests.

Still keeping an eye on him she flicks on the kettle and takes mugs from the cupboard. 'The supermarket was manic and would you believe, when my back was turned your favourite biscuits just jumped into the trolley. They didn't even ask!'

His expression remains serious as she fills the teapot. It's one her aunt in Jamaica gave her after her father died. She must video call her later. Albert liked to hear about the island where his family came from too. It was one of the reasons Femi had wanted to foster him. They share a similar family history. The social workers had matched them up well.

'Did your trainers turn up?'

Albert nods.

'Do you think they were taken out of your bag?'

Albert shrugs. He looks defeated and beaten, the other kids are always teasing him it's no wonder he hates going to school. When he gets home he spends most of the time hiding in his room and playing computer games.

'Will we call Auntie Sharisha later today?'

Albert slides onto the chair opposite her and lifts his mug.

'How many hours difference is there in Jamaica?' she asks.

'Six.' Albert's voice, unlike his gangly frame and long arms, is small and there's barely a hint of his lisp since he's been going to a speech therapist.

'So, what time is it there now?'

Albert glances at the large wall clock. 'Ten in the morning.'

Femi smiles brightly. He's doing well at school. She believes it's because they read together most days that he's made so much progress.

She nudges the biscuit packet across the table, closer to him. Today she's determined to stick to her diet. She wants to lose two stone by Christmas. This year she wants it to be perfect. Ricky her oldest foster boy, didn't understand when she told him.

'Why lose weight?' he asked last night with all the sensitivity of a seventeen-year-old. 'You never go out anyway.'

'If I lost weight, I would.'

'You wouldn't look right if you were thin.'

'I want to lose this.' She'd grabbed a handful of flesh on her hips.

'Voluptuous,' Ricky had said laughing, reminding her of their museum visit, he'd added, 'Like a Rembrandt.'

She'd grinned back at him. Not because of his back-handed compliment but because he knew the artist and had used the word she'd taught him. She's convinced he'll pass his A levels but she keeps up the pressure of taking them out at weekends when she can; museums, art galleries and theatre treats. Femi firmly believes in a rounded cultural education. She would have liked one herself and now, by educating her boys, she is fulfilling her own needs too.

Albert coughs, puts his hand to his mouth and crumbs scatter onto the table.

'What's wrong?' Femi asks. He doesn't reply. 'Is this about meeting your father? It's best we speak about it because then I will understand and I can find a way to help you.'

Albert sips his tea. At thirteen, he is gawky but gaining confidence. Today. Femi thinks, his vulnerability is wrapped around him like an invisible cloak.

He sighs and pulls on his bottom lip. It's a nervous tic.

'There's nothing we can't fix between us, we've been able to sort everything else out, haven't we?' she says encouragingly.

Albert nods.

Femi doesn't have to remind him about the bullying at school and how she went to the headmaster, or how she's replaced his stolen Adidas trainers or even how he'd lost concentration in class one day and been shouted at by the teacher. He'd come home and cried. That was the first time Femi had cuddled him. He had sobbed in her arms, heart-wrenching gulping sobs as if the entire sadness of his being was finally unleashed. He'd been twelve years-old then and had been with her only two months but this is now — today.

'Come on,' she giggles. 'Or do I have to hold you by the ankles and shake it out of your pockets.'

Albert laughs.

Femi's heart lifts at his smile. It can't be that bad she thinks.

'Dad phoned me again.' He looks down at the table and wraps the biscuit wrapper around his index finger.

She breathes slowly. 'How does that make you feel?'

Albert shakes his head. 'I dunno. We talked computer games.'

Albert was placed in foster care because his parents were drug addicts. Albert's mother died of an overdose when he was six, and Delroy put him in care while he went into Rehab five years ago. Albert has been diagnosed with chronic developmental trauma caused by repeated and prolonged domestic violence from when he was a baby. Albert had been placed in various foster homes around the country until he had eventually arrived in Kent. Now, Femi didn't want to let him go.

'Did he ask how you are or about your school?' she prompts kindly.

Albert nods.

'Try and speak to me, Albert, and tell me how you feel, can you do that?' Her tone is gentle and calm. She'd done well on her course and she taps into the resources and training stored in her head.

'Are you looking forward to seeing him?'

Albert raises his eyes to her. 'What about you?'

'It's no problem,' she says. 'This isn't about me. This is about your relationship with your father and it might help you.'

Albert shrugs. It's the indifferent attitude of a teenager but Femi knows it matters to him. It matters to him very much.

'I can understand that you might be curious and that you

want to see him.'

Albert's face brightened. 'You can?'

'Of course. I'll take you into town. We can walk together —
with Peanut.'

Albert nods emphatically then his eyes turn dark and serious.
'You know what happened the last time?'

'Yes.'

He flicks the crumbs on the table with his index finger.

Femi continues, 'Your Dad didn't turn up, but that's in the
past. Let's give him another chance tomorrow. This might
be a great step forward for you, Al.' Femi says with more
conviction than she's feeling.

Albert smiles brightly.

Femi knows he desperately wants to see his father and she
feels a pain in her chest. She's not alarmed. She's a paramedic.
It's not a heart attack but it's searing pain — it's as if her heart
is being sliced apart.

* * *

The following morning, after Ricky leaves for his football
game, Femi and Albert are leaving the house when they see
the new neighbour. He's throwing out boxes and she calls out
and waves. He glances up, raises his hand and disappears back
inside his house.

'I don't think there's any children,' Albert sighs.

'I agree, Albert. I think he's living on his own.'

It's a bright morning and Westbay's beach huts look stunning and so picturesque, all aligned along the promenade like
colourful huts for toy soldiers.

'This is my favourite colour,' Femi says pointing to a pink

one.

Albert looks along the row. 'I like navy.'

They're early and so Femi pauses for a moment to sit on the steps of the beach hut and she pats the small space beside her.

'We always sit here on our way into town.' He smiles at their usual habit and he wiggles in and takes his place.

'Well, we're not doing any harm and it's not for very long.' Femi sniffs appreciatively at the sea air and this always makes Albert giggle. He mimics her, before they both explode laughing.

'I held my breath longer,' she teases.

'Let's go again,' Albert replies.

'Best of three.'

They both know that on the third one, Femi will lose control and laugh helplessly as she tickles Albert.

Peanut sniffs happily under the steps, uninterested in their silly game, hoping there maybe remnants of a last night's discarded fish and chip supper.

Albert says, 'I wish we knew someone who owned one of these.'

Femi smiles. 'Why?'

'Then we could get a fish supper one night and sit on the little balcony and watch the sunset.'

'When the summer comes, we can get some fish and chips, anyway, and we can sit on the beach, would you like that?'

Albert nods, and Peanut looks up hopefully. Femi's heart skips. She sincerely hopes that Albert will still be with her in the summer.

'Come on, then.' She smooths down her orange and black dress and offers Albert the dog lead. He smiles and Peanut follows obediently as they walk around the pretty harbour, past the fishing boats and the small shops along the quay.

'The tide is out,' Albert says, as they wait patiently for Peanut to sniff appreciatively at the lobster pots and fishing ropes from the working boats.

'Yes, the boats are right down in the water, aren't they?'

'It's amazing how much the tide goes out.'

'Yes.'

'Do you ever get frightened going out on the lifeboat?' he asks.

'Sometimes, but I'm trained and I'm always with the best people.' Femi brushes off his question, more recently she's become more frightened and she knows that it's a combination of her own PTSD from her experiences but also because she doesn't want anything to happen to her. The boys need her. She has to be here for them.

'I wonder what it's like to be a fisherman.' Albert pulls at his bottom lip.

'Cold and wet, and very dangerous, I'd imagine.' Femi links her arm through Albert's. 'I thought you wanted to be a computer programmer.'

'Gamer,' corrects Albert.

'Do you want another game of Minecraft with me tomorrow?'

Albert grins. 'Yes. You need the practice.'

'You won't be upset if I win?'

Albert laughs scornfully. 'As if!'

'I almost defeated the Ender Dragon last night, didn't I?'

'No. Not even close.' Albert punches her playfully on the arm.

'Come on, we'd better not keep your Dad waiting.'

They are still smiling as they walk under the old sixteenth-century clock tower which straddles the road like Colossus stood in front of Mandraki harbour at the entrance to the city of Rhodes. The colourful shops of Harbour Street look resplendent in the April sunshine as the clock chimes quarter to the hour. 'We still have plenty of time,' Femi says.

The pedestrianised street is lined with an assortment of brightly coloured shops and outside the Turkish barbers a queue has already formed. Albert shades his eyes from the sunshine. 'The Grooming Room – Esquires of Westbay,' he reads, in his poshest voice. 'That's where Ricky goes, isn't it?'

'Yes.'

'Can I go there next time?' He pulls on his tight curly hair.

'Maybe?' Femi laughs playfully.

The flower shop, Darling Buds and Blooms has a bay window filled with colourful plants and flowers and outside two wheelbarrows with a floral arrangement that's so beautiful, even Albert stops to look.

'That's pretty,' he says.

Femi nods but her attention is already on Taylor's Art Gallery next door. She's drawn to the magnificent photographs on display in the window; a colourful Chaffinch and a peacock blue Kingfisher

'It must be a male,' Albert says, following her gaze. 'They're more brightly coloured. It's got a blue-grey cap and it's belly is rusty-red.'

'It's stunning, isn't it?' replies Femi, pleased with his knowledge of birds, and they spend a few minutes admiring a water-colour painting of a Toucan.

Then, from across the road, Femi waves to Sanjay reminding herself she won't be ordering a takeaway Indian meal anytime soon. Although the boys love it, she's determined to diet this time.

'Can we go to the zoo again, maybe in the summer?' asks Albert. He holds Peanut on the lead and he leans down to rub him gently round the ears. 'I love animals.'

Femi smiles but her heart is heavy. 'Of course.'

'The Bistro is open,' Femi mumbles to herself, remembering what an eye sore it had been. Now it's a lovely looking restaurant, painted in cream and burgundy. Femi pauses to read the menu in the window and her mouth is already watering. She wants to visit it but with this new diet, she decides, it will have to wait.

'Can we go in the Harbour Cafe, again?' Albert asks, following her gaze.

'Maybe next week?' Femi raises her hand to Karl, the cafe's manager, who beams back at her. Today his dreadlocks are tied up and she can see how handsome he is, in his long French apron. Come on, Al, we don't want to be late.'

They pass the butchers and the pet shop before crossing over by The Ship and into the square. It's busy and there are lots of people milling around, drinking coffee from styrofoam cups and carrying fish and chips in the direction of the beach.

They head past The Ship, on the corner, where Ricky washes up two evenings a week in the kitchen, and then Femi stops beside the fountain in the square. Waiting outside the Italian restaurant, is a small, skinny man wearing a Rastafarian cap, a worn jacket and denim jeans. He stands smoking but when he sees them, he smiles, waves, drops his cigarette on the pavement and crushes it with the pointed toe of his boot.

'Off you go then, Al. Have a good time.'

But Albert doesn't hear her. He's already half way across the square.

Femi turns away deliberately. She doesn't want to see how Albert throws himself into his father's arms or if they stand awkwardly in silence. She has to let go. She doesn't turn back.

She walks quickly down Harbour Street trying to quell the rising fear inside her heart, hoping all will go well for Albert but fearing he may leave her. She spends a few minutes staring in Jane's Jeweller's window, trying to distract herself, then her mobile phone rings.

'Hi sweetie.' Freddie's voice rings out cheerfully. 'Did it go okay?'

'I'll let you know tonight when he's home.'

'Nitesh is cooking his new chicken dish, do you want to come over?'

'Not tonight, thanks. I want to be at home for Albert.'

'Oh, okay. Now, I've covered your shift for your meeting next week.'

'Brilliant. You're a star, thanks.'

'Okay, sweetie. Nitesh says hi, he's on call all week.' Freddie is referring to his husband who like Femi volunteers for the RNLI.

'Me too.'

'Love ya!' Freddie calls.

'Love you more. Bye.' Femi hangs up thinking about Freddie. He's the best admin, receptionist she's known and she feels lucky that he befriended her on her first day working in the clinic. He's supported her through all her fostering and when he married Nitesh two years ago, she was the best woman at their wedding. It had been a lovely day and although Ricky had been with her, she couldn't help but feel very alone. She'd been surrounded by lots of couples; all glamorous and good-looking, slim and beautiful — all of them had looked like they were in love.

It had been the one time, Femi had wished she had someone special by her side; someone who loved her, someone who desired her, someone who could share her life.

She catches sight of her reflection in the jewellery shop window and sucks in her tummy. Perhaps if she lost weight, she might finally find the man of her dreams and fall in love.

* * *

Ricky throws the flinger and the ball flies high into the sky. Peanut chases after it, running along the shore line, a slow loping gait, but eager and excited. 'He's such a dope,' Ricky says as Peanut changes direction, thrown off course by a more interesting scent.

Femi smiles.

Albert is crouched down, on the sand, wearing his trainers, hunting for oyster shells on the beach. He's occupied and content in his own world.

It's Sunday morning and Femi has dragged the boys down to the beach for some fresh air. Ricky didn't score in the football final but his team won and he tells her about the game. She pulls her jacket across her stomach and watches Albert, engrossed on the beach, concerned that he has been shut in his bedroom since being with Delroy yesterday afternoon. Femi wants to make sure he's okay but she can't ask him outright, she will have to wait until he's ready to talk.

Peanut drops the ball at Ricky's feet, pants and wags his tail.

Ricky scoops up the ball and flings it across the stones again. They both know Peanut will never tire of this game and Ricky laughs. Femi can see the change in him. His body has filled out and he looks broader and stronger across the shoulders. So different from the pale, skinny waif-like skeleton that arrived on her doorstep almost four years ago. He's transformed into this confident young man who enjoys sport, works hard and loves life. Long may it continue, she thinks, remembering Peter's conversation with her last week about how teenagers can suddenly become estranged from their foster carer.

'How was your shift last night?' she asks. 'Did you enjoy it?'

Ricky laughs. 'Washing dishes in the pub?'

'I thought you were more important than that. Haven't you been promoted to stacking the dishwasher?' she grins.

His eyes screw up in concentration. 'Paul said he might take me on as bar staff when I'm eighteen.'

'Great. Only another year.' Femi's wondering where the four years have gone, since she had opened her front door and welcomed him with a big smile saying, 'My name is Femi but you can call me whatever you're comfortable with.'

'Auntie?' he'd mumbled.

'Auntie is perfect.'

He'd stepped forward then and she had taken him into her arms. Femi would never forget that moment. His body had shaken but there were no tears — just relief. He'd been exhausted and confused, pushed from home to home for over six years. He'd never known stability. He'd never known what it was like to make a mistake and to be forgiven. When he'd run away, he'd simply been moved somewhere else, another home, another school, another part of the country.

Now, here in Westbay, he seems settled and happy. He isn't always the quickest or the cleverest but he is determined to do well for himself and when he was sixteen, they had chatted about his future. Femi has said that she wants to see him through his A levels and hopefully through to university. This has visibly shaken Ricky. He knew that at eighteen he should move to independent living, but Femi firmly believed that Ricky needed support to finish his education. After being put through foster care, experiencing trauma at birth, failure, rejection and a breakdown — Ricky knew this was his golden opportunity.

He knows Femi has every intention of supporting him for as long as possible, to give him the best chance in life.

He has piercing blue eyes and there's a dark shadow already growing on his chin and it makes Femi smile. A few weeks ago, Ricky came into the kitchen and talked about growing a beard.

'If you're doing it so you don't have to bother to shave, like you don't bother to tidy your room or open the bedroom window, then it's a mistake.'

'Why?' he'd looked genuinely confused.

'Because, quite simply, my darling — you will smell and that's not a good thing for any of us.'

He'd grinned at her then and she'd booked him an appointment at the Turkish Barber's in Harbour Street. The two brothers, Ozan and Yosef, taught him how to self-groom and unlike many teenage boys, Ricky now smells nice and clean. He's even taken to ironing his shirts and, on rare occasions, he even remembers to leave his trainers outside to air.

He's grown so quickly. Where has the time gone? She looks at him as Peanut drops the ball at his feet and waits expectantly.

'This is my piece of heaven,' she says aloud, savouring the wind on her face and the noise of the sea lapping on the stones and she walks over to sit on the steps of the pink beach hut.

Ricky throws the ball again for Peanut and she moves so there's enough room and he sits on the steps beside her, just like Albert did yesterday.

Ricky says, 'Al's very quiet today. He's hardly said a word.'

'He's processing,' Femi replies quietly.

She knows that talking outside in the fresh air, beside the sea, is therapeutic. She'd shown the boys how easy it is to speak clearly, openly and honestly without judgement while they made pictures from stones and driftwood, or after the tides went out they would score letters into the sand. Conversation came easier to them all when they were pottering about, doing something else, concentrating on the beauty of the beach or playing with Peanut.

'I tried to talk to him.' Ricky rubs his cheek.

'I know and you're very kind. Just give him some space and some time.'

'He didn't even want to play Animal Crossing, last night.'

'He will.'

There's a pause and Femi can feel the tension in Ricky's body beside her. Eventually he says, 'Will Al go and live with him?' Ricky's voice is a croak.

'We can't rule it out but it will have to be what's best for Albert.'

'Being with us is best for him.' Ricky's tone is sulky. 'We're family.'

'Delroy is his father,' Femi replies evenly but her heart is thumping with fear. She knows how Ricky feels. They're like a proper family and for Albert to leave them now would be heart-breaking — for them both.

'I'm really pissed.' He kicks a stone. 'I'd miss Al, if he left.'

'I know.'

'It's not fair.'

Femi doesn't answer, the wind whips up a tear and she wipes it quickly away. She'd have to keep an eye on Ricky and mention this to Jenny. She didn't want Ricky to go off the rails again. When emotions become too overwhelming for him he often gets angry or runs away and Femi didn't want to lose him too.

'Do you think that tanker on the horizon is moving?' She nods with her head.

'No. It's been there for days.'

'Really?'

Ricky bursts out laughing. 'Of course it's moving!'

Femi nudges him playfully with her elbow. Albert hears them laughing and looks up, then he picks up an oyster shell and runs toward them. As they head home with Peanut sniffing at every blade of grass and trailing behind them, Femi is reminded that, like the seasons, nothing lasts forever, including her own close-knit family. Everything changes. It's life's evolution that is both exhilarating and frightening.

3

Chapter 3

Femi has changed into her pyjamas and is brushing her teeth in her en-suite bathroom when her iPhone rings. It's Sunday. It's late. She spits out toothpaste and hurries into her bedroom.

'Hello?'

'Hi, Femi. I know its short notice,' Peter says. 'But I wouldn't ask unless it was an emergency. There's a refugee here in Dover and he needs somewhere to stay tonight. I know you've been approved for two children and we can get a change to your approval for a third child. You've had all the DBS checks and it will be quicker and easier if you can take him.'

'It's almost midnight.'

'It's just for a couple of nights.'

'Oh, Peter—'

'I can get the paperwork done quickly. We could be with you in a few hours.'

'I don't know—'

'You've got a spare room.'

'Yes but—'

'He needs a home. I wouldn't ask Femi, unless I was desperate. He's in a pretty bad way and I want to make sure he's looked after. Femi, please... help me.'

'I thought lots of families had signed up to house Ukrainian refugees.'

'Not all of them have been verified and not all of them can take a child. Besides, he isn't Ukrainian. You know that all sorts of nationalities come over on the boats from Calais: Afghans, Sudanese, Pakistanis and Vietnamese. We've had four hundred crossing today — and you know how the process is, Femi. It's so laborious. Please. He's fifteen and he's been through hell getting out of Syria. His country has been decimated. His father and brother were killed in front of him. He's suffered so much—'

'Oh, Peter—'

'He's broken his ankle on the crossing so he can't go far. He needs physio but we can get him all that help once he's settled.'

'Has he any family?'

'His mother and sister have been taken— they're somewhere in Syria still, we're trying to locate them but it could take months.'

Femi has seen the news and read the papers about the wars in the Yemen and in Syria. More recently, she and the boys have been horrified at the bombings, mass graves and war crimes inflicted by the Russians in Ukraine. Their discussions usually take place over dinner and it provides a topic of conversation, as well as allowing them to formulate their opinions and develop discussion skills in a safe environment. It's important to Femi that the boys learn to have their own opinions, and listen to others, even though they may disagree.

Femi wanted to help but the thought of taking in a refugee tonight, concerns her. Although she is qualified to help, she's unsure how the boys will react to another person in the house — another boy — a refugee. Should she ask them?

'Femi, it has to be tonight.' Peter shouts away from the phone to someone in the background and Femi can hear muffled noises. It sounds chaotic where he is. 'You can arrange cover, change your shift, can't you?'

Femi thinks of the boy, if it's been as awful as its been shown on television, then she wants to help. She *must* help. Besides, she wasn't working tomorrow.

'Of course, I'll take him. Bring him here.'

Peter sighs heavily. 'Thank you. I'll get all the documentation ready. He can't claim benefits or anything until he's eighteen. We'll have to verify his asylum claim and until that's successful the council will have to provide him with accommodation and foster care. He says he's fifteen and so you'll be paid your usual fostering. He'll also get a few quid for a SIM card —'

'I thought you said it's just for a few days.'

'It is. I'll email you the details so you have it in writing. See you soon. Oh, and by the way, his name is Ahmed.'

That was Peter, brisk and to the point and — he always got what he wanted.

When Femi throws the phone on the bed, she looks at her reflection in the bedroom mirror. Her eyes seem older than her years and she shakes her head at her bewildered reflection.

'When will you learn?' she whispers. 'You're such a soft touch. Never,' she replies, slipping off her pyjamas and pulling on her leggings and jumper. 'Absolutely never.'

* * *

Ricky and Albert have their own bedrooms in the converted attic on the top floor of the house but Femi always keeps a spare room for Sandra, her best friend who stands in for her when she goes away for respite or for the occasional evening out.

She's careful not to wake the two boys who are upstairs sleeping on the top floor. It's a requirement that each child has their own room. It's imperative that they have their own space and until now, it has worked well with them upstairs and her and Sandra, or any guests beside her bedroom, on the first floor.

Sandra's room is the small box-room at the back of the house beside her own bedroom and communal bathroom. It's been a dumping ground for a few weeks for all sorts of mess; numerous clothes that have been abandoned that she's been meaning to take to the charity shop; clothes that once fitted her but are now too tight. She shoves them into a bag, makes up the bed with fresh sheets and tidies the shelves. As she draws the curtains she sees a light on in the garden next door. There's someone walking around in the dark, using a torch and she frowns. It must be the hippy, walking around his garden and she wonders if he's lost something, or maybe he's just stoned and he can't find his way back inside the house. She draws the curtains and flicks on a bedside light. She stands at the door looking at the cosy room; single bed, small desk, orange and lime green curtains and matching duvet. She glances around the room once more and wonders how a Syrian refugee will feel arriving here.

Downstairs in the kitchen she makes a hot chocolate and

then sits in the quiet breaking of the dawn, imagining how their lives might now change, hoping it will be positive.

What new dynamic will Ahmed bring to their home?

Femi takes a deep breath, wraps her hands around the mug and stares out of the window into the dark garden waiting for Peter's car to arrive.

Now, rather than thinking of the new arrival, her thoughts turn to her boys. Albert seems particularly quiet since meeting his father and Ricky, in the vital teenage years when he could so easily go off the rails, needs security. Femi knows that teenagers start to question who they are, where they've come from and how their identities have been formed from their past.

Ricky was born in Liverpool and has had no contact with his parents for over ten years. He was abused and beaten and he kept running away. Then at seven, he was caught shop-lifting, he broke rules, missed school, and just couldn't conform. His parents separated and his mother went abroad with another man. Ricky told Femi that his father was a bully and that when he remarried, Ricky was thrown out of the house. He lived on the streets for a while and was subjected to physical and mental abuse. The social workers moved him from place to place but he had no stability or security. He was thirteen when he came to Femi. It had been a rotten start in life for him and Femi knew she had to keep him safe and protected.

Femi had had several other foster children prior to Ricky but they had all been short-term. She knew Ricky was going to be different. Ricky always says, he knew from the moment she opened the door to him and he called her Auntie, that he felt safe. At first, Ricky couldn't settle. When there were problems with friends or school, or if things didn't go right, he ran away.

It was his PTSD, the fight or flight scenario that triggered this reaction. She knows that where there's been neglect and abuse, the brain develops differently. These children are wired differently but Femi also knows she will never give up on him. He doesn't want to see his birth family again. He knows what they did to him and when he has periodic episodes of anger or running away, he's always upset and repentant. He always hugs her and is pleased to come home — more importantly, she knows he has no one else. She is his rock.

Car headlights swing across the room and Femi feels her body tense and her mouth is dry in anticipation. She is confident with developmental trauma. She knows and has seen X-ray images of two brain scans; one with a child with appropriate development and a second scan of a child with chronic neglect that showed parts of the brain was under developed. She has been taught and trained to repeat positive actions and she knows that the brain can re-wire itself over time. She understands the process. Fostering is about changing behaviour, and she's proud of being a foster parent, someone who is trained to look after neglected children with problems.

She stands up.

The car parks on the gravel alongside her Volvo. The headlights go off and Femi wonders what this poor refugee must be feeling. She would look up her notes tomorrow and find out how best to help him. In the meantime, it was important to make him feel welcome.

She opens the door and smiles brightly.

'Hello, Ahmed. My name is Femi, my boys call me Auntie but you can call me whatever you're comfortable with.'

Peanut is curious and walks to the door, wagging his tail in greeting.

The young boy glares at him. 'I don't like dogs,' he says.

* * *

Albert isn't asleep. He's been trying to stay awake for hours. He's been worrying about lying to Auntie. His father gave him a phone. 'It means we can stay in touch whenever we like,' he'd said.

Albert didn't think it was allowed but his father had laughed.

'Rules are made to be broken, son. Besides, we're not doing anyone any harm, are we?'

Albert had shaken his head.

Delroy had continued, 'Look, I know how tough it's been for you, living away from me but I want to make it up to you. I want to be a good father and I can't do that if the social workers are on my case the whole time, looking over my shoulder, can I?

Albert had agreed.

'It's our secret, son.' He'd pressed the old phone into his hand and Albert had managed to hide it in his bedroom.

Now, he keeps looking at it. His father had promised to text him before eleven o'clock now, it's almost four o'clock in the morning.

His phone pings and the book he is reading, falls to the floor with a soft thud waking him up. To his surprise there are noises outside in the driveway so he throws off his duvet and pads over to the window. There's a boy on crutches getting out of the car and he also recognises Peter, Auntie's social worker.

What's going on?

Distracted by his phone pinging again, he crosses the room and jumps into bed to read his message.

Sorry, son. Busy nite. You ok?

He types quick. *Fine.*

Wanna come and see ya on Saturday but got no cash. Did you get some?

Albert thinks about their conversation in the Italian restaurant. He was relaxing and enjoying the garlic bread and bolognese, happy to be with his father at last, trying to see the similarities in their faces; same broad nose, black eyes and wide mouth and that's when his father had said he was short of money. He said it wasn't a problem and he had every intention of getting another job but it was to be their secret. He said he needed money and then Albert could move back to London to live with him.

His fingers type quickly. *I'll try.*

Gotta know before I make the journey.

Okay.

Don't tell anyone, will ya?

No.

Promise?

Yeah.

Our secret son. We'll be together soon. Promise.

Albert imagined living with his Dad. He said he had a big flat overlooking a lovely park. When Albert said he would miss the sea, he'd said that there was a lake in the park and when he said he'd miss Peanut, his Dad promised to get him a rescue puppy. He'd loved the way his Dad had laughed and said they had the same habit of eating spaghetti with a knife and fork. He said they were from the same stock. He said they belonged together now but that he just needed a bit of time and a little luck to push him along.

'I need kindness, son.'

Albert had replied with his mouthful, 'Like Auntie is with me?'

His Dad had smiled then. 'That's a perfect example.'

Albert had smiled back.

Afterwards, they'd sat on the beach talking about their perfect lives together in London and after Delroy was gone and Albert was walking home, he paused to sit on the steps of the pink beach hut. With his knees tucked under his chin, gazing out at the sea for what seemed like a long time, Albert mulled things over until it was dark. He knew something was not quite right but he couldn't work out what it was.

Now, as he hides his phone, he can hear the boy on his crutches banging up the stairs and Auntie fussing over him. Albert pulls the duvet over his head. It was all too much and he wanted everyone to go away. He wanted to be on his own.

4

Chapter 4

Ahmed looks exhausted. He has a thin face, narrow nose and delicate chin and there are dark circles around his eyes. His black hair is lank and dirty and it flops over his forehead, defeated, just like the frame of his fragile body.

'Would you like something to eat?' Femi asks. 'I have some lovely fruit cake?'

From the lounge there is scratching at the door. Peanut is unhappy not to be petted with love or involved with the stranger's arrival.

Ahmed shakes his head. He looks dehydrated so Femi pours a glass of milk and cuts a large slice of cake.

'Let me show you upstairs to your room.'

He clatters up the stairs, unused to the ungainly crutches that seem too big for him.

'The bathroom is here and this is your room.' Femi opens the bathroom door and then the bedroom. He places the crutches beside the bed, sits down and swings his legs up, sinking back against the pillow. He has olive coloured skin and his bloodshot eyes close. He covers his eyes with his arm.

Femi places milk and cake on the table beside him but he doesn't open his eyes.

'There are clean pyjamas here, a toothbrush, towel and flannel...'

His eyes stay closed.

'Goodnight, Ahmed. Relax and sleep well. You're home now,' she whispers but he continues lying very still and he doesn't reply. It looks like he's already asleep but it could also be shock or fear. He has no clothes, no bag, no belongings.

Nothing.

Downstairs the sun is rising and Femi sorts through spare clothes that she keeps for an emergency. She often rummages in the second-hand shops and buys good clothes — sometimes designer makes — for the boys.

Westbay is an expensive town and the second-hand charity shops often have brand names that she looks out for. She knows they are popular with the boys and sometimes Freddie and Nitesh also give her clothes.

She finds a pair of baggy trousers and two shirts that Ricky has worn a few times before he started playing rugby and filling out. She also finds a new packet of boxer shorts she keeps for emergencies. Ahmed is small for his age, barely bigger than Albert. He's like fine-bone china with his long slender fingers and he has a starved body on a skeletal frame. She'd offered to take Ahmed's thin jacket but he'd refused and he'd climbed onto the bed fully dressed as exhaustion had dragged him into a deep sleep. She goes up to check on him. He's eaten the fruit cake. His breathing is shallow but regular and his thick hair is heavy across his brow and his long eye lashes seem to cast shadows over his cheeks. She would let him sleep for as long as possible and then take each day as it comes. Laying his clothes and underwear on the bedside table, she then closes the door softly behind her, aware that this will be a challenge like no other.

* * *

Ricky helps himself to cereal and toast. Although it is early, Femi is already texting on her phone and seems distracted. He knows that she likes to be around when the boys go to school but so far this morning Albert hasn't appeared and Ricky feels unsettled; Albert might be leaving and now this new boy has arrived in the middle of the night.

'So you didn't know he was coming?' Ricky asks.

'It was after midnight when Peter phoned and they didn't get here until almost four o'clock.'

'And, he's from Syria?' he says.

'Ahmed. Yes.'

'He came across the Channel in a boat?'

'Yes, in a small dingy.'

'Is he Muslim?'

Femi frowns. 'I think so. He hasn't woken up yet and we haven't had a chance to speak. He was exhausted last night.'

Ricky butters toast, adds Marmite and takes a bite. He focuses his blue eyes firmly on Femi's face.

'How long is he staying here?'

'That all depends.' Femi puts her phone away and sips her coffee. 'I'll find out more later today.' She remembers the email that Peter sent and then decides to scan through it. The information she needs might all be written in it. 'I'll go to the butchers today and buy some halal.'

'What?' asks Albert coming into the kitchen. He bends down.

Peanut is in his basket and he tickles his tummy.

'Don't say what, say pardon.'

'What did you say?' Albert asks, deliberately.

'Halal,' replies Ricky. 'It's meat that Muslims eat. It's blessed before it's killed.'

'Yuk!' Albert's face screws up.

'Are you Vegan today?' Ricky teases, Albert never seems to be able to make up his mind.

Femi throws the eggs into the pan and scrambles them for Albert. He seems brighter today and more willing to engage in conversation.

'How old is Ahmed?' Albert asks sliding into a chair at the table.

'Fifteen.'

Albert smiles. 'Near my age then.'

It might be in numbers, Femi thinks, but there's so much more than age that can separate two people.

'Does he like animals? I bet he loved Peanut, did he?' Albert is stroking Peanut's ears.

Femi forces a smile. 'He was tired but he will get to know him.'

'We can play Roblox or Fortnite, later, if you like?' Ricky says to Albert, and Femi is pleased that he's trying to engage with him.

Femi empties the pan and passes the scrambled eggs to Albert. 'Thanks, Auntie.'

'You look tired,' she says. 'Did you sleep well?'

'Yeah.' He doesn't look her in the eyes.

'Did you hear Ahmed arriving last night?'

'I heard something.'

'He's a refugee from Syria. He has nothing; no clothes, no

home, no family, no country, so we must be kind to him and make him welcome.'

Albert nods seriously, his mouth is full.

Ricky stands up and puts his dirty dishes on the counter. 'I've got football practice after school. See you later.'

'I'm off today, Freddie has found someone to cover my shift.' Femi glances at her phone thinking of the list of things she has to do with Ahmed and wonders what time he will wake up.

Ricky grabs his sports bag and jacket. 'See you later.'

'Bye,' she calls.

Albert finishes his breakfast. He's managed to deflect the conversation and managed to avoid telling Auntie he's been awake most of the night. He's also seen her handbag on the counter so while she goes into the utility room, he moves closer with his dirty cup and plate in his hands. He can see her purse sticking out. It looks like there a note, is it a twenty?

'Are you putting that in the dishwasher?' Femi's voice startles him.

'Y.. Y...Yes,' he stutters, not turning around.

'Thank you, Al,' she adds, smiling but inside she's concerned. He only stutters now when he is stressed and he hasn't stuttered for ages. She would speak to him after school when there's more time.

Albert dumps his plate on the counter, pushes past her and runs upstairs. He hates school but today it would be a relief to get away from her.

* * *

Femi calls Sandra who was once her social worker and is now her best friend and she tells her about Ahmed's arrival.

'He's so young and vulnerable, yet his eyes are wary and he seems so... jaded. I hope I'll be able to help him.'

'You'll be lovely with him. You just have to remember that refugees have a different trauma to the children here in this country, you know the ones who are often filled with despair —you're familiar with developmental trauma and what it does, aren't you?'

'I did a course.'

'So many kids have no opportunities and they've been ignored by our government,' Sandra says. 'There's been lack of investment in social care that will take generations to recuperate. There will be ripples of poverty related trauma for years and years, even if there is the will from the government to sort it out—'

'So many children need help.'

'But the refugees are different.' Sandra argues, 'They generally don't have developmental trauma. Most of them have post-traumatic stress disorder and it will take counselling and years of support to help them. They don't even have the basics; clothes, money, a phone. Even if they have family back in their own country, they will probably never even see them again.'

'What about the Red Cross?'

'The Red Cross and the Kent Refugee Action Network - get involved and help and they will try to find families. Some stories are beyond sad; one Sudanese girl had been trafficked for sex and she's not the only one. Some kids have had a traumatic journey and sometimes it's taken them years to get here to England.'

'It's overwhelming,' Femi says. 'Do you ever get over something like that?' Femi frowns. She's familiar with abuse;

social, mental, physical and emotional with her experience as a foster parent but being a refugee somehow seems so much more traumatic.

Sandra replies, 'Generally speaking, if a child sees death and they experience losing family, it's less challenging for them to recover than it is for a child who has suffered serious and constant neglect. If they've had good formative years in their country of origin and, if they want an education, you know —if they want to learn, want a job and a better future like they had in their own country or their families had, they may well succeed. Unlike some of the foster children in this country and that's because most of the refugees arriving here, haven't experienced neglect as an infant.'

'So, you're saying that developmental trauma is harder — much more difficult to change to help the child move forward?'

'Yes, the boys like you have; Albert and Ricky have been traumatised through their early, formative years and that is what stays with them. Boys like them are much harder to fix.'

Femi has faced difficulties with both of these boys and she knows that her problems with them aren't over yet but she loves them and she's willing to do whatever it takes to help them towards a normal, happy and successful life. She would do whatever it takes. They're not someone else's children - they are hers.

5

Chapter 5

It's lunchtime when Ahmed thumps down the stairs with his crutches. They seem too big and clumsy for him and they clatter noisily on the tiles as he hobbles into the kitchen.

Femi is sitting at the kitchen table studying her laptop. She has spent the morning researching Syria, and in particular Aleppo. She's also gone over her notes from the course she did for fostering refugees.

She smiles. 'Hello Ahmed, come in.' She stands up. 'Peter told me you speak good English but if there's anything you don't understand, just ask. Why don't you sit down, those crutches look awful. Do you think you need them?'

Ahmed frowns and leans them against the table and one of them clatters to the floor.

Peanut raises his head from her bed and stretches.

Ahmed hobbles, backwards, and sits at the table furthest away from the dog.

'It's alright,' Femi says soothingly to him. 'Peanut won't harm you. He's a softie and he loves cuddles.' Femi picks up his crutch and takes them both into the utility room. 'Your plaster cast is dry now. You may find it easier to manage without these, especially at home. I did when I broke my ankle.'

'You did.' It's not a question but Ahmed's voice is so soft that she has to lean forward across the table to hear him. As she does this she can see him appraising her for the first time.

He looks at her half-black features; heavy breasts, wide hips and her generous smile with purple lipstick. She stands up, straightens her skirt and wonders what he makes of her as she prepares toast and tea. She knows from experience that it would be too much to ask what he would like to eat. The decisions that he has to make must be important ones and she can take away the stress by managing the rest.

As she moves around the kitchen, she gives him time to take everything in; the long dining table with eight chairs, the shelves of books, the different orchids she's trying to tend on the long window sill above the sink. Then there's a view of the garden.

As she reaches for the tea, she sees him straining his neck to see into the utility room where there's a pile of washing including sports gear (Ricky) and neat grey trousers (Albert), and an assortment of boys' shoes and boots stacked on racks. Sometimes the room smells of the boys' feet, typical teenagers and this morning she's deliberately opened the door to let in the fresh air.

She places tea and toast in front of Ahmed, thinking in order: first steps are clothes, food, medical and emotional.

He's washed and has changed into a navy shirt and pulled baggy trousers over his cast. They look too big on him and it makes him appear even more vulnerable.

'I'll take you shopping later,' Femi says. 'But at least they're clean.'

Ahmed nods.

'I'll wash your clothes after breakfast if you bring them down to me.'

'Yes.' He flicks his fringe away from his deep-set tired eyes.

'There's peanut butter, Marmite and marmalade. Help yourself.'

This time Femi has a chance to study him. He's delicate, gentle and slow moving. He's thoughtful and he seems to look at everything as if seeing it for the first time. His mouth is wide but his face is gaunt with hollow eyes underlined by deep dark circles. He pushes his thick heavy fringe across his forehead again and his eyelashes flicker. A woman would envy those lashes, thinks Femi.

'You slept well?' Femi smiles. 'I looked in on you a few times.'

'Sorry. I didn't hear.' His English is halting but faultless.

Femi shakes her head. 'Don't apologise. You needed rest. Sleep is good for you.'

He seems reluctant to eat, so Femi grabs a plate for herself, butters toast and adds a layer of peanut butter. Her diet would start tomorrow.

She speaks with her mouth full. 'This is probably a lot for you to take in, so please ask me anything and don't ever be afraid to speak to me. I'm here to help you.'

Ahmed copies her and he spreads peanut butter on his toast.

Femi continues, 'I'm a foster mother and I already have two boys living with me. Albert is thirteen and Ricky is seventeen. They have gone to school now but you will meet them later.' Femi chews her toast giving him a chance to say something but he doesn't say anything, so she continues, 'I don't know if you remember what Peter told you yesterday but you are an unaccompanied asylum-seeking child — a UASC. This means that you have been separated from your parents or those people looking after you and, while your papers are being processed here in England by the authorities, you are cared for by the local authority. The council take parental responsibility for you.'

Ahmed eats slowly. He watches her but doesn't reply.

'I'm employed by the council to look after you and you will stay here. I will help you organise your paperwork and get you a phone and SIM card, buy you clothes and look after you. I'll also arrange a medical check up and we can make sure that your ankle is healing.'

He nods.

'You have been allocated a child social worker. Her name is Lily, and she will help look after you. She will also help you settle in. Does that make sense?'

'Yes.'

'I believe you are fifteen. When you are sixteen we can work with KRAN - The Kent Refugee Action Network, they are an independent charity that helps refugees. They aim to provide safe, positive space and they support asylum seekers to succeed.'

Ahmed nods. 'Soon.'

'Soon?'

'Soon I am sixteen.'

'I think your English is very good.' She smiles. "Where did you learn it?"

'At school.'

'In Syria?'

'Yes.'

'Aleppo?' she asks.

His face darkens.

'Ahmed, I'm sorry but I will have to ask you some difficult questions and this is only because I want to help you. Is there anyone you know, anyone who *you trust*, who I can contact?'

Ahmed frowns.

'Can I let anyone in your family or any friends know you're safe?'

Ahmed shakes his head. 'Maybe.'

'Family?'

He scratches his forehead. 'An uncle but I don't know…'

Femi waits patiently. She knows she must listen. She must listen to everything the child will tell you, if you don't listen to the small stuff now, they won't tell you the big stuff later.

'It was a long time ago,' he adds.

'When did you leave?'

'I think, maybe fourteen months.'

He was so young when he left on his own. 'We can try and find your uncle,' she says optimistically.

He shakes his head and tears well-up in his eyes so she changes the subject.

'Don't worry now, but give it some thought. We need to sort out your paperwork and get you a phone. Perhaps a little later we might go to the beach? What do you think?'

Suddenly she feels completely insensitive. Ahmed has spent hours on a small boat crossing the English Channel, the beach is probably the last place he would feel safe. Femi chides herself for her own thoughtlessness. She'll have to be more careful in future.

'Cake,' he says.

'You want some fruit cake?'

Ahmed nods.

* * *

A week later Femi is leaving the house and the new neighbour is having a big delivery of furniture. She smiles and waves but the hippy with the beard, barely looks at her as he helps two other men unload the van.

She's reversing her car into the street when there's a sudden shout and she brakes quickly.

'Mind!' The hippy picks up a box. 'You almost ran it over.'

She winds down the window. 'Sorry, but I—'

He scowls at her and turns away. Femi hasn't seen anyone else yet, no woman in the house and certainly no children. It's a shame. It would have done Albert good to make friends outside of school.

Femi meets Sandra inside Harbour Cafe.

She has wild and unruly lime green hair and round owl-like glasses. 'So, Ahmed's staying in my room, is he?'

'For the time being.'

Sandra has bagged a window table and Karl, the manager, comes over.

'Hello, beautiful ladies.' Karl has Rastafarian hair, a beautiful complexion and a cheeky smile. He's also far younger than them.

'Hi, Karl.' Femi returns his smile. 'How's Molly?'

'Still beautiful and still my girlfriend, so in case you older ladies want to elope with me, you can't. I'm spoken for.' He grins.

'Aw shucks,' Femi teases, as she places her order. 'I'll have to find a plan B.'

Sandra smiles. 'How's Amber doing in the Bistro across the road?' Sandra nods her green head in the direction of the street. 'That building was such a mess. Do you remember there was a big to do about it last year because the woman who used to run The Ship wanted to turn it into an amusement arcade?'

Karl interrupts, 'Yeah, thank goodness Amber bought it. She's renovated it now and she's got a top chef.'

'I've never eaten there,' Femi says wistfully.

'We must go sometime. A latte and a scone for me, please.'

'I'm on a diet. I want to lose 5 kilos before Christmas. Just black coffee and a scone for me too, please Karl.'

'You're beautiful, Femi. No need for that sort of talk in here. No one needs to lose weight.' Karl takes their menus and flaunts across the room. Femi howls with laughter and Sandra grins.

When Femi first began fostering six years ago, Sandra was her social worker. Social workers can't be your friend but when Sandra moved on to work in the private sector they carried on meeting up and developed a firm friendship. Sandra is also Femi's relief worker who stands in when Femi goes away; on holiday or on a training course. She's very knowledgeable and because of her vast experience Femi doesn't mind that she still insists on explaining most things to her.

'So, tell me about Ahmed,' Sandra urges and Femi brings her up to date just as Karl returns and places their coffee and scones on the table.

Femi says, 'He's exhausted. I've bought some clothes for him online as he didn't want to go shopping with his leg in plaster. He has a phone now and— '

'Where is he?'

'He's sleeping. He spends most of his time in his room. He's still a teenager.' Femi grins.

'When young asylum seekers arrive in the UK, they check their ages and they go into a holding centre until their age is assessed. Most of the Pakistanis, Sudanese, Albanians and Afghanis have no passport or birth certificate. The Afghanis don't even register a child's birth as it's not a culturally important date.'

'Syria is different,' Femi says. 'Before the war, he told me that it was a very educated country and all the kids there went to school. There was massive infrastructure like in Germany.'

'It's decimated now.' Sandra shakes her head in exasperation.

'He's struggling to come to terms with everything.'

'Well, you know about Maslow's Triangle,' Sandra says in her abrupt, no nonsense manner and Femi is occasionally taken aback by how strident her friend can be, to the point of being very bossy.

'Do you remember from the course?' Sandra insists, watching Femi who is busy scraping out her pot of cream to put on her scone. 'For heaven's sake, Femi. It's the cream first and then the jam.'

'I prefer jam first.' Feeling rebellious, Femi smiles. 'And, yes, I remember, there are five stages of the triangle: Physiological like breathing, food, water, sleep, excretion and sex. Then Safety; security of your body, a job, family, morality. Then there's Love and Belonging; family, friendship—'

'You don't have to list them all.'

'I want to,' Femi replies, biting into the scone. She wipes cream from her chin and giggles. When she's finished her mouthful she says, 'The last two stages are Esteem and Self-actualisation.'

Sandra nods seriously. 'That's why you've done so well with Albert and Ricky. You've helped them with their self-esteem and their confidence. They've developed respect, and,' she pauses dramatically, 'they have problem-solving skills, lack of prejudice and have established morality.'

Femi shakes her head. 'I just don't want *their* foundations to be shaken.'

'They won't,' Sandra says confidently. 'They have different traumas. Have you managed to get Ahmed to open up at all yet?'

'Not really. The first few days he was so exhausted he slept most to the time but he's staying with me for a little longer now.'

'Good.'

'But it's been difficult because Albert's father let him down again last Saturday but he's promised he's coming tomorrow to see him.'

'Delroy didn't turn up?' Sandra asks.

'No. He messaged Albert on Saturday morning to say things hadn't worked out as he'd expected. Albert was gutted.'

Sandra shakes her head. She'd seen it all before.

'He got really angry and there was an episode at school and he threw his book across the room, then shouted at Mrs Grey and stormed out.' Femi sighs remembering how she'd left work early and gone to speak to his teacher. 'Poor Albert. It's not fair Delroy putting him through this.'

'He's Albert's father.'

'I know but it isn't easy dealing with the fallout when he continually messes up.'

'Did Jamie speak to Delroy? It's up to him to sort it out.'

Sandra finishes her scone and wipes crumbs from her mouth with a serviette. Sandra knows Jamie, they have worked together before.

'He spoke to Delroy and said that it wasn't acceptable and told him Albert was upset. Delroy apparently told Albert he was at an important interview and now, supposedly he's got a job in a garage. Jamie thinks this job might sort him out. It's the opportunity he's been looking for—'

'Does Delroy want Albert to live with him?'

'Jamie says that's his plan. I think Delroy will have to be in the job for a while, certainly until he's more settled, can evidence his stability and arrangements can be made.'

Sandra stares at her friend. She's aware of the difficulties of foster carers and she knows that they need looking after sometimes as much as the children. It's hard to care for a child and then have to let them go. The emotion can be huge. The sense of loss can be devastating.

Sandra says softly, 'You know that if Albert goes to live with his father and it doesn't work out then Albert could be put back in foster care somewhere else.'

'I know.' Femi stares out of the window at the busy street. Standing in the doorway of the art gallery across the road she recognises Ben Taylor, the handsome owner. He's chatting to Eva from the flower shop next door and Femi is happy to be distracted for a while. She watches them laugh together.

Sandra exhales with a sigh of resignation. 'Albert is also starting his teenage years and we both know the statistics for that, don't we, Femi?'

Femi glances at her. 'Let's not be too glum.'

'One third of people currently in prison have come from the care system,' Sandra announces. 'We've failed them,

Femi. At sixteen they can end up in these squalid places with undesirables and they never stand a chance. These places are often ripe with paedophiles praying on them. Many of them haven't got the basics to cope; they don't have the education, the opportunities or the survival techniques. They haven't got a clue how to live or survive on their own. The government really doesn't care for the vulnerable members of our society, Femi. These children are more at risk and exposed than anyone else. They are the hardest hit and suffer the most. Our care services are disastrous.'

'It's the same as the NHS with doctors and nurses,' Femi adds. 'They are seriously underfunded, often badly organised and there's not enough staff and those who do work in it are paid a low wage. This has been going on for decades.'

'There is a chronic lack of funding for our social services and with the closing of Sure Start — our situation is drastic.'

'We can only do our best.' Femi glances out of the window. This is an old familiar bug bear that they have discussed for many years and it never improves. The only thing it does, is to make Sandra angry and fill Femi with despair.

'How does Ricky get on with Ahmed?' Sandra asks quietly, her good temper suddenly restored.

Femi shrugs. 'Fine. The boys all do their own thing. Albert spends most of his time in his bedroom reading and only wants to play computer games. Ricky is out at football practice and badminton and then on Friday and Saturday nights, he washes dishes at the local pub.'

'You've told Jenny?'

'Yes, it does him good to earn some pocket money — then Ahmed sleeps all the time.' Femi casts her hands wide. 'That's boy for you.'

'Does he have any hobbies?

'He said he likes photography. When his leg is better, he says he wants to move to London.'

Sandra smiles. 'Of course, where the streets are paved in gold.'

'That's what Ricky told him.'

'Deliberately?'

Femi shrugs.

Sandra adds, 'You'll have to watch that, Femi. Make sure Ricky doesn't mislead Ahmed because he wants him out of the picture. Ricky can be quite protective of you.'

'Not me, but maybe his position in the house. He likes to be top-dog.'

'Does he still want to go to University?'

'Yes, and he knows he can stay with me under the 'stay put' scheme while he's doing his A levels. Once he's decided on where he goes to uni, he can stay under the supported lodgings arrangement or he can go into independent living.'

'Housing is provided until he's twenty-one,' Sandra says.

'I know but it isn't always decent, is it? I've explained that he can go to uni and I will help or he will have to get a job.'

'What does he want to study?'

Femi smiles. 'I think he wants to study Sports Science — and maybe even become a teacher.'

* * *

It's Saturday and the first weekend in May. Femi finishes her afternoon shift and when she comes home, it's not yet six o'clock but the house is extraordinarily quiet. She knocks on Ahmed's bedroom door but there's no answer so after tapping again, she opens it and peers inside.

'Hi Ahmed, how are you?'

He's sitting on his bed. 'Fine.'

'If you're not too busy I thought we could give it another go and check to see if we can find your uncle?'

Ahmed shrugs. 'There's no point.'

'I know we've checked Facebook and Instagram but we can try LinkedIn. Didn't you say he was a successful business-man?'

'Maybe.'

'He imported clothes?'

'I think, maybe.'

'Shall we take a look and see if we can find him? He might have news of your family.'

Ahmed rubs his cheek.

Femi continues, 'Come downstairs and we'll make tea? Have you seen Albert?'

'Maybe upstairs.' Ahmed swings his legs off the bed.

'I'll just go check. Will you please go and pop the kettle on?'

Ahmed nods. He walks better now and he swings his leg with the cast down the stairs. He seems to be able to move more easily and Femi has a date in her diary next week to have his cast removed.

Femi goes up to the attic floor and she can hear Albert on his computer. She knocks and then walks in to find him lying on the bed, on his stomach, with his headphones over his ears. She taps his feet and when he turns around taking his headphones off, she smiles.

'Hello stranger.'

'Hi!'

'How did you get on today with your Dad?'

'Fine.'

Femi perches on the side of his bed. 'Did you have a good time.'

'Yes.'

'Where did you eat?'

'Chips.'

'In the shop?'

'On the beach.'

'Wasn't it cold?'

Albert shrugs.

'Do you want to come downstairs, Ahmed and I are having tea?'

'No.'

Femi knows it's not the right time to have a conversation with him and that he will continue gaming.

'You know I'm going out for dinner? Ricky will be here and I've left you some bolognese in the fridge.'

'Okay.'

'Is that alright, with you?'

'Yes.'

'Ahmed will also be here so will you make an effort to speak to him or show him one of your computer games?'

'Yes, Auntie.'

'Thank you. Night, night, and remember to finish your game by nine o'clock. That's curfew for gaming, then you can read a book, remember?'

Albert nods.

'Night then.'

'Night, Auntie.'

She's meeting Freddie and Nitesh for an early dinner in town and she's looking forward to adult company and some fun.

6

Chapter 6

In the kitchen, Ahmed moves round, avoiding Peanut lying on his bed who is half asleep but watching the boy navigate past him. Ahmed walks the long way around the table to get the mugs and then the milk from the fridge so that he doesn't have to pass the dog.

'Let sleeping dogs lie,' Femi says brightly coming into the kitchen.

'He's awake — I think.' Ahmed frowns and looks at the basket.

'It's a saying we have in English, it means to leave things alone and not disturb them. Is that what you would prefer to do?'

Ahmed looks unsure.

'Do you understand what the phrase means?' She smiles.

'Yes.'

'It's rather like your situation with your uncle but I think it's best if we look for him or someone in your family, rather than to leave things as they are, don't you?'

Ahmed's eyes darken and Femi knows he understands but

she must be supportive and try to help him. She has no wish to remind him of his past but it's healthy for him to speak about things when he's ready and she is hoping he will open up to her.

He places a teapot and mugs on the table, and opens the cupboard to lift out the fruit cake. Femi realised early on that this cake was his favourite so now she's added it on her weekly online shopping. He cuts a big wedge. 'You want some?'

'I'm going out for dinner, so I shouldn't really but it does look delicious. Just a small slice,' she says and she doesn't complain when he cuts a piece equally as large as his. Her diet isn't going well. There's always something happening and it's just so hard to lose weight when she's encouraging the boys to eat. She's a natural feeder and that's her comfort zone.

Femi takes a sip of her tea. 'You're getting very good at making English tea, Ahmed. I'm very impressed.'

He gives a shy smile. 'Maybe I work in a restaurant.'

'Would you like that?'

He turns his mouth down. 'I like to photograph.'

'Take pictures? Really?'

'Yes, with my iPhone.'

'What sort of pictures?'

Ahmed reaches into his pocket and pulls out his phone. He scrolls through the pictures and he selects the ones he likes the best and turns his phone to show her.

'These.'

'This is the garden.'

'Swipe them,' he says.

Femi swallows her mouthful and stares at the photos on his phone. They are lovely pictures that he's taken; a tiny ant on the stone path, a spider caught in its silver web, a ray of sunshine on the fence, and one of a blackbird with a pointed yellow beak. 'These are lovely. You have an incredible talent, Ahmed.'

He smiles and takes back his phone. 'I like to take faces.'

'You want to take photographs of people?'

He smiles shyly. 'Maybe.'

'I'll have to see if I can get you a proper camera.'

'Really?'

His face is so animated and he looks so happy that Femi feels she has offered him the world. For some unusual reason, he looks happier to have a camera than he does to find his family. That's very unusual, but Femi is happy to roll with this idea, purely to see the change in him. His shoulders are a little straighter, his eyes a little brighter and, he eats his fruit cake now without shyness.

'That's your favourite cake, isn't it?' Femi smiles.

'I like,' he replies.

He's fitting in to the family and Femi breathes a silent sigh of joy. Everything will be alright. That's when her bleeper goes.

'I have a shout,' she says, standing up. She texts Sandra quickly.

'Shout?'

'An emergency with the RNLI. I have to go. Sandra's phone number is on the fridge but she's on her way over here now.'

As she leaves Ahmed is already cutting another slice of fruit cake.

Five minutes later, when she arrives at the station Nitesh is already in the changing room wearing his woolly bear suit similar to a onesie and is pulling on his dry suit.

He grins at her. 'Thought you weren't coming.'

'You know me, I never like to miss an adventure.' Femi is fast, she's clumsily pushing her feet into steel-plated yellow wellies before grabbing her helmet with its earpiece and radio, and thermal gloves.

'Hi, Jeff,' she calls out to the tractor driver. 'Who's the Helm?' she asks, as they climb into the lifeboat.

'Max.'

'Let's hope it's not too serious.'

'Jetski - someone's in the water.'

Femi secures her life jacket, all thoughts of dinner in town now quickly forgotten. 'A risk of hypothermia,' she mutters. 'Do you remember the last time, we had to ditch the jetski and go back and find it?'

* * *

The following morning is warm and sunny, the magpies, wood pigeons and squirrels are all living in harmony in the trees at the bottom of the garden. There's a deep blue sky and a sliver of a fingernail moon reflected in the sunlight and Femi sighs contentedly. She's happy to sit at the terrace table in the early morning sun, knowing the rest of the day will unfurl at its own pace and, for the first time in a long time, she has nothing urgent to do.

Femi breathes in deeply remembering last night's emergency, crossing the sea in the dark, rain and fog and rescuing a drifting jetski with its exhausted driver. She'd returned home cold and tired but with a sense of satisfaction. After Sandra had gone, she had wondered why she volunteers at the RNLI, why she works in the clinic and why she fosters children but she's come to terms with the fact that she just wants to help people. She wants to solve everyone's problems and make sure that all is well with the world. It's frustrating when it doesn't always work out and sometimes she gets exhausted just from trying.

The shrill sound of a drill and then hammering from the house next door breaks her thought process. She can't see into the garden. Both houses are very private but she hears whistling and it grows louder so the neighbour must be standing on the other side of the fence. It's not a tune she recognises. She wants to call out and say something welcoming but then it stops and a door bangs and he's gone.

Normally on a Sunday, she would take the boys out to a museum or a gallery or perhaps even the zoo but today there's a relaxed atmosphere at home that she doesn't want to upset. Besides, the boys are growing up and taking on new hobbies and interests. Today, Ricky is at a football match, Albert is in his bedroom gaming on his computer, and Ahmed is probably upstairs sleeping so she's content to kick back for a while and she even feels quite guilty that she doesn't want to tidy the garden.

Peanut sits at her feet in the shade, happy after his early walk on the beach, and he stretches contentedly before yawning loudly followed by soft snoring.

A little while later, Ahmed hobbles outside onto the patio.

'Goodness, you're up early, Ahmed. Have you a bus to catch?' She grins.

'Bus?'

'Just an old colloquialism, a silly saying,' she adds.

He smiles but it doesn't reach his eyes.

Peanut stretches and snorts.

'It's peaceful,' Ahmed says, slipping into the chair furthest from Peanut.

'It's perfect.' Femi is happy to sit in companionable silence, drinking her coffee.

Ahmed makes a rectangle with his long fingers and he stretches out his hands as if they're a camera. Femi watches him silently for a few minutes. Both of them engrossed in their own thoughts.

There's banging in the garden on the left and Ahmed flinches as if he's been hit. The neighbour is hammering nails into wood.

'Take no notice,' Femi whispers, 'There's nothing to worry about. He's an old man and he's a bit strange - maybe a hippy.'

'Hippy?'

'A throwback from the sixties.' Femi explains knowing she's not doing a good job. 'Someone with long hair who probably doesn't work. You know, someone who you don't want to get involved with.'

Ahmed whispers back, 'What he do?'

Femi shrugs. 'I don't know. He moved in last week. I've hardly seen him.'

'He likes birds.' Ahmed points to the bird boxes perched in the acacia trees in the next door garden.

Femi looks up. She hadn't noticed the bird houses. 'It's the first time I've sat out here this year.'

'What's that?' Ahmed points to the garage at the bottom of the garden, hidden by overgrown bushes and shrubs.

'It's a garage, where I can keep the car. There's a small driveway round the back of the house that leads to the road.'

'You don't use it?'

'No.'

'Why?'

Femi pauses with her cup at her lips. 'There's lots of boxes in there.'

'Boxes?'

'Stuff from when I moved here?'

'What's stuff?'

Femi feels guilty. She knows that Ahmed arrived with only with the clothes on his back. He owns nothing so it's hard emotionally for her to explain the things she's saved.

He insists. 'What stuff?'

'Things from my past.'

He frowns. 'So much... stuff?' Ahmed flicks his fringe from his eyes.

Femi agrees. 'It must seem like a lot to you.'

'Will we look?' Ahmed stands up. 'Show me?'

Femi swallows hard. It's the last thing she had on her mind today. She really doesn't want to get tangled up in her past. She's not ready for all those memories and certainly not today when she feels so peaceful.

'Come?' Ahmed says excitedly, already hobbling down the path. 'Come, come. Let's see inside.'

* * *

Ahmed ducks under the flourishing and untamed twisted willow that needs cutting back, past the overgrown hedge, a fig tree and a massive rosemary bush. Ahmed is revived and filled with enthusiasm. He pushes the door. 'It's locked.'

'Yes.'

'I break the door?'

'No.' She laughs putting a restraining hand on his arm. 'Steady on, Tom Cruise, there's a key, somewhere.' She fumbles along the ledge on top of the wood and finds the key. She holds it up triumphantly in the air. 'Ta da!'

'You leave the key outside?' He's surprised and he frowns.

Femi can't tell him that she didn't even want the key in the house and if she is honest, a part of her is surprised it's still there.

The padlock is rusty but the key turns and she pushes the door open. It creaks loudly and a rush of cold air escapes past them as if it's been locked up too long and needs to be free.

Femi finds a discarded rock in the garden and props open the door and warm sunlight floods into the dusty, old garage

'Wow!' Ahmed whispers, peering inside.

Femi wipes a cobweb from her face and is about to step inside when Ahmed puts his hand on her shoulder and then pulls his iPhone from his pocket. 'I have light,' he says, moving quickly past her. 'This is—'

'Careful,' she cautions, standing behind him, in the doorway, looking over his shoulder.

'So many...,' he whispers.

She had forgotten how many boxes she had and now she couldn't possibly imagine what is inside them all. How could she have so many memories all boxed up and hidden at the bottom of the garden?

'And this?' Ahmed bends to pull at a cloth and, as it falls to the floor, spiders scatter and dust fills the air. He coughs and covers his mouth and nose with the back of his arm. He crouches down and hunches over the boxes, removing and wiping dust with his hands. 'They have names.'

'I labelled them.'

Leaning against the wall are copies of a few old paintings and he carries one to the door, lifts it up and tilts it toward the natural light.

'Picture?'

When he looks at Femi, he sees her eyes are filled with tears — but he doesn't yet know if they are happy or sad ones.

She picks up the smaller one from the floor and brushes off the dust with her sleeve, quietly looking at it as if for the first time, seeing the details of the country scene.

'You paint it?'

'It's *The Haywain*.' Femi's laugh echoes in the close confides of the dusty garage. 'John Constable — he's a very famous artist.'

'And this?' He asks holding a portrait in his hands.

'That is Frieda Khalo.' Femi remembers it hanging on the wall in her last home. 'She's one of my favourite artists.'

Ahmed isn't listening. He's already disappeared back into the garage and he's busy hauling out a big box, dragging it across the concrete floor.

'More,' he exclaims delightedly as if he's just stepped into Aladdin's cave. 'There's many more.'

Torn between his excitement and her own curiosity, Femi crouches down beside Ahmed as he taps the top of the box.

'We open? Let's put outside.'

Femi watches him, surprised by his strength and determination.

'We can't. We need scissors.'

'I have.' Ahmed pulls a penknife from his pocket and Femi blinks wondering where he'd kept that hidden. He rips the brown masking tape and pulls off the lid in one easy movement and Femi is suddenly confronted by her past. She gasps and covers her mouth. There are photographs, books, notebooks, diaries and something wrapped partly in yellow tissue paper.

'This?' asks Ahmed lifting it carefully in his delicate hands. 'What is this?'

Femi takes it from him. Her throat has seized up and she cannot speak, she cannot swallow. She can't do anything except try to quell the emotional tsunami rising in her stomach. Her eyes burn, her bottom lip quivers and she feels she's ten years old again. There's suddenly an overwhelming, lurching sense of loss, a void so deep, a depth so profound that she's suddenly frightened of falling... falling so fast and deeply that—

'You okay?'

She nods.

'I take it back? I hide it.'

But Femi won't let the package go. 'No!' She clutches it to her chest remembering her father, and how he had returned from Jamaica with these two small dolls. They were a present for her, a special gift.

She remembers his husky voice, 'These are for you, my beautiful daughter. They will always remind you of your heritage and, one day, I will take you there. We will go together and you will meet all your aunties and family.'

A few months later he was dead.

Tears begin to roll down her cheeks, and she wipes them away as quickly as the memories rush over her in waves. Then suddenly she's frantic. She pulls at the tissue paper and unwraps two five-inch vintage Jamaican figurine dolls mounted on a small slice of wood. They wear colourful native clothes; one a faded yellow bandana and the other a faded yellow scarf. The boy carries a broom and the girl's skirt is torn. They are folk art and a souvenir from her father. They were his last gift to her.

Femi lifts the torn hem of the girl's skirt and sees the scar on the doll's thigh, scored there many, many years ago when she was a small girl, in a different life. So many memories, tumbling together, engulfing her.

Ahmed places his fingers on Femi's hand. His touch is light, his fingers cool.

'Okay?'

Femi's brown eyes meets his worried hypnotic and tired-gaze. This poor boy, standing beside her, has been through so much, and she feels guilty for displaying these complex emotions. Her past has been traumatic and sad but there was no comparison to his suffering— most of which he can't or refuses to talk about.

Pain. Heartache. Sadness.

She clutches the dolls to her chest. There's an abundance of wild emotions between them, yet somehow, Femi feels a sense of strength and power. She could make a difference. She would help him heal — just as she had helped Ricky and Albert, and they could all grow stronger together. She will fight for them all. She will fight for justice and for what is right.

'Hey!' A man's voice calls out and she turns quickly.

A head appears and the neighbour leans his bare arms on the fence. 'You're not going to chop down that twisted willow, are you? Robins have nested in there.'

Femi straightens her back. 'Pardon?'

The hippy neighbour has a long tangled beard and it covers half of his face, the other half is covered by a cap over his eyes. 'I didn't see you. I thought the boy was alone.'

'This is my garden.'

'Well, the branches hang over in my garden and robins have nested.' He points up and Femi follows the direction of his finger. 'You can't disturb them.'

Femi knows it's her garden and he's a new neighbour but she feels the strength suddenly drain from her and the powerful resolution from a few moments ago dwindles. As she grips the dolls in her hands, her resolution falters as she whispers, 'I won't touch the tree.'

7

Chapter 7

Ricky is tired when he gets home. After three hours of washing up in the pub, he's been on his feet, watching everything and trying to learn. He can't wait to be eighteen, he wants to know how to work professionally behind a bar; making cocktails — and everything. Paul, the manager says he might give him a job during the holidays but not behind the bar until he's eighteen. The time can't come quickly enough and Ricky can't wait to earn more money. He wants to be independent. He wants to buy a new cricket bat for the summer season and there's a cricket sweater on eBay that's cheaper than he's ever seen. It's a bargain. He's eager to check his savings to see if he's got enough.

It's just after ten o'clock when he leaves his bike propped up against the back wall, and goes in through the utility room, kicking off his stinking trainers. His feet are hot and sweaty. He'd ask Auntie to get more of that foot smelling stuff that made his feet better.

Peanut wanders in from the lounge to find him standing with the fridge door open, drinking orange juice thirstily from the carton.

'Hello, mate. Don't tell anyone. Our secret.' Ricky wipes his lips on his arm and bends to rub his head. That's when he notices eight large boxes all stacked up in the corner of the kitchen. 'What's that? Where did they come from? Where is everyone?' he asks but Peanut doesn't answer, instead he wanders off in the direction of the living room and Ricky follows him.

He's surprised to find Auntie and Ahmed sitting on the sofa and watching television together.

'Hello, Ricky, did you have a good evening?' Femi smiles.

'What's this?' He nods at the TV screen.

'It's a documentary,' she replies. Ahmed seems engrossed and he doesn't look up. 'It's a David Attenborough documentary. You want to sit with us?'

Ricky shakes his head.

'There's toast and milk in the kitchen. I've also saved you some meatballs.'

'Halal?' asks Ricky.

'Yes.'

'I'll make an omelette.' He returns to the kitchen.

Femi follows him.

'What's this?' he asks. 'Why are these boxes here?'

'They're from the garage.'

'From the garden?'

'Yes.'

'Why?' Ricky reaches for the eggs.

'I've decided to clean it out.'

'What for?'

'I think it would be good for Ahmed to have a studio for his photography.'

Ricky turns to stare at her and his mouth hangs open.

Femi continues speaking, 'They're still processing his paperwork and so he probably won't go to school this term and—'

'School?'

'Yes, he's fifteen, he has to go to school and continue with his education so this will give him a point of focus. It will give him something to do every day. Especially during the summer.'

'He's staying?'

'Yes, for a while longer.'

Ricky moves around her, making toast, pouring milk and beating eggs saying nothing but Femi feels as though she can hear his brain whirling and the tension building. She continues, 'I think it will be good for him. It will occupy his mind and he will have something to focus on — something positive. I've found an old camera in the garage and I've managed to get some old photographic equipment from eBay so he can develop his own photographs.'

'No one does that any more. Why can't he go to Tesco's like everyone else?'

'Because this is more fun. I remember watching my Dad develop photographs. We had a dark room for a while at home and it was great fun to see the images coming to life in front you.'

Ricky stares at her.

Femi reaches for a biscuit and says patiently, 'It's the process, Ricky. It's the fun of waiting for the photograph appear — to be developed right in front of your eyes. It's like magic.'

Ricky pours the eggs into the pan. 'It's stupid.'

'It's interesting for Ahmed. He likes photography and I think he'll be good at it.'

'He should play football.'

'Not everyone likes sport and Ahmed is different.'

'At least you've worked that one out,' Ricky mutters.

'What do you mean?' Femi stands closer to him. Challenging what he has said, she insists, 'Ricky, there is no prejudice in this house, remember that. Everyone can be who they want to be. Remember how Albert was bullied at school?'

Ricky doesn't look up.

'Do you? Well, there will be no bullying, jealousy or anger in this house. You are all my boys and I will treat you all equally. You know that.'

Ricky flips the omelette.

Femi whispers, 'Please don't be jealous, Ricky. You know Ahmed arrived with nothing but the clothes on his back. He's lost everything. He's seen his family killed in front of his eyes and he's watched his country bombed and destroyed. He's traumatised.'

'Why didn't he stay to fight?' Ricky tilts his chin at her. 'I would have.'

'He's only a boy.'

'I would have stayed.'

'I'm sixteen now,' Ahmed stands in the doorway. His face is dark and tense.

'When was your birthday?' Femi moves toward him trying to dispel the angry atmosphere in the room with a cheerful voice. 'You didn't tell me.'

Ahmed shrugs but he stares at Ricky with unashamed hatred.

Femi continues speaking using a calming voice, 'Ricky,

Ahmed is only a year younger than you now. Look, why don't you two go to the cinema together. Get to know each other and become friends? It would be great if you could get along and get to know each other properly. What do you say?' Femi reaches for her purse and frowns. She'd taken out a hundred pounds from the cashpoint and now there's only sixty in her purse. She counts the three twenty-pound notes. Money has never gone missing from her purse or her home before.

'What's wrong?' asks Ricky.

'Nothing. Please, Ricky. Take Ahmed to the cinema tomorrow and I'll pay.' She hands him twenty pounds.

Ricky pockets the money and tips his omelette onto his plate. 'I'm eating this upstairs in my room.'

* * *

The next day, after Ricky and Albert come home from school, Sandra now with electric blue hair, Freddie in a bow tie and Nitesh in an old sweater, arrive in a swirl of excitement. They all gather in the kitchen and there's an air of anticipation as they take off their jackets and make a fuss over Peanut.

'Ahmed is in the garage, he's sweeping it out,' Femi tells them, 'but I'll text him now you're all here.'

'Is that why he has a SIM card?' Freddie laughs.

'Of course.' Femi smiles and sends a quick text to Ahmed.

Can you come to the kitchen, please?

He replies: *Now?*

Yes. Immediately!

'Is that really how you communicate?' Nitesh laughs, looking over her shoulder.

'It's easier than me trekking down to the bottom of the

garden.'

'It would be good exercise,' Albert says.

'What's happening?' Ricky asks impatiently, coming into the kitchen after changing out of his school clothes. It's one of the only nights he doesn't have any sports activities on after school or not working in The Ship, and he's mildly irritated. He had been asked to take Ahmed to the cinema and now everyone's gathering in the kitchen perhaps this will be a good excuse not to go to the cinema with Ahmed.

'It's a surprise,' Femi says.

'Surprise about what?' Ricky greets Sandra with a smile. 'Nice hair, is there a colour you haven't used yet?'

'She's going through the whole rainbow, at our request, aren't you sweetie?' Freddie says.

'What's going on, Auntie?' Ricky asks. 'What's all the fuss about?'

'I know.' Albert grins. 'I know, don't I, Auntie?'

'Well tell me, you idiot.'

'No name calling,' Femi admonishes.

Albert digs Ricky in the ribs. 'Yeah, be nice.'

'I'm always nice to you.' Ricky nudges him back.

Femi smiles. 'Do you want to get it out, Al?'

Albert goes over to the fridge and very carefully he pulls out a large chocolate cake. He balances it in his hands and places it carefully on the table while Femi pulls plates, knives and napkins from the drawer.

'Where are the candles?' Albert asks excitedly.

Femi hands him a box of candles and he begins to insert them into the top of the cake, counting sixteen.

'Birthday cake?' asks Ricky.

'It was Ahmed's birthday last week and he didn't tell us, so

I thought it would be nice if we celebrated with him.'

'Why? His birthday has gone now.'

'Don't be miserable,' Sandra chides him, she nudges his elbow. 'Besides, I happen to know that chocolate cake is also your favourite, isn't that what you always ask for?'

Ricky gives her a slight smile. 'Maybe.'

'Well then, be kind to Ahmed.'

'It's a good excuse for cake,' Nitesh declares, patting his flat stomach.

'He's coming. He's coming,' Albert whispers excitedly spying Ahmed approaching through the kitchen window. 'Let me light them.'

Ahmed is surprised to see so many people gathered in the kitchen. He stands for a moment in the doorway wondering if he's done something wrong and why are they all staring at him? It's not just Auntie and Albert but Ricky looks like he could kill him. They were supposed to be going to the cinema together and Ahmed was dreading it. Now, he recognises Sandra — Femi's best friend, and the two men. He remembers Freddie works at the clinic but can't remember his husband's name. Ahmed wants to run. There's a sense of expectation in the air and he's suddenly scared. He feels a sense of panic rising in his chest, the helplessness of his situation, caught in a trap, the familiar fear of judgement, what will they do to him?

Suddenly, they all start to sing.

'Happy birthday to you...'

Albert points to the table and Ahmed sees a massive chocolate cake, bigger than anything he's ever seen before and it's on fire, but it's not really. He looks closer, they're candles on top and the flames are flickering and it looks so pretty just like ones he's seen on television, in the films, when there are happy families and no war and everyone is laughing and celebrating and clapping. He stands still, unable to move. He can't speak. Why are they doing this?

'Happy birthday, dear Ahmed…'

He looks around at them all; he's met Sandra and Freddie and Nitesh before, once or twice, and they're alright. They don't ask him many things and they're friendly and they seem kind but now, to his utter amazement, they're smiling at him. Albert is singing heartily but Femi is singing the loudest in her church voice. Even Ricky's lips are moving and then suddenly the song is over and they're all clapping and they seem to be waiting for him.

Ahmed stares at Freddie. He looks so out of place in red trousers and a multicoloured striped shirt and a bow tie.

'It is a little camp, darling but I do love these colours.' Freddie tugs on the lapel of his shirt.

'Blow them out.' Albert pulls Ahmed forward and into the kitchen nearer the counter. 'It's your birthday cake. You have to blow out the candles. Quickly.'

Ahmed doesn't know what to do. He's never had a cake before and he's suddenly overwhelmed. He feels as though he's going to cry and his eyes begin to burn. He's flooded with a memory, an old one, from his past life: his mother and sister, and of a birthday when he was very, very small. Then there's another fragmented memory, in a camp he can barely remember and he's trying to grasp at it, trying to remember faces but it evades him and then Albert is dancing in front of him.

'Come on, Ahmed. Blow them out!' Albert pulls on his shirt sleeve and pushes him closer to the table. 'This is for you.'

Albert claps his hands, he's so happy and excited and Ahmed feels tears fall and he doesn't understand why he's crying. He's happy to be here with this lovely family and these kind people but he's frightened to say anything. He can't blow out the candles. He hasn't got the breath. His chest is tight and feels taut in his stiff body but then he feels Femi's warm reassuring hand on his shoulder.

'It's alright,' she says softly. 'But if you don't blow them out, Albert will.'

He rubs his eyes with his sleeve.

They all laugh but it's kind laughter and Ahmed doesn't know what to do and then suddenly he's wrapped his arms around Auntie's waist and his head is buried in her warm soft bosom and all he can hear is the sound of his own sobbing. It sounds so deep, guttural and wretched that he wonders if there's an injured animal that's found its way into the house.

Femi wraps Ahmed in a big hug. She rubs his back reassuringly and waits for his body to stop convulsing in wretched tears. She can't imagine his sadness, his conflicted emotions and his deep-seated trauma. All she can do is hold him and she leans down and kisses the top of his head.

Ahmed slowly pulls away and wipes his eyes. 'Sorry,' he says but he's smiling though his tears.

'Nonsense, we all understand, don't we?' Femi asks.

'I've started crying on my birthdays too,' says Freddie. 'They come around far too quickly.'

'You're such a drama queen,' replies Sandra.

'Ready to blow out the candles?' Nitesh asks.

Ahmed nods and gets ready to blow out the candles. 'I've never had a birthday cake,' he whispers.

'Well, it's tradition in this house, isn't it boys?' Femi smiles.

'Yes,' squeals Albert waving the cake slice in the air.

Sandra nudges Ricky. 'You love birthday cake, I know you do.'

He replies grudgingly and with a smile, 'Yeah, you're right.'

'You can make a wish,' Albert says, 'but don't tell us what it is, or it won't come true.'

Ahmed looks at Femi. 'Is that true?'

She nods encouragingly. 'Make a wish as you blow them out.'

Ahmed closes his eyes.

Goodness, thinks Sandra, his eyelashes are amazing. 'What I wouldn't give for eyelashes like those,' she mumbles.

Albert hops excitedly from one foot to the other wishing Ahmed would hurry up and Ricky sighs, he's confused and annoyed.

Why is this new boy getting so much attention?

Femi claps her hands excitedly. Her diet would have to start tomorrow. 'Let's cut the cake then, Ahmed. Come on, before Albert decides to scoff the whole lot by himself.'

* * *

The following week all the boys have finally gone to the cinema. They have gone to see the new Tom Cruise movie that's getting rave reviews and Femi has asked Freddie over to keep her company at home. Freddie has dyed his hair white blond. He's wearing a mustard-coloured shirt and navy chinos.

'Sandra, persuaded me,' he says. 'So, I did it last night when I got home.'

'What does Nitesh think?'

'He wants a divorce.' He laughs. 'No, really. He doesn't like it. He says it ages me.'

They're sharing a bottle of New Zealand Sauvignon Blanc at the kitchen table. The terrace door is open and although it's a lovely evening the wind makes it too cold to sit outside.

'So, how's it all going?' he asks, watching her take a handful of salted crisps.

'Do you mean my day, my diet, with the boys, or generally in my chaotic life.'

'Oh, you're snappy today, you do need a break. What's wrong?'

Femi sighs. 'I'm tired, sorry.'

'Well, the boys have all gone to the cinema tonight, so that's a result.'

'That took some persuasion, I can tell you. It's taken over a week to get them to go together.'

'Problems with Albert?'

'Actually, no. He seems much happier. He saw his father again last weekend.'

'That's good.'

Femi raises her eyes to the ceiling. 'It will be if Delroy can sustain it.'

Freddie nods and sips his wine. 'So, these boxes are still in the kitchen, what's this all about?'

'They're from the garage—'

'I know. All your memories.'

'Ahmed is going to use the garage as photographic studio. I've found him some developing equipment on eBay. Will you help me carry it down later?'

'Of course, and that's wonderful, Femi. So, are these boxes staying here forever?'

'No, I need to go through them but it will dredge up my past and I'm dreading it. I'm not ready to go through them all yet.'

'Well, then, don't put yourself though it all, Femi. It's not worth it. The past is the past and you must concentrate on the future. Is that what's bothering you? Is that why you're like a demon?'

Femi shakes her head. 'I don't know. There's this under-current all the time. I feel that Ahmed and Ricky don't get on and there's this tension simmering between them. I'm also frightened that Albert's father will let him down again and that everything will go pear-shaped and he'll have another episode—'

'And?'

'And Ahmed rarely speaks. He doesn't seem to want to find his family and he doesn't want to talk about his past — and to be honest, I don't blame him.'

Freddie sighs.

'The only emotion he's shown was when we gave him his birthday cake.' Femi sips her wine and reaches for the cashew nuts. 'But I also have another more worrying problem. Money has gone missing from my purse twice.'

'Ah, that's serious.'

'After the first time I asked the boys and they all thought I blamed them but I didn't. I know something isn't right.'

'Nothing like this ever happened before Ahmed arrived, did it?'

'No, but then Ahmed doesn't go anywhere. He doesn't need money. This is his first outing since the cast came off his foot. I've always paid for everything.'

Freddie sighs. 'It's a difficult situation.'

'Well, there's a procedure to follow. The last time I filled in my diary record and I spoke to Peter. Then I spoke to each child individually with their child social worker — and all of them deny any knowledge of taking money.' She sighs. 'It's just that it creates this awful tension on top of the resentment Ricky already feels for Ahmed. It's like an underlying jealousy although I try to spend time with Ricky. I even went and watched his football game last Saturday in the pouring rain.'

'Did he win?'

Femi shakes her head. 'He didn't play well and he was furious with himself, so there was all that to contend with as well.'

'He's a teenager. I was a nightmare at that age too. Imagine, knowing you're gay but not able to tell anyone.'

'That must have been awful for you.'

Freddie shrugs. 'It's in the past but it wasn't easy. Luckily when I did tell my parents they said they already knew. You can't always hide these things.'

'Not when you're so camp, I suppose.' Femi smiles.

'Umm, that was a bit of a giveaway,' Freddie throws his head back in laughter. 'But I was lucky I had them to speak to, especially after my break up with Graham before I met Nitesh. I was suicidal.'

Femi reaches over and pats his hand. 'Everyone has a story and when everything else is stripped away, it's kindness that's the most important thing.'

'You're kind to your boys. I know that and I saw Ahmed's reaction to the cake.'

'Do you think he could be gay?' Femi asks.

Freddie shrugs. 'He's a delicate boy.'

'He's come a long way, travelling on his own,' Femi says, 'He's been subjected to all sorts of abuse that he doesn't talk about, and I can't seem to get him to open up.'

'Everything takes time.'

'He needs friends and someone to talk to.'

'Remember how Ricky was when he first came here? He ran away more times in the first three months than I can remember and you were beside yourself.'

'But he always came back.' Femi picks up the bottle to refill the glasses but Freddie covers his. 'Not for me. I have an early start tomorrow, let's take these boxes you've bought Ahmed, down to the garage.'

Femi smiles. 'Studio, darling, photographic studio.'

8

Chapter 8

On Saturday morning, after Ricky has gone to football and Albert has gone to meet his father, Femi wanders down to the studio. She was called out on an emergency early this morning with the RNLI to one of the fishing boats. One of the crew had suffered a heart-attack. It had been a difficult rescue as the sea had been particularly rough. Fortunately, after several minutes of securing the boat she'd managed to climb onboard and made the fisherman's condition stable. They had managed to get him ashore to the hospital and she's pleased to have been the one on board who was trained as a paramedic. It was difficult climbing from the lifeboat to the fishing vessel. She had managed it but not without difficulty. She needed to lose weight or one of these days she wouldn't have the strength to haul herself over the side of the boat.

Femi takes her time in the garden, stopping to admire her flowers and the changes she's made by cutting back the rosemary, fig tree and willow. It's the first week in June and the purple clematis is flowering, the poppies have burst and their petals are bright red in the sunshine and the Acacia tree is in full bloom. She must cut the grass this week, it hasn't been done for three weeks as she's been working a few extra shifts at the clinic while one of her colleagues is on holiday. She should remind Ricky to do it. She checks the cable running from her house to the studio and she must think about getting a proper electrician to sort out the power so that it's more permanent.

The studio door is open.

'Can I come in?' she calls out.

'Yes.' Ahmed's voice is quiet.

She pokes her head around the door and blinks in the darkness. 'How's it going? Have you set everything up?'

'I think so.'

'Was it difficult?'

'No.'

It takes a while for Femi's eyes to adjust to the darkness. There's a small lamp in the far corner and he has trays and bottles of chemicals lined up on the shelf. He seems to know what he's doing and Femi's impressed. It reminds her of how her father had organised himself.

'I've bought you some clothesline for your photos as they dry.'

'Thank you.'

'And, here are a couple more plastic trays, and a roll of paper towels.'

He takes them from her and while he looks for somewhere to put everything, Femi looks around admiring the photographs that Ahmed has already pinned to the wooden walls. She's surprised and pleased that he's taken so many, lots of the garden; flowers, a small beetle, a bumble bee and then she spies a familiar face.

'Goodness, you've taken one of Albert, how lovely.' She moves closer noticing how Albert seems quite self-conscious. He's sitting on the grass holding Peanut in his arms. Ahmed has caught that uncertain smile that Albert has when he's supposed to do something but doesn't always get it right. It's almost an apologetic smile.

Femi smiles. That's a considerable improvement in Ahmed's relationship with Peanut. Normally they both avoid each other but to see Peanut in the picture with Albert, warms her heart. He looks happy and Femi realises that converting the garage was the best thing she's done for him.

'I think you're good at portraits,' she says. 'You should take more.'

'Can I take yours?'

'You can when I've lost 5 kilos—' She stops. 'What the—? Who—'

There's a picture of a grizzly-looking man staring at her. He's leaning his tanned and well-muscled arms on top of the fence. His chin is resting on his wrist and although is face is covered in a cap, sunglasses and long beard, he's staring straight at the camera and when Femi peers closer, she knows it's the hippy neighbour.

'How did you get this?' she asks.

'He often leans over the fence.'

'Why?'

'He likes to talk.'

'Why does he talk to you?'

Ahmed shrugs. 'Maybe he has no friends.'

'What do you speak about?'

'The garden and the birds that are nesting.' Ahmed replies. 'All sorts of stuff.'

Now, she experiences a sudden swell of fear. The neighbour has access to her vulnerable boy. Femi wonders what they talk about and just how much contact they are having at the bottom of her garden.

* * *

It's late afternoon and Femi is waiting for Albert to come home after another visit with his father. She's cleaned the house and changed the sheets on her bed and vacuumed the kitchen. These visits are now happening weekly and Albert seems very confident and mature about the growing relationship with his father.

Although Femi is happy for him, she can feel a distance growing between them that wasn't there before. She assumes it's because he's now transferring his emotions onto his father and although that makes her sad, she understands how this will all play out in the long term. She must prepare herself for the inevitable.

The back-door bangs and Ricky strides in dumping his football bag on the floor.

'Hi, did you win? How was it?' Femi tries to engage him in conversation but he doesn't reply. Ricky's mood is foul so she leaves him to go upstairs and shower.

Ahmed wanders in from the garden. He's spent the afternoon in the studio. His foot is now much better and there's barely a sign of a limp.

'Perhaps I cook tonight?' he says, 'I make your bolognese recipe?'

'I was going to have a salad, I'm trying to lose weight.'

'Yes, five kilos, I know. I help.'

'It's just so hard.'

'I help,' Ahmed nods and insists. 'I help. I know good food and you eat too many biscuits.'

Femi giggles. 'You noticed?'

'Everyone, they notice.'

'I bought another fruit cake for you this week,' she says.

'Then don't eat any of it.' He turns his back on her and opens the fridge. 'I like salad too. Let's begin the diet.' He removes the lettuce, spring onions and tomatoes.

'Not you, you're too skinny. You need fattening up, lots of carbs to get some meat on your bones.' She laughs. 'I'll make you bolognese.'

Femi hears the front door and she smiles in anticipation. 'Al? We're in the kitchen.' When there's no answer, she frowns and stands up. 'Albert?'

By the time she's in the hallway, he's half way up the stairs.

'Did you have a good time?' she asks.

He nods but doesn't turn around. 'I'm tired.' He carries on walking upstairs and Femi let's him go deciding that she'll talk to him later.

In the kitchen, Ahmed is chopping the salad when Ricky comes downstairs dressed in dark jeans and a *Marvel* T-shirt. He pulls his dirty football gear from his bag and dumps it in the laundry basket before taking his trainers from the utility room. His actions are quick, jerky and he seems angry.

'What was the score.'

'No goals.'

'Did you enjoy it?'

'Yeah.'

'You're off to work then?' Femi says.

'Yep.'

'What time are you home?'

'Same time.'

'Ten?'

'Yeah.'

'Will you have something to eat before you go?'

'Not hungry.' He stands up and grabs his sweatshirt. He doesn't make eye contact with Ahmed but she sees him eyeing the salad on the table.

'You don't need to lose weight, Auntie,' Ricky says, glaring at Ahmed. 'Not everyone has to be fat-shamed.'

'I'm not fat-shamed. You know I want to lose weight, five kilos before Christmas, remember?' Femi tries to make her voice jocular but it falls flat. 'I'm sick of looking Rubenesque.'

'Suit yourself.' Ricky grabs a banana from the fruit bowl and heads to the front door.

'See you later. Have a good time,' Femi calls but Ricky has already slammed the door as hard as he can.

Femi sits down at the table and rests her head in her hands, feeling suddenly overwhelmed and extremely tired. She has to sort this out. She has to get through to Ricky before everything escalates.

* * *

After the front door bangs shut and Ricky has gone, Femi pours herself a glass of white wine. It's crisp and dry on her throat so she takes another appreciative sip.

'I need to speak to you about the photograph of the neighbour on the wall in the studio.' She gazes at Ahmed and watches his reaction but he looks away and pulls a dish for the salad from the drawer.

'Does he try to speak to you a lot?' she asks.

'Sometimes.'

'Is he alright with you?'

'He's nice.'

'All of my friends who come here are checked to make sure they have no past in hurting or abusing children,' Femi explains. 'It's called a DBS check. Sandra, Freddie and Nitesh, all have them because of the work they do, you know, if you're involved with children you must have it. It's automatic. That's how we can keep our children safe from strangers. We don't want an adult to take advantage of vulnerable children, does that make sense?'

'Yes.' Ahmed stares down at the table.

'Has he asked you for anything?' she asks gently.

Ahmed shakes his head but won't look up.

'Has he suggested anything to you?'

Ahmed shakes his head quickly.

'No?' Femi confirms.

'No.'

'Can you please look at me?'

When Ahmed looks up there are tears in his eyes.

'I want to protect you,' she says. 'Let me speak to him before you take any more photographs?'

Ahmed nods.

'It's alright,' she whispers and places her hand on his, feeling his vulnerability. 'You haven't done anything wrong.'

Ahmed nods. 'He's a friend.'

'I know but I would like you to have friends your own age.'

'They don't like me.'

'You haven't tried.'

'Ricky hates me.'

'He doesn't hate you, besides Albert thinks you're wonderful.'

Ahmed shrugs.

Lily has shared the details of his past. Femi knows now
that Ahmed was sent away by an uncle from Syria who paid
for Ahmed to leave the country. Ahmed stayed in countless
refugee centres and, at one stage in Turkey, he was trafficked
for sex. They found Ahmed abandoned with tears around his
anus and he was hospitalised before being relocated to another
refugee camp. From Turkey, he made his way, illegally, to
France and finally to England as it was the only language he
spoke other than Arabic. It had taken Ahmed almost two years
and even now, he's still a child.

'He's a good man.' Ahmed's shoulders slump and he leans
against the sink.

'I can sort it all out,' she whispers. 'There's no problem.'

A tear slides down Ahmed's cheek and onto the table. 'I
don't do anything wrong.'

'I know.'

'He's kind,' he whispers.

'I'm sure he is,' Femi replies hoping to God that it is true.

* * *

Femi knocks on the neighbour's door four times before he
finally opens it and by that time she feels as though he's
avoiding her and being deliberately evasive. Her tone sounds
more indignant that she would like but she's tired and worried.

'Hello, I just wanted to introduce myself properly, I'm Femi,
your neighbour.'

'I know who you are.' He matches her cold tone.

'Can I come in?'

He stands aside and she's surprised to see his house has been transformed into a light and airy open-plan kitchen and dining room with white walls and big windows into the garden, so different from the house it was before. Outside on the patio there's wood and several toolkits. Femi must have disturbed him working.

They stand in the hallway and he folds his arms.

'I just wanted to explain that I'm a foster mother to three boys.'

His dark intent eyes stare at her and his forehead is creased in a frown. His clothes look dirty and shabby.

'Do you live alone?' she asks, 'Or do you have family?'

'It's none of your business.'

'I was thinking if you had children, they may get to know my boys.'

He shakes his head dismissively. 'I don't.'

Femi feels her anger and concern rising and she continues, 'These boys are very vulnerable and all my friends are normally DBS checked. I'm sure there's no problem but I have seen that Ahmed has taken your picture. You speak to him over the fence. He said that you didn't mind, and, to be honest, I don't have a problem with it but,' Femi pauses thinking of her words carefully but she's unnerved by his steady gaze, and she feels his anger rising — it's almost palpable. The muscles in his jaw are working hard to keep still and his large hands hang at his side. He begins clenching his fists but Femi stands her ground. 'The thing is, I have to be careful with who they mix with.'

'What are you trying to infer?' His voice is cultured, educated and his tone is measured.

'I'm not inferring anything. I just want to make you aware of the circumstances. Ahmed has transformed the garage into a photographic studio. He's only sixteen and he can't go to school yet until his papers are sorted, which will now be in September. He's a refugee and—'

'He already told me.'

'He told you?'

'Yes.'

So, you speak to him a lot?'

'Is that a crime?'

'No.'

'Then what's your problem?'

'The problem is...' Femi can feel her anger growing inside. Why can't this stupid man realise what she's trying to say? 'Is that he's vulnerable. He's been through a terrible time and has a past that would probably make any normal person cringe with shame. And, I'm also saying that it might not be healthy for him to meet you at the bottom of the garden.'

'We don't *meet*!' The man stands with his shoulders straight back. 'I live here. This is my house and sometimes I happen to see this young boy taking pictures of the birds in the garden — he doesn't know their names, he doesn't know what they're called and so I help him. He asked me—'

'Oh, well thank you but—'

'But what?'

'Please understand, I have to be cautious—'

'Listen lady, I'm a respected ornithologist. I don't appreciate you coming here and accusing me of whatever it is you're thinking. I also lecture at the university and, if you'd bothered to ask me in first place, then you wouldn't be feeling so stupid or awkward now.'

'Oh?' That's a lot of information for Femi to suddenly take in.

'Now if you'll excuse me, I'm in the middle of hatching ducklings.' In two strides he's opened the front door. 'I'm busy.'

Femi leaves without speaking. She's furious and, as the door closes behind her, she exhales loudly and thinks she'd hate to be a student in one of his classes.

9

Chapter 9

Femi's chin has dropped onto her chest and her breathing is calm and regular. She's fast asleep on the sofa when her mobile rings.

Peanut wakes from his sleep, yawns and then curls up to sleep again.

'Femi? It's Paul.'

Femi sits bolt upright as her mind springs into action. Paul from The Ship.

'Is everything alright? Where's Ricky?' she says urgently.

Paul, the manager of The Ship, never phones her unless there's a problem. Femi's heart thumps heavily in the cavity of her chest. Social services know that Ricky works there. Some of the governments rules are strict but it's important Ricky has the same opportunities as other boys of his age, as a result, Ricky can earn some pocket money and develop confidence, self-esteem and a sense of responsibility.

'He's fine. Well, he's got a black eye but I wanted to let you know. He's on his way home.'

Femi checks her watch. It's not even ten.

'What's happened?'

'I don't know exactly. I was behind the bar. Ricky went to the Gents and there was an argument and a fight broke out with one of the customers.'

'A regular?'

'No, some guy from the north.'

'What about?'

'Ricky said, he was a pervert and he tried to accost him in the toilet.'

'Oh God.' Femi places her hand across her eyes. 'But he's okay?'

'Yes, nothing happened. There was another local guy in the toilet who I know well. He's a regular. Do you know Ben Taylor from the Art Gallery?'

'Vaguely.' Femi remembers that Amber from the Harbour Cafe and Ben Taylor are often seen together.

'Ben says that it was Ricky who picked a fight with this guy. Presumably this guy was washing his hands and he looked at Ricky in the mirror, and Ricky said, what's up with you, mate? And then he accused him of wanting to fuck him.'

'Oh, no.'

'Ben broke it up and played it all down. He brought Ricky out to me but not before the other guy had punched Ricky back — probably harder than he was expecting.'

'I'm sorry, Paul. Thanks for letting me know. I'm sorry.'

'No one else, knows. The other guys gone and he's not calling the police but I thought you'd want to know.' Paul sounds concerned. 'Has anything happened to Ricky recently? He seems a bit out of sorts. You know, a bit tense.'

Femi sighs. 'I don't know what's wrong. I'll speak to him.'

The only thing she could think of was his jealousy of Ahmed

and she fears it is increasing and now he's unable to control himself. She'd have to speak to Peter and Jenny and work something out with them. She couldn't afford for anything to happen.

'That's the door now, I'd better go,' she whispers.

'Okay, speak tomorrow.' Paul hangs up.

Femi heads to the hallway where Ricky is moving quietly like a stealthy cat, up the stairs, two at a time.

'Come in the lounge, I have to speak to you, Ricky.'

'I need the bathroom—'

'NOW!'

Ricky turns, clearly shocked by her tone. She points at the open door her tone slightly softer. 'Now, please.'

Ricky turns meekly back downs the stairs and she can see a big shiner on the side of his left cheek.

'That looks sore,' she says.

* * *

'What happened?' she asks.

'It wasn't my fault.'

'I need the truth.'

'This guy started on me—'

'What did he say?'

Ricky stares at the floor.

'You have to be honest with me, Ricky. I want you to have these opportunities but I can't lie for you. Jenny will see your bruised eye, but beside all of that, I'm worried about you.'

'Don't be.'

'Did you start it?'

He doesn't answer so Femi asks softly, 'What on earth were

you thinking?'

'He started it.'

'Not according to Paul or to Ben Taylor.'

'So, you believe them more than me?'

'I want the truth from you — not from someone else.'

'You don't trust me?' Ricky's eyes blaze.

'I want to trust you. I want to know that you'll be honest with me.'

'I am,' he shouts.

'Keep your voice down, unless you want the boys to come down here to see what's going on.'

Ricky flings himself onto the sofa and throws his leg over its arm. He swings his leg quickly back and forth.

'Tell me what happened.'

'The pervert picked on me in the Gents.'

'What did he say?'

'Say?'

'Yes, what did he say to you?'

Ricky opens his mouth but nothing comes out.

'What makes you think he was a pervert? What did he actually say to you?' Femi asks calmly, but her head is thumping and her heart is hammering. She has to sort this out — quickly.

'He stared at me.'

'What did he say to you?'

'He looked at me.'

'And, do you hit everyone who looks at you?'

'No—'

'Then what did he say to you?' Femi insists.

Ricky fidgets and takes his leg off the sofa and leans forward gripping his fists.

'Did you hurt yourself?' she asks.

Ricky shakes his head.

'Let me look.' This is Femi's opportunity to sit beside him and she takes his hand. She can feel his tension and hears his measured breathing. His hands are clean, no cuts or bruises.

'Wait here, I'll get some ice.'

She leaves him for a few minutes so he can collect his thoughts and calm down. When Femi returns, she notices now that Ricky seems frightened.

'Will Jenny find out?' he asks.

'We can't keep it a secret,' Femi whispers. She dabs his eye with a damp cloth and ice, and he flinches. 'Paul was doing you a favour. Why did you do this?' He doesn't reply so Femi continues quietly, 'You must promise not to let me down.'

'What will we say to Jenny?' he says. 'Can we tell her it was an accident, in the garden or with Peanut?'

'I can't lie, Ricky.'

'It has to be our secret.'

'And I have to be sure this isn't a result of something else.'

'Like what?'

'You tell me?' Femi stares at him. 'What's bothering you?'

The lounge door opens and a dark head appears around the door. 'I heard voices,' Ahmed says, 'Oh! What happened to your face?'

* * *

Ben Taylor is far better looking up close than Femi had imagined and, self-consciously, Femi stands straighter and pulls in her stomach as she enters the art gallery. To her delight Ben is affable and his smile is friendly.

'I'm Ricky's foster mother, Femi,' she says, by way of introduction, holding out her hand.

Ben takes her hand. 'I thought I'd seen you together in town.'

'Thanks for helping Ricky out, last night,' she says. 'I really appreciate that.'

Ben tilts his head and smiles at her. 'He's a good boy.'

'Well, he wasn't last night.'

'That was an unfortunate incident.' Ben shakes his head.

'He said the man in the toilet propositioned him but Paul said you were there and I need to know what happened. I also have to investigate for the CSW.'

'CSW?'

'Child Social Worker - all my kids have one and as their foster carer, I have to keep a diary of all these sort of events.'

'I guess you have to cover your back,' he says.

'That's true, of course, but it's also a reminder that the children are the responsibility of the local government, they just happen to live with me.' Femi hopes that her voice doesn't sound too resentful but today she can't hide her emotions. It's been a long night.

Ben nods. 'Of course. Well, I was there and I didn't see anything unusual. The guy was washing his hands, I was drying mine and Ricky was spoiling for a fight. It's a shame he picked on such a tough-nut. I'll be honest, Femi, it did seem almost deliberate.'

'Deliberate?'

'You know what teenagers can be like, they puff out their chests, strut and hold their arms wide like gorillas.' He grins. 'Ricky walked in to the toilet, looked around and then said to the guy, what are you looking at?'

'We're lucky then that the guy didn't want to press charges.'

'Well, he'd had a few drinks and he'd slugged Ricky back, so I think he was pleased with himself. And, besides, you know what Paul is like. He's a magician when it comes to sorting out problems like that.'

'I guess he's probably had lots of practice.'

Ben smiles. 'Yes, probably.'

Femi looks at the floor, then she looks around the gallery surprised at the art work on the wall. Most of the paintings are of Westbay and the pretty Harbour Street, beach and beach huts but on the near wall are the most beautiful photographs of wildlife. Perhaps they've been taken at the zoo, but the animals don't look like they're in captivity.

'Are you okay?' Ben asks.

Femi nods. It's the worst news she could have expected. Ricky caused the fight. He had often used his fists as an answer to his problems and the last time it was after he'd been dropped from the cricket team. He'd had a go at the boy who was made Captain but he hasn't behaved like that for over a year. Femi had to make Ricky see that this wasn't the way to behave. It's always hard to watch him regress to his old ways. Fight or flight. With Ricky, you never knew which way he'd go.

'I'm sorry, Femi.'

'That's okay, Ben. I need to know the truth, then I can deal with it. Ricky can't behave like that.'

'If you need me to speak to him, I will.'

'Thank you but I'll speak to him again tonight.'

'How long has he been with you?'

'Almost four years and I thought he was getting better. I'm hoping he'll go to university and I don't want him to go off the rails now.'

'Teenage years can be difficult at the best of times.'

Femi smiles. 'Thanks again.'

'Well, if there's anything I can do, just let me know. I've worked with boys like that before.'

'You have?'

'I still do, I teach some of them carpentry. There's a charity in London which helps some of the boys found on the street. You know, homeless boys with nowhere to go.'

'That's what frightens me. Ricky is getting to that age and I don't want him to make a mistake now and end up like them.'

'I'm sure he'll be fine. You're doing a brilliant job. I admire you.'

'Thank you.' Feeling suddenly self-conscious, Femi makes her way out. She's wondering how she will deal with Ricky. Perhaps he still feels threatened by Ahmed's presence. She must speak to him. Her kids are all so special and wonderful and she has no favourites. and Ricky must understand that. She's so lost in thought, Femi bumps into a man coming into the gallery. He's tall and strong and he steadies her with his hands on her shoulders.

'Careful,' he says.

'Oops sorry.' She looks up and she meets his eye. 'Oh gosh, it's you.'

She's shocked to discover that it's her neighbour holding her and she steps quickly back as he releases her.

She almost didn't recognise him. He looks cleaner. His beard is trimmed and he wears glasses that make his eyes look large and intelligent. Now, he doesn't look like a hippy. He actually looks like an attractive and clever college professor. She sidesteps him quickly and dodges out of the door, not realising she was holding her breath.

'Am I going absolutely mad?' she whispers to herself. 'What's wrong with me?'

That's when her phone goes and she's called out to an emergency at sea.

'Thank goodness for the RNLI,' she mutters. 'Just the distraction I need.'

10

Chapter 10

Femi is exhausted. The captain of the yacht was young and inexperienced and he'd lost all sense of direction when his wife went into early labour. Fortunately one of Femi's colleagues, had experience in midwifery, but Femi gave a helping hand and the little girl was born within minutes. Back onshore, it took the ambulance longer to arrive than anticipated and it was late by the time Femi came home but she was compensated by the fact, the baby's parents called her Sirena — she was their mermaid of the sea.

Now, in the lounge, Femi sips her coffee and tries to stay awake while Jenny crosses her legs and smiles encouragingly at Ricky.

'So, you got that bruised eye playing football?'

'Yes.'

'And, you didn't tell the teacher?'

'It didn't come up swollen until I got home and by then it was the weekend and I'd forgotten about it.'

'You have to report these things,' Jenny admonishes him, and she frowns at Femi as if to say, you should know better.

Femi shrugs back as if to say, you know what teenage boys are like.

'Do you remember who did it?' she asks.

'There was a scramble in the penalty area and I didn't notice.'

Jenny looks doubtful, writes a few notes then says, 'I'll check with the teacher anyway.'

After she's gone, Ricky smiles at Femi. 'I think we got away with it.'

'Don't even say that.' Femi frowns at him. 'I'm not happy with you about that whole incident. I spoke to Ben Taylor and he said you'd provoked that man and basically, you got what you deserved.'

Ricky stands taller with his shoulders back. 'You can't trust a word Ben Taylor says. He's done time. He's been in prison,' he shouts.

'That's not the point.'

'You prefer the word of an ex-con to me?'

'If he's done time, then he's paid his price. We all need a second chance and if he's taking his, then he's doing well. I'm sure if he's as bad as you think he is then Paul, and Amber and most people in the community wouldn't give him the time of day. But he's a successful businessman now.'

'A leopard never changes—'

'This isn't about Ben. This is about *your* behaviour. You can't go around picking fights with people. I mean it, Ricky. I won't stand for you being aggressive. This is a thin line you're walking and if it's because you're jealous of Ahmed, then I'll tell you now — there's no need to be. You're *all* my boys and I'll help you *all* the best way I can. You are all different and you all have different needs. Do you understand me?'

'Yes, Auntie.'

'Now, I spoke to Paul and he's agreed that you can go back to the pub next Friday. But that's only on the condition that you behave yourself. Before that, you must apologise to Paul and to Ben —in person. You have to take responsibility for your actions. I've taken a great risk letting you work there and you're not going to jeopardise everything. You have some grovelling to do Ricky, if you want to keep your job and more importantly if you want to grow into a decent human being.'

Ricky shuffles toward the door. 'Thank you.'

Femi can see her words have made a difference but how long it will last — she has no idea. She has to tread warily but she must set her standards and he must rise to them.

'Now, I also expect you to make amends with Ahmed. Please make an effort with him. Play a video game or try and do something nice— at least have the decency to have a conversation and treat him like a proper friend. He's been through a different sort of hell to you and he's vulnerable and sensitive. We are all he has in this world.'

'Yes, Auntie.'

* * *

The next few days pass without incident and on Thursday night, they're all eating dinner together. Ahmed insisted on a large salad with avocado (his favourite) and beetroot and, Ricky and Albert tuck into fried chicken marinaded in soy and Teriyaki sauce and garlic bread. Femi notices Ricky making an effort with Ahmed as she goes upstairs to change. She has been invited to Sandra's birthday dinner in town and because they are being polite with each other, Albert suggests they play Animal Crossing together after dinner.

Femi is pleased to have a night off. The boys don't have much in common but at least the resentful atmosphere seems to have abated. As she slips into a colourful red, yellow and black dress and checks in the mirror, she realises that it's still very tight on her. Perhaps the salads that Ahmed has insisted on eating each evening for the past fortnight, are not having any effect at all.

'You look lovely, Auntie,' Albert says, when she comes downstairs.

Ahmed looks up and smiles with approval.

Femi picks up the gift and flowers for her friend, she'd bought earlier. 'Do you approve, Ricky?' she asks smiling, 'You're allowed to pay me a compliment.'

'Yeah.' Ricky looks away.

'I'll take that,' she says.

'Whatever,' Ricky replies, but Femi is pleased that he has a lopsided smile on his face.

Femi enjoys the walk into town, past the rows of beach huts and she notices the pink one has a For Sale sign taped on the side. Knowing the price of the beach huts are extortionate, she walks on hoping that regardless of who owns it, she can still sit on the steps any time she likes — when no one is around.

Harbour Street is busy with people heading to and from the beach, some with fish and chips and others carrying weary children home after a day out. Harbour Cafe is closed and there's a queue outside Harbour Bistro, inside the restaurant she catches sight of Amber, the owner looking poised and elegant as she seats a couple at the window.

The Ship is busy, and rock music floats over the wall from the patio at the back followed by a round of clapping. Femi feels energised and happy to be out for an evening with no responsibility.

Sandra has reserved a table in the Italian and Femi is one of the last to arrive. She greets Sandra with a kiss and massive hug and hands her the pretty bouquet of purple freesias and crisp white roses and a small gift.

'Love your purple hair,' Femi says.

'Mum loves it,' Sandra whispers, 'and Bob hates it.'

Bob is Sandra's other half. He's small and stocky and an accountant with no sense of humour. He rarely goes out with Sandra and sometimes Femi forgets her friend is even married. They are happy together but lead separate lives.

He kisses Femi formally on both cheeks. His lips are wet and she wonders how Sandra is attracted to such a man. She moves toward the faces she recognises and Freddie pats the seat beside him.

'I've saved it for you, gorgeous girl.'

Femi slides into the seat. 'Well, if she's not around I'll sit here.'

'You're gorgeous, Femi. Tell me how your week off has been,' insists Freddie filling her wine glass with Pinot Grigio.

'No way, I'm having a night off.'

Nitesh has a twinkle in his eye. His moustache is trimmed and his dark straight hair is parted meticulously and he leans across his husband and waves his phone.

'I'm going to check Tinder for you. We'll soon hook you up with some sex god.'

Femi laughs. 'Yes, he'd really fit in with my life at home.'

'You never know,' says Freddie.

'I like the idea of meeting someone but not on Tinder, and besides, it would have to be someone very special who understood the love and commitment I have for my boys.'

'They're someone else's children, you need a life.' Freddie raises his glass.

'They're not someone else's - they're mine.' She grins.

'Until social services tell you otherwise,' quips Nitesh.

As the first course arrives, Femi begins to relax and the wine has a soothing effect. It's a happy, fun evening and Freddie and Nitesh are good company. They've been to the theatre in London and, as they all love musicals, Femi begins thinking about taking the boys to the Christmas Panto.

'I'll book tickets as soon as they come on sale. It will be Ahmed's first panto,' she says.

'It's only June, Femi.' Nitesh laughs. 'Don't encourage Freddie, he's already looking at costumes.'

Freddie claps hands together in delight. 'He will love it!'

'You're right. Ahmed will love it. They all do. Ricky's face was a delight last year, he pretended to be too old for it, but he couldn't help joining in.'

Nitesh laughs at the memory.

Femi waves her wine glass as she speaks. 'It was Albert who loved it the most. He was using a coat hook for his hand and getting Peanut to be a pirate with him for weeks afterwards.'

Freddie laughs. 'It's Cinderella this year, goodness knows what he'll get up to— '

'Don't,' says Femi, suddenly overcome with a wave of sadness. 'There's no telling what might happen. He might not even be here with us at Christmas.'

Nitesh reaches over and fills up her wine glass. 'I think we should get Freddie to dress up as one of the ugly sisters anyway, what do you say?'

'Great idea.' Femi laughs. 'But he's not wearing any of my

clothes again. He looks much hotter in them than me.'

Just before it's time to go home, Femi grabs her handbag and heads to the toilet. It's done her good to get out and to have an adult evening for a change. They don't happen too often and she hasn't laughed this much for a long time.

She passes a table with a single diner and he's reading a book. When she looks more closely she recognises her neighbour. He doesn't look up and he doesn't see her. Femi goes quickly into the bathroom and a few minutes later, as she returns to her table, she's emboldened by the white wine and she stops at his table.

He looks up and she pulls out the chair and sits opposite him. It's a clumsy effort and she's not too sure what she's doing. To her relief he doesn't frown or look angry. He actually looks quite amused and there's a smile hovering on his lips.

'Is anyone sitting here?' Femi asks.

'There is now,' he replies, matching her gaze, and she notices his grey green eyes behind his glasses. He also looks younger than she initially thought.

'I want to apologise. I was rude and I'm sorry.' She holds out her hand.

He takes her fingers and she's surprised by his touch and a small shiver runs down her spine. She blinks and suddenly feels very self-conscious.

'Apology accepted.' He nods seriously.

'I shouldn't ask but I have to,' she says. 'If you work at the uni, are you DBS checked?'

He smiles. 'Yes.'

'Phew!' she says dramatically and they both laugh. 'Thank you.' She goes to stand up but he says, 'Ahmed's a good boy and he's a fast learner.'

'I know.'

'I've told him the names of all the birds, the flowers, the plants and the trees and he remembers them all — unlike many of my students.'

'He is a clever boy,' Femi agrees. 'What happened to your ducklings?'

'They all survived and are back where they belong.'

'Albert would have liked to see them. He adores animals.'

'Maybe next time.'

Femi stares at him, wondering what next time means. Her head is foggy with the wine.

The neighbour strokes his neat beard. 'I don't think it could have been easy for Ahmed growing up in Syria.'

'No, the war has been awful, and he's suffered a great deal, although he doesn't talk about it.'

'It's what he suffered to get here and I'm not referring to the war,' he pauses.

Femi raises her eyebrows.

The neighbour appears to choose his words carefully. 'Homosexuality is not tolerated in middle eastern countries.'

'You think Ahmed is gay?'

'There is a possibility. Have you spoken to him about it?'

'No.'

'Perhaps you should.'

Femi frowns. She's not sure now if she likes this man that seems to know more about Ahmed than she does.

'Has he spoken to you about it?' she asks.

'He doesn't need to.'

'Are you gay?' she asks.

The neighbour smiles. 'No, not at all. I'm sorry if I gave you that impression.'

Femi waves her hand in the air. She's suddenly confused and feels slightly drunk. She's not even sure why she's sitting at this stranger's table and she certainly can't make out why or how she's in a conversation, discussing the intimate details of her foster boy. She stands up quickly.

'Lawrence.'

'Pardon?' she replies.

'I thought you were going to ask me my name.'

'I wasn't.'

'Well, now you know anyway.'

'Well, good night,' she says pausing, 'Lawrence.'

'Goodnight, Femi.'

As she walks away, she's conscious of him staring at her back and she wonders if her dress is too tight, and worries that her bum looks too big and, why on earth the name Lawrence seems to suit him, when he doesn't look like a Lawrence at all.

* * *

Femi makes coffee and stares out of the kitchen window, pleased with how the garden seems less overgrown. It's a quiet morning. Ricky is at football training and Albert is doing his homework upstairs in his bedroom and Ahmed is in bed.

It's been an unusual week. Following Sandra's party last night and Femi's surprise encounter with Lawrence, she's now worrying that Ahmed might be gay.

She holds no prejudice and she's in no way a homophobe. She's far more worried about what Ahmed might have suffered. Lawrence was right, homosexuality in the Muslim world is unacceptable. It's hardly surprising then, that Ahmed doesn't want to talk about his past and shows little interest in finding his family. Although she wants to help Ahmed, he must feel safe. She wants him to trust her and, more importantly, confide in her.

Femi has already spoken to Sandra about this and now she's ready to try to tackle the issues affecting Ahmed that he might be trying to hide. She reaches for her laptop and makes herself comfortable at the kitchen table and looks back over her training notes.

Half an hour later, Ahmed comes downstairs and wanders into the kitchen. 'I'm making stuffed peppers for dinner tonight,' he says.

'Lovely, there should be everything you need in the fridge and the cupboard.' She doesn't look up.

They both work in silence. It doesn't take Ahmed long and when he's cleaning the pan, scratching at the sticky rice that's stuck to the bottom, Femi looks up and regards him closely. He's a calm and quiet boy, very self-contained and watchful. He speaks good English and he's very sensitive and kind. She's noticed that when they watch programmes on television together he gets absorbed very quickly. Last week, in one episode of a nature programme, a baby elephant died and she noticed tears cascading down his cheeks. She had reached out for his hand and he hadn't pulled away. There was a sensitive side to him that needed her and she wondered if that was because he wanted to distance himself from his previous life.

'Come on, let's look for your uncle,' she says, enthusiastically, tapping her laptop.

Ahmed turns around and looks surprised.

'Come on, sit here beside me. Let's just have a few minutes.'

'I'm not sure,' he says.

'We must let someone know you're safe,' insists Femi. 'Your family must be so worried about you.'

Reluctantly Ahmed finishes drying the plates and hangs up the tea towel. He barely has a limp now and he moves with graceful ease and as Femi begins searching her computer, he slides into the seat beside her.

'Now, we need to get on to the Syrian websites. You can do that, here take this.' She pushes her laptop at him and after looking hesitant, he begins to type. His fingers moving quickly across the keys.

'You can change the keyboard,' he explains, bringing up the Arabic letters.

Femi sits at his shoulder as he scrolls through the names and photographs, all written in Arabic.

'It's such a different language,' she says. 'Unlike any of our European languages.'

Ahmed is concentrating and he doesn't reply.

'Wait. Look. Isn't that Aleppo?' Femi points to an image she remembers from earlier searches. The buildings are decimated and the streets empty.

Ahmed grunts.

'Come on, do you want to talk me through it? Let me help you.'

Ahmed grows quiet as he scrolls through images; one shot after another of the city that was once his home, now in ruins.

'It must be very difficult but do you recognise anything at all?' she asks gently.

Ahmed doesn't blink. He continues to stare at the screen and as he becomes lost in his own thoughts, Femi imagines that he's transported in his mind, back to his own country, in a different time and place.

'How long ago was it?' she asks.

His fingers begin to shake.

'Ahmed, stay with me. You're here. You're safe now. You have nothing to worry about.' She moves closer to him.

He bites his bottom lip and flicks his fringe, scrolling faster through more images of the bombed city.

'There's nothing,' he whispers.

'We need LinkedIn. The business pages. We need to find your uncle. Don't torture yourself, looking at these images, please, Ahmed.'

Ahmed's fingers work swiftly. He takes a deep breath and his eyes harden. He shakes his head and begins to mutter under his breath, in Arabic.

'What are you saying?' Femi whispers. 'Let me help you. This can be a positive experience for you. If we find your uncle, the one who helped you escape, someone you trust, then that will be the link for you to find the rest of your family.'

Ahmed ignores her, scrolling faster and she can feel his shoulders tense.

'We can do this together, Ahmed.'

He shakes his head, muttering words that she can't understand.

'I know you miss your country and your family,' she says softly. 'I want to help you. Do you remember the name of your uncle's business?'

He ignores her.

'Ahmed?'

He scrolls fast and the screen makes her dizzy.

'I want to help you.'

'You can't,' he says through gritted teeth.

'I can.'

Suddenly he slams the computer lid shut.

'You can't.' He covers his face with his hands and rubs his wet eyes.

'Talk to me, please, explain?'

Ahmed shakes his head.

'Please?' she asks.

'You'll hate me.'

'No, I could never do that,' she says honestly. 'You're safe here. Nothing will happen to you.'

The kitchen is quiet apart from the slow, regular breathing of Peanut tucked in his bed in the corner.

'Will you send me back?'

'Not if you don't want to go.'

Ahmed speaks slowly and quietly, 'My uncle sent me away.'

'I understand that. It was a difficult time—'

'It was nothing to do with the war.'

'Okay,' she pauses, 'then why?'

He turns to look at her but then he looks down at his slim, soft hands. 'It's because I like boys,' his voice is barely a whisper and Femi doesn't dare to move. She waits for him to continue, 'It was dangerous for me, for all of them. It's illegal. They hate us. They hate me.'

'Ah, now I understand.'

He turns on her angrily. 'What do you understand? How they beat me? How they tortured me? How I begged my uncle to help me when he despised me? He hated me.'

'Oh, Ahmed, I'm sorry.'

'Sorry for what? That they killed my father and brother because of me?'

'No.'

'That they took my mother and my sister and raped them

because of who I am?'

'It wasn't your fault.'

'You don't know that.' He wipes his silent tears and begins sobbing quietly. 'You don't know anything.'

11

Chapter 11

It's Saturday and Albert is excited. He sits silently in his bedroom thinking. It's quiet downstairs. Auntie is on an afternoon shift and she won't be back for another hour. Ricky is at football practice, Ahmed is in his studio at the bottom of the garden and Sandra is probably scrolling through the news on her phone.

He looks at the photograph on the wall that Auntie insisted on framing. It's one that Ahmed took of him a few months ago and, in it, he looks confident and smart in his school uniform. He's smiling at the camera. Albert tilts his head and looks quizzically at his own image. He looks much older now than when he arrived here eighteen months ago. It was also lucky that Ahmed had caught him on a good day. He'd captured his puzzled smile and flat nose. When Albert had first arrived he had been overwhelmed with Auntie's love, generosity and kindness and he had thought at one time he might live here for years just like Ricky. He thought he'd go to grammar school next term and then hopefully go on to university. He liked that about Auntie, she was a real go-getter and she encouraged you to be a better person. She had pushed him and now he wasn't so scared — he certainly wasn't frightened of the bullies at school and he sometimes even quite liked going to class, especially the science one where he learnt about animals. She pushed Ricky too, not in a bossy pushy way but in a way that meant she could get the best out of him. Auntie had that knack of getting the best out of all of them — including Ahmed. He liked Ahmed. He understood his silence and how he kept things to himself.

Albert lies back on his bed with his hands behind his head. His room is a mess: clothes, bags, trainers, books, school books and computer hardware that he collects are all piled up on his desk. He thinks of his father. He rolls the word around in his mouth like a marble or a Malteser. 'Father,' he says, 'Father.'

'There are more opportunities in London,' Delroy had said. 'Loads of opportunities to get into programming and gaming.'

Albert smiles up at the ceiling. Last week when they were sitting on the beach talking, Dad promised they'd go to the theatre and to shows and museums just as Albert does now with Auntie — they'd already taken Ahmed to the museum and to the art gallery and next they were going to the zoo. Delroy said there was a good school nearby and that Albert would be happy there. 'Life in London will be exciting. You and me, together at last.'

They had been sitting on the steps of a random beach hut with pretty maroon paint and yellow and blue mermaids stencilled on the side.

'Just the two of us,' Albert had said happily.

'For a while,' Delroy had replied vaguely.

Albert frowned. 'You and me, no?'

'Well, how about if we had a proper family?' Delroy had smiled then. He was rolling a cigarette and he licked the cigarette paper.

'How do you mean?' Albert fidgets, his legs jiggling.

'What if I told you, I've a lady-friend and she has a couple of kids too? And we might all hook up and live together, share costs and things so that we can be a real family.'

Albert thinks about it. 'How old are her kids?'

'Younger than you, five and seven. You'd be the big brother. The eldest boy. They'd look up to you. You could play with them and keep them company.'

'Company?'

'Yeah, well, not often but if me and the Missis wanted a night out sometimes, we'd leave you pizza and you could stay up a bit later. You'd be in charge. You'd like that wouldn't you?'

Albert had stared out to sea then. He liked pizza but he wouldn't want to share it nor would he want to be looking after babies. He sat looking at the scene around him. He hadn't noticed the children swimming, nor the dog barking, not even the ding-dong of the ice cream van up on the road until now. He'd been so happy to be with his father. Then suddenly Delroy had flung his arm around Alberts's neck and hugged him close. 'Don't worry about any of that now though, son. That's all *way off* in the future. Right now, it's about you and me and getting you home so that we're together.'

Albert felt reassured so he says, 'Tell me about the park again, Dad.'

'Park? What park?'

'The one near where you live. Where we will walk Oscar.'

'Who's Oscar?'

'Didn't you say we could get a puppy and that we could walk him in the park near the flat?'

Delroy had stared at him blankly and then burst out laughing. 'Of course, my son, of course. I didn't realise you're going to call him Oscar.' Delroy wiped his palms on his jeans and screwed up his eyes to look at the fishing boats making their way back to the harbour. Albert followed his gaze and watched the flock of squawking seagulls eager for the discarded catch from the back of the boat.

Delroy placed the rolled-up cigarette behind his ear and checked his watch. 'One step at a time son. Now it's nearly time for me to go. Did you manage to get me anything this week?'

Albert had been waiting for this moment and very carefully he reached into his pocket. He was pleased to help his Dad but he didn't want to do it anymore. It's as if the money was burning a hole in him. Besides that, Auntie is careful with her purse now, she's been hiding it in the utility room but he managed to find it yesterday.

He holds out two ten-pound notes and Delroy takes them and pops them quickly in his back pocket.

'Thanks, son. This is good. We're saving well together and at this rate we might be together by next year.'

'Next Year?' Albert wails. He thought it would be much sooner than that. 'Didn't you say I was going to school in September, near you?'

Delroy rubs his mouth with the back of his hand. 'Well, son, it's not a lot of money, is it? Ten pounds won't get us far.'

'Twenty pounds and I gave you forty before that and twenty before that.'

'I know you did, but it all costs money. The train fare to visit you and—'

'But you're working now.'

'I am son, but I have to pay the rent and now with all the costs going up. It's expensive to keep coming down here.'

Albert feels tears pricking at his lids. 'It's taking ages,' he mumbles.

Delroy squeezes his shoulders. 'But it will all be worth it. Can you get more money?'

'Maybe.'

'What about at school? Kids have cash, don't they?'

Albert nods. He'd nearly been caught last week and that had frightened him. Then there had been the interview with Auntie and Jamie about the missing money and he'd lied.

'If I get caught, Auntie will be furious. I don't know what they'll do—'

'Well, don't get caught son, then Auntie won't know. Come on, let's get an ice cream.' Delroy stands up and brushes down his trousers.

'I thought we were saving,' Albert wails.

'Don't look so glum boy. Of course, we're saving but an ice cream won't ruin the bank will it?'

Albert walked beside his father and for some reason it was niggling him that he called him 'boy'. He much prefers it when he calls him 'son'.

* * *

It's happening again. Even though Femi has been cautious and hidden her purse, she thought it had stopped. She hoped it would all stop but the thief is more brazen now — or more desperate, Femi isn't sure which but she's not happy. She'd hidden her purse deliberately after being called out to another RNLI emergency this afternoon which involved a twelve year old boy on a dingy caught in the under currents of a receding tide. They found him ten miles off the coast and got him back safely before he became dehydrated — now she's worried about her own boys.

So much can go so wrong and so quickly.

She walks down to the studio with Peanut at her heels who stops to sniff in the undergrowth while she taps on the door.

'Ahmed?'

He appears quickly and she's sad to see him looking tired and pale.

'Are you alright?' she asks.

'I didn't sleep well last night.'

Femi perches on the chair beside him. 'That's normal, Ahmed.'

He potters at the big table where his photographic equipment is laid out.

'Did you speak to Lily this morning?'

'Yes.'

'Good, it always takes time, especially when you relive memories and you shared some with me yesterday which will have upset you.'

Femi makes a mental note to speak to Lily again and also to Peter. Perhaps Ahmed needs more counselling. She would keep her eye on him.

'Ahmed, some money has gone missing from my purse again and I need to know if someone here at home has taken it. I'm not accusing you but I need to know if you have taken any money from my purse.'

He shakes his head. 'I don't spend money.'

'I know. You rarely go out either, but I need to ask you. I'm asking all of you.'

Ahmed shakes his head. 'No.'

Femi spends a few moments looking at his photographs and he shows her his latest one of Peanut and it makes her smile.

'I think you quite like him now, don't you?'

Ahmed gives her a shy smile. 'Sometimes.'

As she leaves the studio Peanut is waiting for her, sitting outside patiently.

'You can stroke him, if you want to, he'll never hurt you,' she says but Ahmed looks unsure and Femi smiles.

'Well, one step forward at a time and that's progress.'

She makes her way through the garden to the kitchen where Ricky is sitting at the table eating cereal. His elbows are on the table and he's slurping the milk noisily.

'Ricky, I need to ask you, something. I'm not accusing you but money has gone missing from my purse again, did you take it?'

He looks at her and regards her for a few moments before answering. 'No.'

She nods and turns away.

'But I know who did.'

She turns back to listen.

'Ahmed took it.'

'Why do you say that?'

'Because he's got all that equipment and he's always paying for those bloody frames and canvasses—'

'I bought the frame for Albert's photo and I would have done the same for you, only you weren't interested.'

He pauses with his spoon to his mouth. 'Where does he get his money from?'

'That's no concern of yours. He's a refugee and he gets different financial help to you—'

'Like what?'

'It's none of your concern.'

He tips the remaining milk from the bowl into his mouth and stands up. 'It's your problem, then. You're the one who's missing money.'

* * *

After Ricky goes to work, Femi goes upstairs to check on Albert. It's been a very warm day and after she's knocked on his bedroom door and stepped inside, she's almost knocked out by the smell in his room.

'Albert, you must open a window,' she says, pulling back the bedroom curtains to let in the late evening sunlight. 'It's hot in here, and it stinks!'

Albert's wearing headphones and although he watches her from the corner of his eye, he can't take his concentration from the screen. This is the best bit of the game and it's the worst time for Auntie to come into his room. She throws open a window and a rush of warm air fills the room.

'It's too hot,' he complains.

'Well, it maybe be warm outside but at least it's fresh air, Albert?' She waits patiently at his elbow watching his progress on the screen until he finally looks up and removes his headphones.

'We're changing your sheets tomorrow.' Femi is standing with her hands on her hips. 'And, I'm not taking no for an answer. Every two weeks, we agreed.'

Albert nods.

'You'll also have to put the vacuum around. It's your turn.'

Albert bites the inside of his left cheek.

'And, when you come downstairs, please bring down your dirty plates and mugs.' Albert follows her gaze to the stack of dirty dishes on the table beside his other computer. They were in his way anyway, so he'll take them down next time.

'Yes, auntie.'

She smiles then her face turns serious and she perches on the bed beside him. 'Do you know where I keep my purse?'

Albert frowns. 'No.'

'I'm asking because more money has gone missing and I will have to report it.'

Albert shakes his head. His brown eyes are big and round.

'I have to ask you and I'll speak to Jamie again.'

Albert nods and after Auntie has closed the door he breathes a heavy sigh. Jamie was quite a nice social worker, he'd had worse and Dad was right. He would have to be more careful. He'd have to focus on the kids at school.

12

Chapter 12

It's the beginning of July and it's very hot. The windows are open and the sun is relentless; beating though the open kitchen window and there's not a breath of fresh air. Femi can hear voices at the bottom of the garden and she pauses folding the washing and listens.

For the past few weeks, she's watched Ahmed from the window upstairs talking over the fence to Lawrence. She's not worried. Not now that she's googled him. Lawrence MacNeal is a lecturer at the University and she's impressed by his credentials; working abroad for the World Wildlife Fund for ten years, doing extensive research and important studies, most of which she didn't understand but he seems to be well respected by the academics and that has put her mind at rest. Now, he seems to spend a lot of time talking to Ahmed and when she hears Ahmed's soft chuckle she's both pleased yet concerned. Ahmed never laughs like that with her. He's always very serious.

Later that evening, Ahmed is in the kitchen and she's making his favourite, bolognese, for a change.

He shakes his head. 'We should eat salad.'

'We need a change of diet and besides, Albert and Ricky will be here for dinner and they're growing boys too. Do you want to make garlic bread?'

'You'll put on weight.'

'I won't. Pasta isn't fattening. Haven't you seen Sophia Loren?'

'Who?'

'She's probably one of the most beautiful women in the world. She's probably in her eighties now, beautiful, Italian and she swears she's kept her figure by eating pasta...' Femi's voice trails off because Ahmed looks sceptically at her and she adds lamely, 'She was one of the greatest movie stars of all time.'

'Bigger than Lady Gaga?'

'They were from different times. Back then there was no social media to make people famous like there is today.'

Ahmed grunts. Even though he's a refugee, he's part of a generation that can't understand not having social media.

She asks him carefully, 'What do you and Lawrence talk about?'

Ahmed shakes his head and turns his mouth downwards. 'Nothing really.' He opens the tin of tomatoes for her.

'He seems knowledgeable about wildlife...' Femi is fishing.

'He knows everything.'

'I know, but it's time you met some more people from Syria.'

'That's what Lily says.'

'Social workers are here to help and support you,' Femi replies. 'I spoke to her and she says she wants you to go to the refugee centre. The charity has a meeting place in Canterbury where you can go and meet other refuges from your own country. I've mentioned it to you lots of times and I think you should go.'

'I don't want to meet anyone.'

'You may meet people who knew your family—'

'I don't want to.'

'I understand your fears Ahmed, but I'm sure even if you did meet anyone who knew your family, they wouldn't know about you or the reason your uncle got you out of Aleppo,' she adds gently. 'In this country there's no problem being gay. You don't have to be frightened. It's not illegal here and neither is it a sin.'

Ahmed raises his head. 'Do you think I wouldn't change if I could? It's not my fault. I was born this way.'

'I understand and I'm certainly not asking you to change, neither is Lily. What we're saying is that there is help and support here for you.'

'What if they send me back?'

'They won't. Your life is in danger over there. They can't send you back.'

Ahmed frowns. 'We don't tell anyone.'

'Of course not. It's up to you to tell people what you want them to know.'

'I don't want Ricky to find out.'

'He wouldn't have a problem with it and besides, it might be good for you to tell Albert and Ricky straight out and then deal with any questions they may have. You don't have to hide. You are your own person.'

Ahmed shakes his head. 'No.'

'Are you frightened they might not accept you?'

Ahmed doesn't reply.

'Do you think Ricky might be homophobic?'

Ahmed tips the tomatoes into the frying meat. 'He doesn't like me.'

Femi stirs the pan. 'I'm sure he does. And, what about speaking Arabic? It would be good for you to speak your native language again, wouldn't it?'

Ahmed shrugs.

'Lily thinks it's a good idea and she told me she's talked to you about it.'

'I said I would consider going.' He stares blankly at Femi. 'I consider and I don't want.'

'Think of it as an opportunity. You may meet lots of interesting people, they will understand what you have been through, what you experienced.'

He shrugs. 'I will talk to Lily, she's going to collect me tomorrow at midday.' Ahmed's face clouds over and his eyes darken. He bites his lip and frowns.

'You can't spend the rest of your life hiding at the bottom of the garden, talking only to Lawrence. You must meet people your own age, and people who speak your language, it will be good for you—'

'You don't know that.'

'Can you give it a try, for me?'

Ahmed throws the tin in the recycling bin. 'Alright. I go then.'

'Good.' Femi is relieved, at least it will get him away from the neighbour. 'Lily will be pleased.'

* * *

Ahmed is taking apart an old camera that he bought on eBay for five pounds. He wants to see the mechanics behind it and see how it all fits together but he's not very good at this and he's already lost two small screws and he can't find out how to fit the cartridge for the film.

Lawrence might help him. He knows about everything.

He likes Lawrence and he wonders if he'll lean over the fence today. He hasn't seen him for a few days and he misses him. There's something very soft and gentle in the way he speaks to him and in the way that he explains everything. It reminds him of his older brother Mohamed, who had always seemed to know everything. He knew the quickest way back from school, he could always get hold of a football and he always cooked lovely food. He was quick, efficient and he always had time for Ahmed. If anyone could multi-task it was Mohamed. He would eat a sandwich, kick a football in the air twenty times and explain life to him. Mohamed was fourteen when he explained about girls, marriage and sex and although Ahmed was only ten at the time, he thought he understood everything, enough to know that he wasn't interested in girls. He asked Mohamed one day, walking back from school, what would happen if he didn't like girls and Mohamed had laughed and rubbed his head.

'You will, Ahmed. Believe me, you will.'

But Ahmed was resolute. 'What happens if you like boys?'

Mohamed had stopped still. He'd taken Ahmed by the shoulders, leaned down and looked severely into his eyes. 'Never. Ever. Say that. Never ask those questions.'

'Why?'

'Because it's forbidden. It's illegal.'

'I don't understand.'

'You don't have to understand, Ahmed. You only have to obey. It's in the Koran. Never tell our father or uncles or any of our family, do you understand?'

'So, I can't love a man? What about you?'

Mohamed's serious face breaks into a grin. 'Phew! You had me worried then. That's a different type of love, Ahmed. We're family, like with our uncles, we can love our family — even the men.' He laughs aloud. 'You really had me worried then, Ahmed.'

But it was Ahmed who was worried and by the time he was twelve, he realised he loved Faarooq and he wasn't family. He was his best friend.

* * *

Albert doesn't hate school as much as he used to. He's learnt how to avoid the people he hates. He hides during break time and he reads so he doesn't have to speak to anyone. Now, he puts up his hand and excuses himself from the class to go to the bathroom.

Mrs Johnson gives him a strange nod but continues speaking to the class. It's English, and she's reading from one of the romantics that Albert finds so boring. It's full of emotions, tears and regrets and love and Albert thinks girls have little to worry about if they keep going on about it all the time. They should just shut up. They should keep their thoughts to themselves. No one cares how they feel. He certainly doesn't.

He walks quickly along the corridor, past the toilets and into the cloakroom where the class above him, the older class, are out on the sports field. He peers around the changing room door and he's in luck. It's empty. He runs to the far window and there's no one nearby. They're all on the cricket pitch or playing rounders and some are sitting in groups under the trees. He turns back to look at the sports bags and jackets hanging on the pegs. He picks the expensive brand-named bags first and he rifles through clothes; smelly socks, dirty trousers, and school books. He's amazed at what people keep in their bags; food, sweets, pictures and magazines. He doesn't stop. He works quickly as his Dad told him to do. He finds a wallet with a few notes, he's careful not to take everything; a rolled up note here and there and a bit of change and soon his pockets are full. There's a noise outside and voices. He freezes. Then suddenly, he swings into action. He kicks the bag under the bench and disappears back into the corridor just as the door to the playing field opens. His heart is hammering and his hands are perspiring but he's filled with elation. As he slides back into his seat and Mrs Johnson's voice continues to drone on, he's filled with euphoria.

He's done it.

13

Chapter 13

'Think of it as your birthday present,' Femi says. 'I did the same for Ricky when he was sixteen.'

'Really?' Ahmed is excited. He's never been to a proper barber before or if he did, he doesn't remember.

Femi was careful to get permission first. She knew she had to check with Lily and she'd agreed. She'd also thought it would do Ahmed good.

They walk under the town clock together and into Harbour Street and Ahmed's eyes are initially drawn to From The Heart Gift Shop where the windows are filled with seaside type gifts: colourful lighthouses, paintings of seahorses, summer sandals, plates with shellfish designs and fishing nets, until he sees the Turkish Barbers.

He stares at it. '*The Grooming Room — Esquires of Westbay*,' Ahmed pronounces with awe just as Albert had done a few months ago.

'Come on, we have an appointment.' Femi takes his arm and pushes him past a small queue of young men, sitting on the bench outside. It's luxuriously designed with three steel and black leather grooming chairs in front of wall-sized-mirrors. On the far wall is an expensive array of wet shaving sets and an assortment of colourful beard brushes as well as a variety of creams, gels and hair sprays.

Ozan and Yusef, obviously brothers, are dressed in long black shorts and neatly ironed immaculate white Polo shirts.

'Hello gorgeous Femi. You look beautiful and I love your dress. Oh, so who do we have here, today?' Yusef, the slightly taller brother calls out. 'You must be the lovely, Ahmed. You're very welcome. Take a seat.' He claps his hands and indicates to one of the black leather chairs in front of the mirror.

Femi smiles.

Ahmed blushes.

'And what about you, pretty lady,' Yusef continues, 'will you wait for this handsome young man?'

'Hello, Yusef.' Femi laughs and she nods at Ozan who is busy styling a gentleman's hair at the back of the salon. 'I'll pop back in about half an hour?'

'That would be lovely my darling, and let me tell you, just in case no one has said it to you this morning, you look absolutely gorgeous. I love your natural Jamaican style — so colourful and fun. Such a pretty dress.'

Femi blushes. 'Thank you.'

Yusef puts his hand on his heart and bows dramatically. 'It's my pleasure. Now, what will we do with this young man? Keeping the fringe, sir?'

Femi lets herself out of the barbers and is happy to browse the shops. She pauses at Eva's, Darling Buds and Blooms with its bay window and beautiful floral wheelbarrows filled with colour and fresh flowers. Eva is serving a customer but she looks up and smiles. Jane's Jewellery Shop with its expensive range of fine hand-made rings and Step Ahead Beauty Salon, look busy.

Femi stands aside to let a family with young children and a buggy go past and finds herself staring into the window of the art gallery. There's a picture of a duckling hatching and it's mesmerising. She stands transfixed looking at its soft down and small eyes, and the way it's uncurling from birth, she can feel movement and action as the tiny life begins.

'It's beautiful, isn't it?'

Femi jolts out of her trance and turns to look at the man who's suddenly appeared beside her.

'Oh, hello, Lawrence.' Her heart begins to beat faster.

He nods at the painting. 'I can't believe how good it is.'

'I think it's incredible. You can see the innocence and how unsteady and unsure the little duckling is, it must remind you of your ducklings?'

'Yes.' He smiles.

'Who painted it?'

Lawrence replies, 'I think it's a new local artist.'

'It's incredible. What a talent.' Femi turns to look at it again but it's only to distract her from looking at Lawrence. He seems to be incredibly close to her and she can smell his tangy aftershave. She steps quickly away but so does he and they almost collide as their shoulders touch.

'Sorry,' he mutters an apology.

She shakes her head and wonders why he's apologising. He also seems embarrassed.

'Are you in town alone?' he asks.

'I've just taken Ahmed to the barbers.'

'Really?' His face lights up. 'That will be an experience for him.'

'Yes, with Yusef,' Femi agrees.

'I was fortunate to have Ozan restyle me. I think he's a little more conservative. I think Yusef would have given me a Mohican.' Lawrence strokes his thin beard. 'Then he would have dyed it purple.' He grins and rubs the back of his head.

Femi looks at his hair and bursts out laughing.

Lawrence holds her gaze. 'It's too hot for coffee, would you like an ice cream?'

She would like an ice cream but she's on a diet. She's also surprised that he wants to spend some time with her.

'I—'

'No problem if you're busy. I understand.' Lawrence backs away, his smile fading, he's about to leave but then Femi reaches out and there's a tingling sensation in her tummy when she touches the soft hairs on his arm.

'I would love to.'

He shakes his head in delight, hardly believing his luck. 'Great. We could go and sit on the beach, if you like?'

* * *

The beach is busy, so they walk along the promenade away from the town and find a beach hut that's closed.

'Let's sit on the steps,' Femi suggests, licking her ice cream quickly before it melts.

'Will we fit?'

'I'll move up.'

His leg is warm beside her as they sit companionably on the beach hut steps in the shade, huddled together with their knees bent, watching the action on the beach; children swimming, lovers cuddling, couples reading as they lick their ice creams. Overhead seagulls squawk and chase each other.

'Some of these beach huts never open, do they?' he asks.

'Not all of them.'

'I wonder who owns them all,' he muses.

'I've often wondered. Some of them are very expensive and it's ridiculous as they have no electricity or water.'

'It's a handy place to keep your beach gear though.'

'Expensive.'

They sit for a while eating until Lawrence says, 'Do you take your boys swimming?'

'I'm going to suggest it tonight, it's the first evening that we've all been at home together for a while.'

'Really?'

'Yes, Ricky's often out at the gym or he has some sports fixture after school.' She doesn't mention the evening pub shifts twice a week. 'What about you?'

'I like swimming but I only like warm water. I think I've been spoilt living abroad in Malaysia.'

'Were you there for long?'

'Over ten years.'

'And, did you take your family with you?'

'Family?' He frowns.

'Wife, children?'

'Ah, no. None of those.'

Femi nods. She hopes it wasn't a clumsy way to ask if he had a partner.

'What about you?' he asks, finishing the last of his cone. 'Anyone special?'

'Actually yes.' Femi is conscious of him watching her, his eyes screwed up in concentration.

'Ah, I did wonder. A beautiful woman like you wouldn't be alone, but I haven't seen anyone...' his voice trails off and he wipes his mouth and beard with a small tissue.

'Sure, you have, you've seen them all. You know them: Ricky, Albert and Ahmed.'

Lawrence's face breaks into grin. He offers her a tissue.

'Thank you.' She wipes her hands. 'That's about the extent of it.'

'Have you always been a foster mum?'

'I trained as a paramedic but fostering is something I always wanted to do.'

'Why?'

Femi thinks for a minute. It's taken her a long time to be able to speak openly and freely. She's had counselling and she has come to terms with her life and in the end she says simply, 'I was fostered.'

Lawrence is surprised.

'My parents died when I was thirteen,' she adds.

Lawrence reaches out and places his hand on her knee which she finds comforting. 'I'm sorry,' he whispers and there's a deep sincerity in his tone that resonates with her.

Femi takes a deep breath. 'Dad died in a boating accident in Jamaica. He went on holiday and never came home.'

'That must have been such a shock.'

'Yes, awful.'

He waits quietly beside her while she forms her words.

'My mum was always fragile but when Dad died, that tipped her over the edge and a few months later she overdosed.'

He reaches for her fingers and he holds her hand gently between his and she doesn't pull away.

'That must have been so hard for you.'

'That's when I decided to be a paramedic. I found her and I couldn't save her. I felt so helpless.'

'But you were only thirteen.'

'I know.'

'What was your Dad like?'

Femi smiles. 'He was a hospital worker and he loved that job. I think it suited him. He was kind and funny and he loved poetry. He used to read to me most nights before he went to work.'

'What sort of poetry?'

'His favourite was AA Milne.'

'Ah, *Christopher Robin*?'

Femi smiles. 'Albert loves *Buckingham Palace*.'

'I liked *Lines and Squares*, even now I don't walk on the lines.' He laughs.

'I preferred *Bad Sir Brian Botany*, Dad used to do funny voices that made me laugh, and then we'd always end with *Vespers*.'

'*Vespers*, yes, it was another favourite,' Lawrence whispers. 'I used to read it too, and I remember reading it often.'

And because he looks so sad, Femi says, 'Don't feel sorry for me. I was in care for a few months but I was very lucky. My experience was good, my foster family were lovely and I'm still in touch with them, although I haven't seen them for ages.'

'Did you have brothers or sisters?'

'A step brother and step sister but the system wasn't so good for them. They were a bit older than me and because of that I think they were harder to place. I think they stayed in care.'

'Are you in touch?'

'No.'

'Do you want to be?'

'No, they weren't kind.'

'I'm sorry.'

'Don't be, they were children of my mum's first husband and they were white. We never really got on.' Femi speaks with a ferocity that surprises her and so to change the subject she asks, 'Do you have brothers or sisters?'

Lawrence's eyes are deep blue almost navy and Femi is drawn to the intensity of his gaze and she feels his body tense when he says quietly, 'I have an older sister.'

'Are you close?'

'We are closer now, now that I have come back to England.'

Femi smiles. 'That's good to live near each other.'

'She lives in Brighton.'

'And your parents?'

'They're in Wales.'

'Do you get on with them?'

'We haven't been close for a long time. There are lots of issues that we don't agree on but things are improving and we get on better now than we did.'

He lets go of her hand and checks his watch. 'Look, I'm having a lovely time with you Femi but I don't want you to be late to pick up Ahmed.'

'Of course.' Femi rises to her feet wishing she was five kilos lighter and that her dress wasn't so short.

'I've had a lovely time.'

'Me too, thanks for the ice cream, Lawrence.'

He smiles. 'My pleasure, Femi.'

As he walks back toward his house, Femi heads in the opposite direction toward the town. She said she'd collect Ahmed and pay the bill for his haircut but instead of wondering what style he's had, she's thinking of Lawrence all the way to

Harbour Street.

*　*　*

'Come on,' Femi calls up the stairs to Albert. 'We haven't got all night. The tide will have gone out by the time you get downstairs.'

Ricky stands bouncing a football outside in the drive, occasionally he kicks it against the wall and it bounces back. He controls it with ease, showing off, knowing Ahmed is watching him. He's also cursing Albert, annoyed that he's taking so long. Ricky's hot and he enjoys swimming. He likes the coolness of the water on his muscles. He's taken off his shirt and his pale skin is already prickling with the heat and he hopes he won't burn.

Ahmed doesn't have that problem. He leans against the wall with his eyes closed enjoying the sun on his cheeks listening to Ricky kicking the ball against the wall. He has naturally brown skin and now that he's had a new haircut, he doesn't want to get wet. He doesn't want to go swimming. He doesn't want to wear swimming shorts but he does want to go to the sea. He wants to get closer to it. He wants to see if it's as scary as he remembers, in the dingy when it capsized and he broke his ankle. He hates being scared of anything but it's because of him that all the scary bad things happened. Syria and Aleppo are from another life and crossing the English Channel was nothing compared to what his family endured. Mohamed would tell him to man-up, and sort himself out. 'Be a man', he would say. So, one day, Ahmed would learn to swim. Today he would watch them all and see how they do it so he would know for another day. It couldn't be that hard, could it?

Femi carries a beach bag and towels for them all.

'Here, Ricky, catch,' she calls.

He collects the football quickly in his arms and catches the sun cream. 'Put some on or you'll burn. It's still hot.'

Femi isn't the best swimmer. She doesn't like to wear a swim suit but the thought of exercising in the water inspires her. It's easier to move in water and besides no one will see her once she's in. She checks her watch, half an hour of treading water, swimming and walking to the beach and back might help her lose weight. Tomorrow she will stand on the scales and see if she's lost a few grammes, the ice cream didn't help, but in the meantime she can lay on her back in the water and look up at the blue sky and imagine she's in Jamaica with her father.

Albert finally arrives.

'Do you need a hat?' she asks.

'N–N–No. I'm f–f–fine.'

Femi frowns.

They all head to the beach but he follows, walking deliberately a few feet behind, knowing they're pissed with him for keeping them waiting but he can't help it. His heart is racing and he's very agitated.

When Auntie came into his bedroom after he said he couldn't find his swimming costume and she helped him look through his drawers, she almost found his stash of cash. He had it in a neat bundle ready for the morning. He'd even counted it. He had eighty. Eighty pounds. He can't believe how easy it had been stealing at school and, he felt happier he didn't have to take it from Auntie. Albert was determined to give his father everything tomorrow. He had to leave here and get to London as soon as possible before he changes his mind.

'Father,' he mumbles softly, all the way to the beach. 'Father. Son. Father. Son.'

Femi turns periodically to check on Albert. He's worried about something and he's stuttering again. She'd have to find out what was bothering him but he's harder to reach now. It's as if he's withdrawn emotionally from her and she'd have to work out what to do. She may also ask Sandra when she's back from Greece.

'Holiday,' Femi mumbles, looking at the shimmering sea. 'Wouldn't it be lovely to be on a holiday.'

14

Chapter 14

After school breaks up, July passes quickly into August. Femi makes sure she spends time with the boys, together and individually. There have been trips to the local zoo (Ahmed and Albert), the Tate Modern, London (Ricky), the Victoria and Albert Museum, London, (Albert), and to local art galleries and museums mostly with Ahmed, but on the whole the boys are happy in their own company, pursuing their hobbies and becoming more confident and independent.

Ricky loves sport and Femi is pleased that he has this release for all of his energy. Since the pub incident, he seems to have calmed down and while there's no real communication between him and Ahmed, there's a truce which makes life comfortable at home.

Albert is the one who fluctuates the most, depending on the visits with his father but their bond seems to be growing stronger. Femi knows this because Albert seeks her out less and less often. His visits with his father are sporadic though Delroy says it's because of his shift work at the garage. The visits are often shortened because Delroy always has to get back to London and it means that although Albert sees his father, it's never quite long enough to have a proper chat and they never have time to discuss *when* Albert will be moving up to London.

On the plus side, Albert is happy that he can make his father happy. When he passed over the stolen money, Delroy had whistled and ruffled his hair.

'You're the best son in the world, Al,' he said.

The problem Albert has now, is that school is over for the summer and his sources have dried up. It's just as well that the summer holiday has arrived because a big problem was developing in the year above him. They suspected a thief was amongst them. They worked out the money was taken from the sports changing room and from the lockers. There had been a furore and the headmistress had spoken to all the classes, telling them the dangers of stealing and that CCTV would be able to identify the thieves next term. This had led Albert to develop a case of the shivers and then he started stuttering. He knew Femi was concerned.

She spoke to Jamie about it and he suggested more counselling but now that school is over for the summer, Albert feels better and things are back to normal.

Ricky is happy. He's pleased to have a break from school and he's working extra shifts in the pub, washing dishes in the kitchen, wiping sweat off his brow most nights. He's been studying hard and he has one last year to complete before heading off to university next year.

Sports Science will lead him into a future that excites and motivates him. Originally he'd dreamed of being a famous footballer, another Ronaldo, then his imagination turned to cricket and he'd dreamt of lifting The Ashes. Now he wants to enter the Olympics as a swimmer, so he's spending much of his time down at the local indoor pool. Sometimes, when the tide is up, he goes into the sea and, to his amusement, Femi is concerned and warns him of the dangers and the currents.

That was until Ahmed chipped in. As usual, he had taken over the conversation, as he always seems to do, and he told them of his experience crossing the channel in a small dingy where eight of the forty people died.

That was the problem with Ahmed, he always knew more, has experienced more, been through more and even though he doesn't want to talk about it — it's like he has Auntie wrapped around his finger. Who knows how many zoos she's taken him to in the past few weeks but she's a sucker for his excitement and his joy of seeing new animals.

There's something about Ahmed that he doesn't trust and when he sees him sitting in the Harbour Cafe with the neighbour that Femi warned them about, Lawrence — he knows he must keep an eye on him.

Ricky doesn't want Ahmed coming into their lives and taking advantage of Femi, besides, Ricky knows stuff. He knows what happens between men, even though he's not that way inclined, he's even seen how some boys behave.

There's a couple of boys in his class who are trans or clearly homosexual and it really doesn't bother him, so why he's so angry with Ahmed, he's not entirely sure. That incident with the bloke in the toilet in the pub, a few months back, continues to niggle Ricky. He was sure the guy was staring at him but after speaking to Ben Taylor and after he replayed it all in his head, maybe the guy hadn't hit on him.

Maybe Ricky had made it all up - but why?

Had he been so obsessed with Ahmed?

Ricky's pleased he's kept his job in the pub, Paul has been good to him and he's determined that he won't let him down again. Besides, Auntie has been amazing. He knows a lot of boys who don't have to work. Their parents are rich and they have summer holidays abroad, but that would never happen to Ricky, and he doesn't care. He wouldn't swap his life now that he is with Auntie. He's already decided that he's going to keep his head down during the summer, enjoy all the sport and go to the gym and the pool, work hard and save money. He was going to stay out of everyone's business.

At home, Albert's too frustrated to play games and he rips off his headphones and tosses them on the bed and rereads his dad's message.

Haven't got the money to visit this weekend, son.

He's irritable and tired. He can't sleep at nights and then he can't stay awake during the day. His emotions swing like a giant pendulum, one minute he can't wait to see his dad and spend every minute with him and then on the other side of things, he doesn't answer his dad's messages. His dad still evades Albert's question.

When?

Delroy was clever like that. He was good at sidestepping questions just as he was good at evading responsibility. It wasn't his fault. He was born this way. His dad was a loser and his mum never cared about him. He went to school but no one paid him any attention and he flew under the radar, barely learning to read or write but it didn't bother him. He managed well enough. He tinkered with cars and pretended he was a mechanic but more importantly Delroy lived on his charm. He always managed to choose a woman who had a bit of money, who was needy and who wanted sex. That was his strength, he was good at that. He was charming. He knew how to pay a woman a compliment, pay her attention and make her feel like she was the only woman in the world for him. Delroy considered himself the consummate actor. He'd sleep with any woman and ingratiate himself with her so that little by little, they would slip him a bit of money. He didn't need a lot. Just enough for cigarettes, a bit of dope, a flutter on the horses now and again and a few drinks in the pub most evenings. Delroy had been surprised and pleased that Albert had been so willing to help him. It was another source of income.

At the bottom of the garden, Ahmed has a secret. He spends most of his time in his photographic studio and today he's studying the images as the face appears like a miracle before him; a blank piece of paper dipped in liquid and then the wide eyes, slim nose and dark hair appear as the image develops.

Ahmed's heart begins to race and he's filled with enthusiasm. He's met someone special but he can't tell anyone. No one must know. It fills him with excitement but also with shame — especially as he's in no doubt that the other person feels the same toward him. It's subtle, a fleeting touch of the hand, that heart-beat of a glance that lingers that small fraction of a second, the blushing of his cheek and the thought of what might happen.

It was a surprise encounter in town and they chatted for hours, the time flew and when it was time to part Ahmed knew that his friend felt the same way. He also said they should be careful as he's also experienced the same negative and violent opposition. He's been repressed, assaulted and he had to run away too — and so he understands Ahmed. For the first time in his life, Ahmed can open up and tell the truth. He's explained what he's been through and, finally someone loves him, despite all the pain, shame, hurt and humiliation. But, how far can they go and, more importantly, what if Femi finds out — or worse still Ricky?

* * *

It's the August bank holiday and the town is busy. Albert is happy when he ducks through the shade of the clock tower and he reaches Harbour Street. It's pedestrianised so it means he can navigate the people more easily, dodging and swerving on the balls of his feet, past families, couples and dogs on leads.

But Delroy isn't waiting in his usual place outside the Italian. Albert can't see him anywhere. He checks his watch, he's only a few minutes late and he wonders if Delroy is angry that he's late and he's left already.

He stands in the square, squinting into the distance, swivelling his head from side to side. He turns around and checks each direction, feeling the rising panic in his gut. His mouth is dry and he nervously bites the inside of his cheek, hopping from one foot to the other.

'Gottcha!'

Albert spins around as Delroy grabs him by the shoulders. 'Ha! Fooled ya!'

'I–I–I' Albert stutters but then smiles with relief.

'Gotta toughen you up, a little bit, son.' Delroy rubs his curly hair. 'Why didn't Femi get you a haircut this week?'

He blushes. 'I'm getting one next week.'

Albert has dressed with care, a white t-shirt, navy shorts and his Adidas trainers. In his pocket he has some cash. He's taken a big risk in getting it from home but he can't let Delroy down. He had to see him this weekend. He needed father and son time.

'Doesn't she care about you?' Delroy teases. He smiles and Albert finds it hard to know sometimes if he's joking but Delroy doesn't wait for an answer, instead he turns around and points to a tall skinny woman with heart-shaped tattoos on her arm and two small children at her side. 'Meet your family, son. This is Valerie.'

Her lips are painted purple and her eyes, rimmed with heavy liner, are dark and intense. Her hands shake as she sucks on a thin, rolled-up cigarette. Beside her are her two small children, mini versions of her, although they're dressed neatly in shorts and t-shirts.

They all stare at him and he stares back.

'That's not friendly, son.' He pushes Albert in the back. 'Give her a kiss and say hello nicely.'

Albert stumbles forward.

'Stop being so clumsy, son. That don't do much for your image. You gotta get a bit of class. You'll learn from Valerie, she'll teach you, won't you, honey?'

Valerie nods but she doesn't smile as she leans down for Albert's kiss and presents her dry cheek to him. Her skin his hard and rough and Albert resists the urge of wiping his lips afterwards with the back of his hand.

'These are your brother and sister; Mal and Sita.' Delroy hooks his arms over their shoulders and he stands proudly between them.

Albert frowns. They don't look like him, are they really related?

'Cat got your tongue?' Delroy laughs. 'Thought you'd like the surprise. It's a hot day in London and I thought we'd all spend the day on the beach.'

'I wanna get a cold drink,' Valerie says, turning her back and she points to The Ship. 'Let's go to the pub, that one there.'

'Come on, then, let's go everyone, and Albert,' he whispers, 'this is your chance to get to know everyone and to get on with them.'

As they all shuffle toward the pub, Albert feels Delroy's arm on his shoulder and his hot breath on his cheek as he says, 'Be a good boy, son. Stop sulking and be good to your family.'

Albert who wasn't aware that he was sulking, is suddenly irritated. 'I thought you were coming on your own.'

'It's the bank holiday, son. What do you want me to do with everyone? They're family. We've gotta stick together. Let's have some fun, lighten up, fella.' He pulls a cigarette stub from his pocket and lights it, greedily sucking the nicotine into his lungs.

They both watch Valerie and the kids walking ahead of them and Delroy whispers, 'Sometimes you've gotta do stuff you don't wanna do to get what you do want, you understand me?'

Albert nods even though he doesn't know what his father has to do or what it is that he's doing that will lead him to get what he wants. Albert's headache is increasing and his temples are throbbing. Why does everything have to be so complicated? He'd taken a big risk to make today a special one — a happy one — and now he was stuck with these strangers.

Delroy places his hand on Albert's shoulder and leans down.

'Have you got me one of your special envelopes, son?'

Albert pauses. He could put it back. He could say no, but then suddenly Delroy pushes his hand into Albert's back pocket.

'Is this what I think it is?' Delroy smiles and Albert knows there's no going back now.

* * *

Femi and Freddie have been shopping and preparing for the BBQ all day. They've bought chicken, Halal steaks, burgers and sausages which Freddie and Nitesh are now cooking with painstaking precision.

'I don't want it burnt on the outside,' Nitesh complains.

'I want it cooked in the middle,' Freddie pulls the tongs from his husband.

Femi walks away leaving them to sort it out. The air is tangy with the hot coals and smoke and for some reason it reminds her suddenly of her father. He loved to cook outside and she had helped him, turning the pork skewers religiously. He'd laughed at the English and how they burnt the meat or undercooked it.

'The secret, honey,' he'd told her, 'is not to have the meat too near the flames and always to cook it slowly.'

She smiles at the thought of him and fleetingly wonders what he would make of her life now. She knows he would be proud of her and she knows that he would have been a major part of her life.

On the patio, Sandra has returned from Greece. She's tanned and her hair is now silver grey. She wears a flowing beige and red caftan and she pours Femi a chilled glass of Chardonnay.

'You look sad, Femi. Are you alright?'

'I'm fine. It's just an old memory.' She dabs her eye with a tissue she pulls from her yellow and black dress.

'Cheers!'

They tap glasses.

'I wish Ricky had time to mow the lawn,' Femi says.

'That's the least of your problems,' Sandra giggles. 'That

Honeysuckle is like a triffid and the Jasmine is out of control.'

'I need to spend more time in the garden.'

'At least the trees give you privacy from your neighbour.'

'Do you mean Lawrence?'

'Yes, the handsome one who was in the restaurant the night of my birthday party.'

'Is he handsome?'

Sandra chokes dramatically on her wine. 'I suppose you haven't noticed?'

'I hardly see him.'

'I've seen him in town a few times. I think he's a friend of Ben Taylor's from the art gallery.'

Femi shrugs and then calls out to Ahmed who is at the terrace table arranging the last of the salad. 'There's cold coke in the fridge.'

'Thank you,' he mutters but doesn't look up.

'Is he alright?' asks Sandra as she watches him head into the kitchen.

Femi frowns. 'I hope so. He's been a bit strange recently so I'm giving him some space.'

'Is he still going to the refugee centre?'

'Yes, and he says he's met someone there who knows someone else, who might know his uncle.'

'Is that good?' asks Sandra.

Femi shrugs. 'Well, as you know, his uncle paid for him to leave the country. I'm sure that he will want to know that Ahmed is safe.'

They watch Freddie carry a tray of roasted meat to the table, enough to feed twice the amount of people. 'Dinner is served, ladies,' he calls dramatically.

Sandra whispers, 'So, tell me about Lawrence from next

door? Didn't I detect a little frisson of some sexual awakening?'

Femi smiles and shakes her head. 'It was just an ice cream.'

'You should have asked him to come for dinner tonight.'

Femi shakes her head. 'No way.'

'Why not?'

'Well, it's not like that, he's a neighbour.' Femi doesn't quite feel ready to tell Sandra that she would like to see more of Lawrence.

Sandra nudges her. 'That's very handy then, he can always jump back over the fence afterwards.'

'Who can?' Ahmed is standing behind them holding a dish of homemade coleslaw which he has spent ages chopping and dissecting, according to the recipe he found online.

Sandra smiles. 'Goodness, did you make that? It looks delicious.'

'Who were you talking about?' Ahmed insists, unmoving. 'Were you talking about Lawrence?'

Sandra sips her wine before replying, 'Do you think Lawrence and Femi would be a good match?'

Ahmed's face clouds over and he thrusts the bowl at Sandra before he turns to rush back into the kitchen.

Femi puts down her glass and follows him inside. The kitchen is cool and Ahmed is busying himself pulling knives and forks from the drawer.

'Sandra was joking,' Femi explains.

Ahmed doesn't reply.

Femi moves closer. 'We have to talk about these things and you know how we all make jokes here; Freddie and Nitesh, and Sandra — we all want to have fun but it's harmless fun.'

'I don't like it.' Ahmed slams the drawer closed and reaches for the kitchen roll.

'Maybe not, but it's what we do to make life a little easier, and quite often it makes us all laugh.'

He turns on her, his eyes blazing. 'Lawrence is *my* friend.'

Femi replies with a measured tone. 'That maybe so, but it would be nice if he were friends with us all.'

'Then you should have invited him tonight.'

'Lawrence is away,' Femi replies.

Ahmed stares at her. 'How do you know that?'

'Because I did invite him.'

Ahmed pushes past her and moves quickly onto the terrace and when Sandra appears she raises her eyebrows in question. Femi shrugs in reply. Ahmed was not himself at the moment and Femi knows she will have to keep an eye on him and speak to Lily tomorrow.

15

Chapter 15

They are eating at the table when Femi sees Albert's head in the window of the kitchen. She beckons him to come outside and join them and when he doesn't, Femi stands up and goes inside to find him. Femi trusts her instincts and she has a hunch when things aren't right with her boys, especially Albert, and she's concerned.

He's upstairs in his bedroom.

'Albert? Are you alright?'

'I'm going to have a shower.'

Femi stands in the doorway, it's unusual for Albert to shower at this time. 'How was your day?'

'Fine.'

'How was your dad?'

'F-F-Fine.'

'What did you do?'

Albert shakes his head and Femi can see that he's upset.

'Do you want a hug?' she asks.

He nods and as she steps forward she feels his skinny arms around her waist and she knows that Albert needs to be reassured. He needs to know that he's safe and that this is his home and that he can tell her anything. She is non-judgemental and she will do whatever she can for him. But she must be patient, sometimes it takes a while for the truth to come out but she will find out, she's determined to know what's going on. Delroy wasn't taking Albert anywhere unless he is going to be absolutely looked after.

She would speak to Jamie about it. He should know what's going on with Delroy and if he's going to upset her boy, then Delroy would have a fight on his hands. She would do whatever was in her meagre power to care for him.

She holds him tightly and kisses the top of his head.

'Have you eaten?'

Albert shrugs.

'Why don't you have a shower and then come down and finish off what's left? They all want to see you and you can give Peanut a piece of sausage.'

* * *

Ricky comes home from washing up in the pub and he's tired. It's been a busy night and he's helped Paul move some beer kegs in the basement. He knows Paul's a decent guy and he treats him well and he's genuinely sorry for what happened but they've moved on from the incident in the pub. Ricky stays out of the way and doesn't speak to anyone.

The house is quiet. In the kitchen, Peanut sits dejectedly in his basket. There's the smell of a barbecue from the garden and it looks like all the guests have left. He opens the fridge. There're leftover burgers, chicken wings and salad.

Femi calls out from the lounge, 'There's dinner, if you're

hungry.'

He grabs a can of lemonade and puts his head around the door. 'I'm tired,' he says.

'Busy evening?' she asks.

'Yeah.' Ahmed and Femi are on the sofa and there's a rainbow flag on television. Ricky heads upstairs to his bedroom and throws himself onto his bed. He stares up at the ceiling with his hands behind his head. He couldn't bear to sit downstairs with Femi and Ahmed watching a gay film. *Pride.* What a load of crap.

Ricky picks up his phone and texts Ashley.

Hey, wanna meet up tomorrow?

She comes back quickly, as if she's been waiting for his message.

Where?

By the clock tower?

Aren't you playing cricket?

I finish by 6

Ok, see ya then.

Ricky likes Ashley. She's one of the girls in his class who isn't simpering, whimpering or constantly looking at herself in the mirror on her iPhone. She likes sport too. She plays hockey in winter and in the summer she's into athletics. She holds the school high jump record and she's training for the Kent Athletics Team.

It had been quite by chance that he'd caught a later bus home from school a few weeks before the end of term. She was sitting upstairs at the front of the bus. He'd sat beside her not realising she also lived in Westbay. He was excited and pleased that she'd even wanted to speak to him.

'They're separated, so I live with my Mum,' Ashley had said

on the bus. 'But I see Dad every two weeks.'

'Do you miss him?'

'I'm kinda used to it now. They split when I was four.' She has short blond hair and two piercings in her ears: a gold stud and a gold dolphin on each ear.

'And your mum's on her own?'

'Yeah, she's a nurse. She works hard.'

Ricky stared out of the window, noticing the bright yellow rape seed and how vivid it was as it stretched over the fields.

'What about you?' Ashley asks.

Ricky is surprised. He assumed everyone knew. 'I live with my foster mum.'

'Oh.' Ashley's mouth is round in surprise.

'Yeah, my parents are dead,' he lies. It's easier than telling the truth. 'So, I was in care and I came here almost four years ago.'

Ashley places her hand on his arm and her touch feels nice on his warm skin. 'I didn't know that. I just assumed that, you know, you're doing well at school and want to go to uni and stuff.'

'You know about that?' Ricky feels his cheeks redden.

'Yeah, I was behind you at that career talk the other week and you said you wanted to study Sports Science.'

Ricky nods and clasps his hands together wishing she would touch him again.

'What do you want to study?'

'I'm going to be a teacher,' Ashley announces. 'An English teacher.'

Ricky smiles and looks out of the window. They were just arriving in Westbay and he imagines what it would be like having a wife who was a teacher.

'Do you want to walk through town with me?' Ashley asks.

Ricky nods quickly and they both hurry to get off at the top end of town and they stroll leisurely down through the square to Harbour Street.

'I've got to go home but maybe another time we could have a drink in Harbour Cafe?' Ashley says. 'I'd love to eat in that Bistro one day, it looks amazing.'

Ricky nods. 'Yeah.'

'My Mum's been there and she says it's expensive but she's never tasted food like it.'

They walk past the beach huts and then they sit on the steps of a navy beach hut and spend a few minutes laughing at a puppy playing in the water for the first time.

'Peanut loves the water, too.'

'We have a Cockerpoo called Bramble, so maybe we could hook up for a dog walk?'

Ricky had smiled then and when they said goodbye, he couldn't help but notice how she had three freckles on her nose and that she tilted her head shyly before saying goodbye.

Since then they had met up a few times; a dog walk, a drink on the beach and more recently she'd waited for him after his shift at the pub and they'd gone and sat on the beach together. She'd even let him kiss her.

They have arranged to meet for a pizza later in the week and Ricky is pleased to have another date with Ashley. He tosses his mobile on the bed and reaches under his mattress and with his other hand, he reaches into his pocket for the cash Paul gave him earlier.

Ricky is saving hard and, now he's met Ashley, he has a purpose. He wants to invite her for dinner in the Bistro.

He pulls out the takeaway Tupperware box and he places

the three notes on top of his stash that was already there. He frowns, it doesn't seem as thick as usual. He counts it slowly and there's thirty pounds missing.

'ARRRRRGGGGHHHH' Ricky shouts as if his lungs will burst. 'I'M GONNNA KILL YOU!'

* * *

Ricky only said a quick hello when he came home. He wouldn't stay and watch the film with her and Ahmed and now, she hears raging shouting from upstairs. Suddenly, Ricky's footsteps are thumping down the stairs; one floor and then down to the lounge and the door flies open and smacks against the wall. He hurls himself into the room.

'You FUCKING thief!' Ricky lunges across the room to where Ahmed is sitting quietly, drinking his tea, engrossed in the film. He grabs Ahmed's shirt collar and the tea goes up in the air, spilling over the sofa.

Femi moves quickly grabbing Ricky by the wrist.

'STOP!' she shouts.

'Steal my money, you fucking—' He has Ahmed by the throat

RICKY!' Femi regains her balance and stands up. She places a hand on Ricky's chest and pushes him backward. 'Stop! STOP, RICKY!'

Ricky relaxes his grip and Femi takes advantage to push him harder, pushing him backwards forcing him away from Ahmed.

'Let go,' she says quietly.

Ricky is panting hard; his chest is heaving.

'Let go!'

He turns away.

'What's happened?' she asks quietly.

He turns back. 'He stole my money. I told you he's a fucking thief—'

'I didn't,' Ahmed says.

'You LIAR!' he looks at Femi. 'He taken my FUCKING money! That's what's happened.' Ricky is panting, his faced is flushed and angry and he's baring his teeth, trying to push past her again.

'Stop, Ricky, stop!'

Ricky tries to push her aside but she's big and strong and she stands her ground.

'STOP!' she shouts.

Ricky pauses and stares at her.

'Sit over there, NOW!' She points at a chair in the corner of the room and pushes him gently away and says, 'We will sort this out but calmly and quietly.'

Ricky moves unwillingly and Femi feels his strong torso under his shirt. He's grown so strong with his football, swimming and gym work-outs and she doubts that she could stand up to him physically now.

'Come on, Ricky,' she says soothingly. 'I understand how you feel. Let's talk about this.'

Ahmed sits in the corner of the sofa. Now he's tucked his legs under his bottom, trying to make himself as small as possible. His shirt is wet and stained from the spilled tea. His trimmed fringe hides his dark eyes. He won't look up.

'I didn't take anything,' he mutters.

'Money never went missing before you came here.' Ricky leans forward angrily.

'It's not my fault.' Ahmed's face is creased in fear and pain.

Femi turns off the TV and tosses the remote on the sofa.

'So, what's happened, Ricky? Tell me everything,' she says calmly.

Ricky's hyperventilating. He's backed away but he won't sit down. Femi doesn't force him but she stands in the middle of the room like a referee.

'My money's gone.'

'All of it?'

Ricky blinks. 'No, some of it.'

'How much is missing?'

'Thirty.'

'Thirty pounds?'

'Yeah.'

'Where was it?'

'I hid it. Ask him.' He points at Ahmed. 'He knows where I hide it.'

Ahmed shakes his head. 'I didn't take it. I don't know.'

'You're lying.'

'I didn't, Auntie.'

'I didn't, Auntie,' Ricky mimics the frightened voice. 'I didn't, Auntie. YOU never call her Auntie!'

'Stop it, Ricky!'

'You'll believe him over me, won't you? You think he can't do a thing wrong but he's twisting you round his little finger. He's manipulating you,' Ricky shouts.

'Manipulating me to do what?'

Ricky frowns. He doesn't know. 'He took my money,' he says sulkily, 'and I want it back.'

'Stay here,' Femi orders. She goes to the door and calls Albert. 'Come down here now.'

Albert shuffles downstairs. His face is wary and he looks

from one to the other, standing with his hands in the pockets of his pyjamas.

'There's nothing to worry about, Albert. But there's a problem and we all need to talk about it, okay?'

He nods and looks at his feet.

'Money has been taken from my purse before and now someone has taken thirty pounds from Ricky's bedroom. I tell you all when you come here that you can trust each other and that this is a safe space for you. If we can't trust each other, then what do we have?' She doesn't wait for an answer. 'I don't know which one of you has taken the money, or why you need such an amount, but I will say, that if I don't know the truth by tomorrow morning I will inform all your CSWs. Now, you know what that means for you all. I don't have to tell you how hard that may make our lives and that you may all be moved to another foster home if this continues.'

Ahmed gasps.

Albert's eyes widen.

Ricky shakes his head angrily.

'This is a serious situation. So, I suggest that whoever has done this, is honest and tells me the truth. We can sort it out between us but I cannot keep this a secret from social services forever. It's far too serious now. Now, if any of you have a financial problem or need money, then please come and talk to me. In the meantime, go to bed, all of you. Go to your rooms and think about it. Don't start fighting, accusing, arguing or anything else tonight. This is our *home* and I won't have bullying, violence or aggression. Now go!'

Femi points to the door, and there's a short silence so she adds. 'I hope you all realise how angry and upset I am.'

Albert is the nearest and the first to go up the stairs, then

Ricky and finally Ahmed who lingers in the doorway, but she won't meet his eye. She turns her back and sits on the sofa, her body is shaking from the encounter with Ricky. She could see how he would have killed Ahmed had she not been there. She thought that his temper, after the last incident in the pub, was well under wraps but it wasn't and sadly she wouldn't be at Ricky's side for the rest of his life to contain his anger. She is upset and frightened, but worse than that. She feels a failure.

Who needs money?

She picks up her phone.

'Sandra? Is it too late, I need to talk.'

16

Chapter 16

Femi's waiting patiently in the kitchen. It's Sunday morning and Ricky is first downstairs. He is quiet but unapologetic. He eats his toast in silence.

Femi uses the time to vacuum the lounge. She has all the windows open as if she wants to get rid of the accusatory atmosphere. She's rubbed the tea stain off the sofa and cleaned Peanuts' dog hairs off the cushion. Her mind is whirling. It does seem a coincidence that money has gone missing since Ahmed arrived but she knows he's honest. He's only spent money that he's been given since arriving here. She's helped him open a bank account and she's made a mental tally of what he's spent on his photographic equipment.

Ricky wouldn't steal his own money or money from her, she would bet on that, so that leaves Albert who was in a bad mood since he came back yesterday after meeting Delroy in town.

Last night, Albert didn't want to talk about his father's visit but he was clearly upset and when he came downstairs after his shower he had eaten some food with them at the BBQ but he'd been very quiet.

Femi polishes the tables and television. She's relieved it's cloudy but she's still warm and feels very tired.

Ricky comes and stands in the doorway.

'I'm going to the gym, then cricket and I might be home late.'

Femi looks at him. 'Thanks for letting me know.'

He comes further into the room.

'Look, I think there's something you should know....' he pauses and Femi waits while he chooses his words. 'I want to be honest with you, please don't think badly of me for saying this but Ahmed's gay. He might not even know it yet but I think he does and, I saw Ahmed and Lawrence having a drink in town together. They looked very cosy, and they spend a lot of time together, I mean a LOT.'

Femi stares at him. Ricky looks tired. He's been working extra shifts at the pub and he's been playing cricket, swimming and also going to the gym most days. His body is filling out and he shaves like a proper man. He's growing up physically but mentally and emotionally he still has some way to go.

'Thank you for telling me,' she says.

Ricky looks disappointed. 'What will you do?'

'I'll deal with it, as I deal with everything else.'

Ricky nods. 'Make sure you get my money back then.'

* * *

After Ricky goes, Ahmed comes downstairs and Femi is folding the laundry.

'There are more strawberries in the fridge,' she says, knowing he loves fruit for breakfast.

173

'I only want milk,' he replies.

'Are you alright?' Femi asks. She sits across the table from him but he won't look at her.

'Fine.'

'What's bothering you, Ahmed?'

'Nothing.'

'Did you meet Lawrence in town this week?'

'Yes.'

'Where?'

'We went to Harbour Cafe.'

'Is there anything you want to tell me?'

'No.'

'You haven't been yourself recently.'

His head shoots up. 'What do you mean?'

'You're very quiet and... very defensive. You don't speak as easily as you did before, has something happened?'

'No.'

'Is this about your uncle?' Femi asks.

'My uncle? No,' Ahmed appears confused.

'Is it anyone at the refugee centre who's upset you?'

'Upset me?... No.'

'I'm here to help you, Ahmed. You can speak to me about anything, nothing will surprise or shock me.'

He stares at her and Femi feels as though he wants to tell her something but he stays resolutely silent.

'I'm here for you, Ahmed whenever you want to speak.' Femi stands up. It has to be in his own time and in his own way. She heads to the utility room.

'I didn't take it,' he whispers. 'On the Koran, I tell the truth.'

'I don't need the Koran or any bible — your word is good enough for me.' Femi pauses in the doorway. 'Thank you,

Ahmed. Thank you for being honest.'

Ahmed nods solemnly and he makes his way quietly down through the overgrown garden to the studio.

* * *

Femi keeps an eye on the time and it's past eleven o'clock and there's no sound from Albert's room so she knocks on his bedroom door.

'Albert?'

She opens it and peers inside. He still has the curtains drawn and appears asleep.

'Come on, sleepy. You've a busy morning.'

She pulls open the curtains as she has done many times over the past eighteen months, and looks at the bundle tucked under the covers.

'Albert?' she calls.

She reaches forward to pull back the duvet from his face when he suddenly throws it off, and sits up.

'STAY AWAY FROM ME!' He jumps up and stands on the bed. He looks wildly around, then he sees his bookshelf and in one swift movement he picks up a book and then another and one by one he begins to hurl them at her.

One catches Femi on her cheek and she raises her arms to cover her face. He throws another that hits her breast, then another at her stomach, they're like missiles and she ducks and swerves from his aim, covering her face with her hands.

'LEAVE ME ALONE!' he shouts.

'It's alright, Albert, please stop,' she says, keeping her voice calm. She glances through her fingers and suddenly Albert has tears falling down his face and his eyes are swollen and puffy.

'Albert, it's alright,' she says calmly, tentatively taking a step forward.

He jumps off the bed and bends to pick up his Adidas trainers and hurls them at her, one catches the top of her head.

'GO AWAY!'

'Albert, please stop.' She holds out her arms to reach for him but he moves fast. He's at his desk. He rips the lamp cable from the socket and he raises it above his head but Femi is quick. She rugby tackles him, grabbing him around the waist, and pulls him down and onto the bed with her arms wrapped around him. The lamp crashes to the floor. They both lay panting, their faces close together.

'It's alright,' she whispers.

Albert is stronger than he was the last time this happened a few months ago and his fingers prize away her hand. He bends back her finger almost breaking it. He wriggles hard but she covers his legs with her own, pinning him to the bed.

'Shush. Come on, quiet now. Calm.'

Albert's chest is heaving. She can feel his anger and his pain and then she feels him sobbing. At first, they are small sobs but then they gain momentum and they swell like the oceans waves getting louder and more primeval. He's hurting so badly that Femi can feel his thin body through his pyjamas shuddering, wracked with grief, gulping tears as he fights the demons in his heart.

She reaches up and very gently, smooths his wet cheek. She runs her hand over his curly hair, remembering her own tears, just like this. She remembers her own pain and the depth of her sadness when her father died. She had been engulfed with a sorrow that had burrowed itself so deeply inside her that now she's shocked at the memory resurfacing.

'Shush, it will be alright,' she whispers, but she's really saying it to herself, convincing her inner child that things will get better. She smooths his hair, waiting for his body to relax and his sobbing to subside.

She lies holding Albert for a long time. She feels his anger gradually diminishing and although his tears fall, they trickle more slowly, dribbling out, wetting his pillow, the sheet and the duvet while Femi continues to hold him. She moves, adjusting her position so that she can rock him in her arms and she runs her hand through his hair, strokes his cheek and little by little she can feel his sense of inner calm return.

She knows about grief. She knows how deep it can bury itself, it's so raw that she can't describe it. It's like a hole in her heart that is filled with darkness that never goes away. All the other emotions and life experiences happen around it and they grow around the heart but nothing can ever touch the hollowness — the sense of loss, so real, so pure and so final.

Femi begins to hum quietly. It was a song her father taught her from a baby, and she remembers his voice, his laughter and his kindness. Tears well up in her eyes but she wipes them quickly away as she hums softly, thinking positive happy thoughts. Her father's death led her to this life and if it wasn't for her, Albert, Ricky and Ahmed would have vastly different lives.

She can make a difference.

She strokes Albert's head and eventually she asks quietly, 'What's happened?'

Femi can guess the answer. The last time this happened was a year ago, when Delroy let his son down. Albert had been looking forward to seeing his father for the first time but, at the last minute, he said he couldn't make it. Femi had to pick up the pieces then, just as she would do now. She'd cheerfully like to tell Delroy what she thinks of him, but she can't. This is how life is and this is how people are and she's not in a position to say anything. The child social worker has the parental responsibility and Femi's job is to support the child and then let go when necessary. It all sounds fine on paper but the reality is so different.

Albert shakes his head and wipes his tears on his pyjamas.

'Is this about you meeting Delroy yesterday?'

Albert sniffs and shakes his head again. He wipes his nose on his pyjama sleeve.

Femi doesn't take any notice. 'You came home late and you said you'd eaten. You didn't want to talk but do you want to tell me now what happened?'

Albert nods and his voice is a croaked whisper, 'He brought Valerie and her two children.'

'Who are they?'

'My new family.'

Femi doesn't miss a beat. 'Are they nice?'

'I told him I didn't want to live with them.'

'And?'

'And, he said, it's all of them or nothing.'

'I'll call Jamie,' Femi says. 'Let's see what he says.'

She knows that Albert will need some help and probably some counselling. 'Come on, let's go downstairs, I've got some of your favourite biscuits.'

* * *

Jamie gives Femi the good news over the phone a few days

later.

'After Albert's outburst, he hasn't been diagnosed with ADHD or autism - but he will get the help he needs to get over his father's awful behaviour. Delroy can't keep letting him down; either not turning up or turning up with a new family.'

Femi sits at the terrace table and strokes Peanut's ears.

'That's good. I'm pleased to hear that. Albert told me that Delroy said he was moving in with another woman who has two children and that Albert would have pizza while he babysat, so I guess it's this Valerie woman who he brought down here last weekend.'

'Yes, Delroy told me about that too.'

'Does Delroy even have an apartment overlooking the park, or is it Valerie's?' she asks.

Jamie pauses before replying.

'You know I can't really tell you these things.'

Femi sighs. 'I know. Data protection. I just worry about Albert.'

'Well, he won't be seeing his father for a while. He lost his job in the garage and was found drunk and causing a fight in the local supermarket, last night.'

Although she's relieved, Femi knows it probably isn't the last of Delroy. 'I hate the thought of Albert living with him.'

'That's not your problem.'

'I know. Poor Albert.'

'Have you spoken to Peter? You need support, Femi.'

'He's on his way round now.'

'You need help too. Be kind to yourself and we'll chat again soon.'

'Thanks for keeping me informed, Jamie.'

Femi hangs up the phone and then she sees Lawrence's head bobbing up and down as he goes down to the bottom of his garden. She thinks he's probably looking for Ahmed.

She leaps up and pulls down her yellow skirt that matches the bandana keeping her curly hair in check. She walks casually down toward the studio, knowing that Ahmed isn't there. He's gone into town again, back to the Syrian centre.

Lawrence calls over the fence to her.

'Morning, Femi.'

'Oh, hi, I didn't hear you,' Femi lies. She holds her hand to her chest as if she's been surprised.

'Sorry.' He grins and she smiles back.

He's shaved off his beard.

'I almost don't recognise you,' she says.

'Ah, yes, the beard has gone. Just for the summer. It's too hot.'

'Yes, I'd imagine it is. Did you have a good trip away?' she asks.

'Just family stuff, you know how it is.'

Femi nods, although she doesn't know how it is at all. 'You missed a great BBQ.'

He leans on the fence smiling at her. His arms are brown and well-muscled.

'That's a pretty colour on you,' he says.

'Thank you.' Femi beams, although she can't think why it makes her so happy.

'Well, let me make it up to you. Do you drink coffee?' he asks.

'I do.'

'Great. What time?'

Femi shrugs. 'That all depends on what I'm doing and who's

around.'

Lawrence checks his watch. 'Great. How about mid-day?'

Femi thinks quickly. She knows Peter will have gone by then.

'Perfect.' Femi smiles.

'I'll be round then. See you later.'

Lawrence waves as he disappears behind the fence leaving Femi mystified. How did he manage that? He's just invited himself to her house for coffee.

17

Chapter 17

Peter arrives a little after ten o'clock. He's wearing lime green trousers and a striped T-shirt, the colours of a rainbow. His hair is like a red squirrel and his beard seems too long in this heat. There's also a sheen of perspiration on his forehead and he looks quite flustered. 'Sorry I'm a bit late,' he gushes. He slings his man-bag on the terrace chair beside him. 'How have you been?'

Femi smiles. 'It's been tough since I last spoke to you. I didn't realise that the incident with Albert would raise the PTSD that I have with my father and his death.'

Peter nods. 'How have you been coping with that?'

'I'm not sleeping.'

'Is that because of Albert?'

'It's because of all the memories. The pent-up feelings and all those boxes that I've stored in the lounge that I know I have to go through at some stage.'

Peter accepts cold water and a frothy coffee.

'Any biscuits?' he asks hopefully.

'I think I might have some.' She heads back into the kitchen and rummages through the cupboards wondering if Albert has eaten them all. She also finds the package from her childhood that she'd kept hidden at the back of the cupboard.

She ventures back outside. 'Here, biscuits.'

'Thank you. Are you losing weight?' Peter asks.

'No, I don't think so.' She pats her stomach. 'I wish I was. Ahmed is making me eat lots of salads but it's early days yet. Look at these, Peter.' Femi places the package with the two Jamaican figures on the table beside the biscuits. 'These were the last gifts my dad gave me, on my thirteenth birthday. He'd come back from visiting his mum in Jamaica, then he was called back again a few weeks later, to help on a fishing trip.'

'They're lovely. Very folky.' Peter turns them in his hands.

'Since I cleaned out the garage, they've been haunting me. I feel as though I've got to go through all the boxes now and I'm frightened of what might turn up.'

Peter nods.

'I don't want anything from my past to upset me. I need to be strong. I don't want to jeopardise my relationship with the boys.'

'What do you think might happen?'

Femi takes a deep breath. 'I don't know, I'm not sure if I'm ready.'

'Is this about you or the boys?'

'Both, I suppose. Things have settled down more now. Ricky is out most of the time and I suspect he's got a crush on a girl—'

'Why do you say that?'

'I saw him on the beach with a young girl. He was sitting on the steps of the beach hut where we normally sit—'

'But he hasn't said they're dating or anything?' Peter asks.

'No, but I have to prepare myself for that day. He's is seventeen, it's inevitable that he's going to want a relationship with someone.'

'What about Ahmed?'

'He goes to the refugee centre now every Saturday. He's gone again today. He seems to like it more than he did, but he doesn't say much. He's very quiet after he gets back.'

'That's probably because he's assimilating the two worlds; the one he left behind in Syria and this one here that keeps him safe.'

'I want to keep him here with me, with us. I want him to go to school in September.'

Peter nods.

'And Albert?' he asks.

'He gets on well with Ahmed. They have been good with each other and they often mess around photographing each other.'

'Does Ricky join in?'

'Sometimes, but Ricky distances himself, I think he feels superior like the man of the family. They sometimes play computer games together but I feel it's all superficial, they do it to please me and so I don't push it.'

Femi doesn't tell Peter about the missing money. She's given Ricky thirty pounds for his savings but she's determined, one day, to find out the truth. At least since the last blow up, no more money has been taken. She doesn't want anything else to rock her fragile boat, especially after the recent episode with Albert.

They chat for a while longer and then Peter stands up to leave.

'Look, Femi, you can always share your feelings and

thoughts with the boys. Tell them about your past. It may help them.'

'I do tell them bits about my past but they're boys. They're not really interested in feelings believe me and to be honest, it suits me perfectly.'

Peter throws his man-bag over his shoulder.

'Look, I'll be moving on soon. Our time is up, but I've enjoyed being your social worker.' He grins. 'You're a remarkable woman, Femi. I'll miss you.'

'Me too, Peter. Thanks for everything. You've been really supportive.'

'I believe Emma is replacing me.'

Femi nods. She's used to not getting too involved with her social workers and she will have to go through the same old rigmarole again. She knows they never have time to read her profile, it takes them all their time to keep up with the children she has staying here. Although they could potentially know so much about her, they're never allowed to be friends. Luckily she still has Sandra. Femi stands up and smooths down her skirt. She'd miss Peter, after all he was the one who brought Ahmed into her life. He steps forward and takes her in his arms and she's comforted by his sad smile.

'Take care, Peter.'

'You too, Femi. Good Luck.'

And that's that, she thinks as she closes the front door behind him, it's all as transient as that.

* * *

At mid-day, Femi opens the front door to find Lawrence, on the step, wearing khaki shorts and a clean white T-shirt. He's brushed his scruffy but clean, shoulder-length hair and his round glasses are cool and very trendy. He seems to have a new 'look' every time she sees him but Femi realises Sandra is right, he is actually very handsome.

'Are you ready?' he asks.

'Ready?'

'Yes, coffee? I thought we'd go down to the beach.'

Femi pauses surprised and then delighted that he wasn't the type of guy who'd invite himself round.

'Can I bring Peanut?'

'Of course.'

A few minutes later, after Lawrence has made a fuss of Peanut and his nose licked twenty times, they are all walking along the promenade. The beach is busy, the tide is high and lots of people are swimming, unpacking picnics on the beach and lying on the stones.

Femi breathes a sigh of satisfaction and enjoys the sun on her skin. Lawrence is happy to walk companionably beside her.

'Isn't it wonderful?' he says.

'I love it.'

'I'm pleased I moved here.'

'It must have been a very different life in Malaysia?'

'The World Wildlife Fund kept me very busy. They have so many projects over there.'

Femi raises her eyebrows. 'And, now you live here?'

'Well, I was tired of travelling and I decided I wanted to have some roots but I don't want to go back home, to Wales.'

'Is that where you're from?'

'Originally but I left a long time ago.'

'So, why did you decide to come here?'

'I met Ben, you know Ben Taylor? He was travelling in the Far East a few years ago and we became friends and we stayed in touch. He came back here and opened an art gallery and fell in love. He's engaged now and he's settled here. Do you know Amber?'

'Ah, Amber from Harbour Cafe.'

'And the new Harbour Bistro, in the building opposite.'

'And, you thought it might happen to you too? Femi teases.

Lawrence shrugs and smiles. 'Fall in love? Well, a man can only hope, Femi. We can only hope,' he repeats staring out to sea.

'I think if you wanted a date, or to fall in love, you'd have more choice in a big city, even one like Canterbury.'

Lawrence smiles. 'To be honest, I'm not in a hurry and I'm happy in my own company. But, this is nice Femi, to be in the company of an attractive lady.'

'Am I to take that as a compliment?'

Lawrence grins. 'I'm afraid, I'm not very experienced with women, too much time with animals, but yes, please. It *is* a compliment. You are lovely.'

'You don't mind that I'm black?'

'Black?' He feigns surprise. 'I hadn't noticed.'

Femi burns out laughing.

'You're actually a lovely shade of brown. Mixed heritage?'

'Dual heritage: a white mother and Jamaican father.'

'Have you been there?'

'Not yet.'

'I'm sorry.' He links his arm though hers and she feels comforted. They don't speak for a while until he stops suddenly and says, 'What do you really think of these beach huts?'

'They're beautiful and very traditional.'

'Do you think I should buy one?'

'What would you do with it?'

'Drink Prosecco and watch the sunset?'

'Then, yes, I think it's a very good idea.'

They both laugh and walk through to the harbour, arm in arm. 'Would you like coffee inside or would you like a takeaway on the beach, Femi?'

'I think you should hurry up and buy a beach hut,' she replies.

* * *

'I'm really sorry, Auntie. They must have been stolen when I was in the sea.'

'Did you see anyone?'

Albert shakes his head. 'I wasn't really paying attention.'

Femi sighs. 'That's another pair of Adidas trainers, how many is that, Albert?'

'I think three pairs.'

'This will be four and if you're not more careful with them, you will have to save up to buy the next pair, is that fair?'

'Yes, Auntie.'

Albert seems upset. He's walked home in bare feet.

'I need to ask you one question,' Femi says quietly moving closer and looking Albert directly in the eye.

He begins to tremble, his heart hammering. 'Y–Y–Yes, Auntie.'

'There's no need to be worried but I need to know that you weren't bullied today, on the beach.'

'No, no, no Auntie. No, I wasn't bullied.'

Femi exhales with relief, pleased that hasn't happened to Albert again but she is miffed that someone could nick his trainers without being seen.

'Okay. I'll order you a new pair,' she says.

'Thank you.' He smiles sheepishly and her heart breaks for him.

He's such a good-looking boy, and so wonderful with Peanut, and even though she knows he may move back to London, she can't help but love him just a little bit more each day.

As Albert makes his way upstairs to his bedroom, he's relieved but uncomfortable. He knew the boy, they were at the same school. He wouldn't pay fifty pounds as Albert wanted him to but he gave him thirty-five pounds instead and Albert has the money stuffed in his shorts. He still hasn't given up on his father.

* * *

'Femi?' Ahmed's voice comes from the lounge doorway.

Femi has fallen asleep. It's been a long day after an early morning shout with the RNLI, but she wakes up very quickly, straightening her blouse and sitting upright.

'Sorry to disturb you,' he says. 'I need to talk.'

'Come in, Ahmed and sit down.' She indicates the sofa.

'In the kitchen?' he replies.

Femi lumbers to her feet. She checks her phone. She made the purchase for a new pair of trainers for Albert. He needs them urgently. They were also his favourites. They'll be delivered tomorrow.

Her body aches with tiredness and she's on an early shift

in the morning. She knows she needs a break and Sandra has spent the summer nagging her to have a few days away but she hasn't got around to it, partly because she feels all her boys are very vulnerable at the moment.

'What is it?' she asks, following Ahmed into the kitchen.

'Will you sit with me, please?'

'Of course.'

'Faisal has arranged for me to speak to a man who can contact my uncle.' He points to the open laptop on the table.

'Faisal?' she asks.

'I met him at the Syrian centre.'

'He's your friend?'

'Yes.'

'Of course.' Femi slides into the seat beside him and waits as he makes a Skype call. They listen to the ringing of the phone and Femi tries to imagine where this man could be and what his life is like.

'Do you know where he is?' she whispers.

'No.'

There is a pause, static and then a male voice. Suddenly the screen comes alive and an old man is hunched over a table. The camera is tilted at an angle that makes his nose and nostrils seem probably bigger than in real life. His face is deeply lined and he has a little grey hair above his ears. He speaks in Arabic and Ahmed replies.

Although she can't understand them, there's an urgency to his voice.

The man's voice is occasionally interrupted by background sounds and he turns away from the screen, and then the picture freezes even though his faint voice continues.

'It's a bad connection,' Ahmed whispers.

Femi nods.

Ahmed and the man speak again and Femi sits close to Ahmed conscious that Ahmed has pulled her into the image and that the man can see them both. He seems to nod often, and he uses his hands as instruments to explain his words and Femi is transfixed until suddenly Ahmed ends the connection.

There seems to be no formality, no goodbye, no sign off.

'What happened?' she asks. 'Does he know your uncle?'

Ahmed stares at the closed lid before turning to her and very quietly, he replies, 'That *was* my uncle.'

18

Chapter 18

Femi makes tea and fusses around by the kettle leaving Ahmed with his thoughts. He's very quiet and it's not until she places the hot black tea in front of him that he actually looks up and remembers that she's there.

'Do you want to tell me what he said?' she asks.

Ahmed shrugs. 'He said, my sister and mother are safe now. They are living in the countryside with a cousin.'

Femi sips her tea slowly. 'Did he say where or how you could contact them?'

'No.'

'That was a long conversation for him to say so little.'

Ahmed's eyes are dark and his hands are shaking. Femi can see he's trying to control his emotions.

'You can tell me anything,' she whispers, 'I know what you went through and I can only imagine the pain you suffered.'

He shakes his head and the pause between them seems to stretch on until he says, 'One night four men raped me,' he whispers, and large tears roll down his soft cheeks. 'They pretend that they are against homosexuals yet they behave like animals…'

Femi cups her mug in her hands so that she doesn't reach out to him. She needs him to talk.

'Mohamed my brother never knew I was gay. I did try to speak to him about it but he wouldn't.' Ahmed shakes his head as if remembering. 'I met Faarooq at school. We were fourteen-years-old and I knew he was different but I loved him even though he wasn't family. We knew there was something special between us. We knew we weren't allowed to talk about it but one night we were alone at home… but then Mohamed came back early.'

'Mohamed?'

'My brother.' He sips his tea. 'He was very angry with us. We were experimenting, I suppose, and he saw what we were doing and he was so angry. He was disgusted with us. I begged him to stay silent. I begged him not to tell anyone, but he did.' Ahmed falls silent. 'A few nights later some men came to our home and, they killed my father and Mohamed. They took my mother and my sister and I never saw them again. That's when they raped me. My uncle found me. He thought I was dead but he risked his life and he took me to his house. My uncle is my mother's brother. He told me he was only helping me because of her. He told me tonight that my mother and my sister have escaped. They have gone to a safe house. He told her that he sent me away.'

'She must be very happy. She loves you,' Femi whispers.

'He didn't want to help me. Even now, tonight, he called me a filthy whore. He told me the only reason he was speaking to me was to tell me never to contact him or any of the family again.'

'What about you mother? Can you contact her?'

'He said I must never try. He said I am nothing to the family and that they never want to see me again.'

Femi says nothing. She has no words.

'They have disowned me.' Ahmed looks up, unashamed of the tears flowing down his cheeks. 'I have no one,' he whispers.

This time Femi stands up, she takes him in her arms, and he rests his head against her waist, and she replies, 'Yes you do, you have me and you have Ricky and Albert. We are your family.'

She feels his arms circle her waist and for the first time he allows her to hold him as he cries silent tears. His grief envelopes them and Femi is fighting back her own tears. She knows what it's like to lose a family and she wasn't about to let that happen to Ahmed. He was hers now and she wasn't going to let him go anywhere without a fight.

'Thank you, Auntie,' he whispers.

* * *

It's the middle of September and Femi is in the kitchen with Ahmed making cottage pie. He's started his new school, a different one to Ricky, because although there is a truce Femi wants them to feel independent from each other. This means they can get different buses to school and engage in school activities without worrying if the other one will be there. They can also make different friends.

Ahmed has experienced his first week of school and, after extra classes with Femi during the summer, Femi knows that Ahmed will be able to keep up with the lessons. He's aiming to attend a photography course in a few years but until then

Femi has suggested that he keeps all opportunities open. She had wisely suggested that he may change his mind.

'It's Lawrence's birthday next week. Can he come for dinner?' Ahmed asks. His eyes are bright and he's smiling more than he has done since he spoke to his uncle a few weeks ago.

He seems upbeat and even relieved that he has spoken to her as well as to Lily.

It all had to go in Femi's diary and even the Skype call with his uncle has been recorded, as has Ahmed's emotional reaction. At Lily's suggestion he has also received extra counselling.

'Can we have a party?' Ahmed asks.

Femi smiles at the thought.

Ahmed continues, 'We can invite Freddie and Nitesh and Sandra?'

'Maybe.' Femi watches Ahmed as he stands at the kitchen table, taking apart yet another old camera that he bought for a pittance on eBay.

Ricky is at the sink peeling potatoes, he's finally around after school to help prepare dinner as he'd sprained his knee earlier in the week. He's resting from his sporting activities and although he's been fed up for a few days Femi is pleased to have him at home and even more excited that he's helping to cook dinner. He tosses a potato into the pot beside the sink causing water to splash out and onto the counter.

'You're a rotten shot for such a sportsman,' Femi jokes.

Ricky frowns, then takes the potato from the water and tries again, throwing it deliberately harder so it splashes Femi.

She grins, leans forward and flicks water at Ricky's cheek and he laughs. He runs the tap and cups a handful of water and looks meaningfully at her.

'Don't you dare.' She laughs.

The water splashes Femi's face and chest and she laughs louder. 'That's so naughty!'

Ricky laughs harder as Femi wipes her face with a tea towel.

'You started it,' he says.

Ahmed watches them play. He's surprised how close they are when they're together and he's even more surprised at how casual Ricky is with her.

'You're not cutting those carrots thin enough, Auntie,' Ricky criticises, pointing with his own knife. 'They should be half that size.'

'According to who?' Femi replies cheekily.

'According to Paul. The Ship do the best roast potatoes, and Paul says it's because everything is cut with precision and presented so well.'

'You're sounding like a head chef.' Femi nudges his shoulder with hers. 'Are you bossing me around?'

'If I must. Just do the job properly or you'll be fired,' Ricky teases.

'So, if we invite Lawrence in for dinner and have a small party is there anyone else you want to invite?'

Ahmed looks at the table.

Ricky concentrates on the potatoes.

Femi raises her eyebrows at Ricky. 'You can invite anyone you like.'

He looks up. 'Anyone?'

'Yes.'

Albert looks up from where he's sitting at the kitchen table, distracted from his school book he says, 'What about that girl?' Albert asks. 'I've seen you sitting with her on the beach hut steps.'

Femi smiles when Ricky's cheeks turn red and he meets her gaze and blinks quickly.

'All of your friends are welcome here, you know that, Ricky. It's the same for all of you. This is your home.'

'What's her name?' asks Albert.

'Ashley,' Ricky replies.

Albert smiles. 'She's very pretty.'

'That's a lovely name,' says Femi. 'And Ashley is more than welcome.'

Ricky's shoulders straighten and he stands taller, more upright and there's a hint of a smile on his face.

'I think we should have a party and invite all our friends then, what do you say, Auntie?'

Ahmed stands gazing out of the window, unmoving and lost in thought.

Albert says, 'I haven't got any friends.'

That's when Ricky flicks cold water at Femi's cheek before dashing out of the kitchen and she chases him with a wet tea towel.

* * *

Ahmed is excited. He's never been involved with organising a party before and he never realised it was such hard work. He's helped Femi shop, unpack the food and drink, and all the extras, and now they have to prepare the house.

It's Sunday lunch time, and although Ahmed wanted the party on Saturday for Lawrence's actual birthday, Femi insisted that Ricky wouldn't be working on the Sunday and everyone would be available to come.

It did make sense and Ahmed made a mental note to remember these types of details for the future.

It's very different preparing for the party at home than it is when they have a get-together at the refugee centre. Here, Femi's attention to detail is far better than Peter's, who, since he isn't Femi's social worker any more, now spends all the time helping refugees.

It is Peter who has also been instrumental in getting Faisal to settle in. Faisal arrived in England a few months after Ahmed and he spoke very little English so Ahmed has been spending a lot of time, helping him to learn English and to understand the difference between their cultures. This also helps Faisal in his job where he stacks shelves in a big warehouse. He works long hours and he's often exhausted but he never complains and he rarely misses a Saturday morning at the refugee centre.

Amy calls Peter to check Faisal's details. She's protective of Ahmed.

'At first Faisal was shy,' he says. 'He doesn't come from Aleppo but from a smaller village in the country and his journey to the UK was worse that Ahmed's. He's kind and caring, Femi. He seems to be good for Ahmed and they laugh together.'

Ahmed never thought that was possible but over the past few months Faisal has opened up to him and now he speaks more freely to Ahmed. Although he is older, he's eighteen, there's an uncertain boyishness to him and Ahmed regards him as being younger than him.

Faisal has told him that he's living independently in a shared house with some very strange people. There's no lock on his door, and the first night he stayed there a man got in and tried to rape him. So now, each night, he has to secure it with a chair and rope. There are also rats and mice in his flat, and there is rarely any hot water but Faisal is grateful to have a roof over his head. Ahmed worries for his friend but Faisal always smiles and raises his fists. 'I will kill them first, if they come near me,' he says. 'Never again.'

This terrifies Ahmed even more. He would hate to see his friend sent to prison or even deported.

It took Ahmed a few days and lots of courage to ask Auntie if Faisal could come to the party. He waited until Albert and Ricky were both upstairs, as if it was a secret, but Femi breezed past all the details, as if having a friend was the most normal thing in the world.

'Of course, Faisal is welcome, Ahmed. This is your home.'

Now Ahmed can see his friend's eyes widen in appreciation. He never knew, nor could he have imagined, that Ahmed lived in such luxury; with a pretty and kind foster mother and he's never seen such amazing food.

He stares at the chicken jambalaya and he can feel his taste buds come alive, screaming out for the rice and the peas but Ahmed nudges him.

'Stop staring at the food or they will think you're a crazy man.'

Faisal grins. 'This food would make me crazy. You are so lucky, my friend, to live here.'

'I know.' Ahmed knows that's the difference of a year in age.

While Ahmed can live in luxury and attend school, Faisal is assigned to a tedious job, to live in squalid conditions with rats, no working shower and rarely any hot water.

'I spoke to Auntie, and she said you can shower here any time,' Ahmed says. 'I think she likes you, but we mustn't tell her or anyone about us.'

Faisal nods. Even though he's only been in the country a short time, he knows what the rules and the system is like. Besides, he loves Ahmed and he doesn't want to ruin anything for him.

Ahmed looks over to where Lawrence is standing with a glass of Prosecco in his hand, laughing with Freddie and Sandra.

Ahmed hasn't taken his eyes off Lawrence and he's pleased the neighbour, his friend, has listened to him and made a special effort. Over coffee in the Harbour Cafe, they had discussed Ahmed's plan. It appears Lawrence has listened to him. He's bought a new checked shirt and with his jeans, he's handsome and confident. At that moment Lawrence turns around and he meets Ahmed's gaze and, for a small fraction of a second, they share a conspiratorial smile.

At the other end of the garden, Ricky is standing close to Ashley. He feels very proud of his family and very grown up and he's also keen to show her off, especially because she's wearing a pretty red dress. He's convinced she'd bought it for him. She's shaved the back of her neck which has turned golden brown in the sunshine and with her short blond hair she looks both studious and rakish at the same time.

Femi had liked her instantly, admiring the dangling sea-horse earrings which Ashley said she wanted to learn how to make one day. Femi had shown her earrings from Jamaica, her favourite ones with Rasta colours and Ricky had felt pleased and confident beside his girlfriend.

Now, when Ricky sees Ahmed and Lawrence share their secret and knowing smile, he shifts uncomfortably on his feet and feels his anger rising. He can see that the guy from the refugee centre is just a smokescreen for his real feelings and he's frustrated that Femi can't see though him and he grips his glass harder.

'What's wrong?' asks Ashley.

'Nothing.' Ricky turns his back on the party and leads her to the food. 'Let's eat. I'm starving.'

Albert plays with Peanut on the lawn. He's stolen a sausage and he's cut it in half so that he can train Peanut to Wait, Sit and Paw. It's a slow process because Peanut is eight now and although he wants to please Albert, he can't be bothered with these games. Besides, there were so many guests that keep dropping food on the grass so that after a while, Peanut barely pays Albert any attention at all.

Albert didn't want to invite any friends. That's because he doesn't have any but also, Albert's decided it's not worth making any new ones. He will be moving to London soon. He's told Delroy that he has to get out of the house by October half term at the latest. Albert's told his father that they are suspicious at school, they suspect he stole the money last term and that he is really worried. His dad hasn't been in contact so much recently but he texted yesterday and said that he was working nights and that it was difficult to get away. He said he would see him *soon*.

Albert holds a piece of sausage for Peanut and the dog sits perfectly still.

'I'm having help,' he whispers to his furry friend. 'I see a special person and they help me process everything... right now, I'm processing my feelings with my father. And I'm allowed to say I'm angry without shouting or raising my voice. You see, I can even whisper it to you, Peanut. I'm very, very, seriously pissed off with my Dad.' Albert smiles and sits back on his heels as if he's achieved a very important milestone.

Femi sees Albert smiling and playing with Peanut and her heart fills with happiness. He hasn't any friends and he hasn't had any problems at school, so far, this term. Femi believes that it's because Delroy hasn't been down. When he's absent, Femi dares to dream that Albert will stay with her.

She sees Ricky with his arm around Ashley and she's happy she spoke with him last week after everyone had gone to bed. That was her opportunity to have the difficult conversation about respect, safe sex, and bringing a girlfriend home to stay the night. She can see by the way they stand that they've probably made love already, and she knows she's done the right thing by talking him through contraception, responsibility and kindness a few days ago. They had talked into the early hours of the morning together.

'Having a sexual relationship should be very special and magical,' Femi said. 'You must take care of your partner, a girl - woman whoever it is, making love is a very intimate part of yourself, especially if it is her first time.'

Ricky nodded.

Femi continued. 'Respect is very important, Ricky. If she says no, she means no.'

'I understand, Auntie.'

'If you get angry, if things don't work out how you want them to, then you must walk away.'

'Yes.'

'You can always come to me, day or night.'

'Thank you.'

'Always be the better person and you can do this by being kind.'

'I learnt my lesson, Auntie. I won't fight again.'

'I hope not,' she whispered, and afterwards before he went

upstairs to bed, he had hugged her very tightly.

'Thank you, Auntie.'

'You're welcome.'

'I will be a good boyfriend. I promise.'

'I know.'

He had kissed her on the cheek before going to bed and she felt it had all been relatively simple. Let's hope it stays like that, she'd thought.

'Oh, to be young and in love,' she mumbles.

That's when she feels Lawrence standing beside her, and the sunlight catches his twinkling eyes. With a slight smile and nod of his head he offers to fill her glass. She has far too much on her plate to even think about having a relationship and not only that, she's not a woman on her own. She comes in a package with three boys and she knows there aren't many people in the world who would want to take on that responsibility.

If only her life was less complicated.

19

Chapter 19

A few days later, Femi is weeding the garden. She's on her hands and knees when Lawrence calls over the fence.

'Are you busy tonight?'

Femi wipes her brow with the back of her hand and leaves a smear of dirt across her cheek. Lawrence laughs.

'It's hot,' she says. 'It's an Indian summer.'

'Far too hot for gardening. Be ready at seven.'

Before she can think or reply, he's already disappeared.

Femi showers and wears a loose cotton dress. She makes a mental note of the boys and their activities; Ahmed and Albert are upstairs gaming and Ricky is doing an extra shift, washing up at the pub. It's still the end of the summer season and they need his help and it gives him a chance to earn some extra money. There's a school ski trip next year that he wants to go on and Femi is encouraging him to do everything he can to get on it.

That evening, Lawrence arrives promptly.

'Where are we going?' Femi says by way of greeting.

'It's a surprise.'

Femi closes the door behind her.

'I haven't seen Ahmed for a while,' he says.

'He's been spending more time at the Syrian Refugee Centre. It's good for him to speak his own language.'

Lawrence nods.

'Any news of him finding his mother?'

'There's one man who thinks he might know someone, who knows someone else... but so far nothing positive has happened.'

Although Ahmed's uncle has said that Ahmed's family want him to have no more contact with his mother and sister, his new friend Faisal thinks differently. He's encouraging him to look for other ways of finding his mother and Femi is pleased. They are both good for each other.

'It's tough for him,' Lawrence agrees. 'I hope it works out.'

'Me too.'

'I like Faisal,' says Lawrence. 'But he's having a tough time.'

'It's the difference between a few years of age. Ahmed gets a family and school, Faisal gets crappy social housing and a hard job.'

They walk along the promenade and Lawrence takes Femi's arm and whispers, 'This way.' He leads her up a small hill beside the beach huts and then up a few steps further onto a lavender and white beach hut.

'Come on.' He smiles offering her his hand.

The beach hut is open. There are two chairs on the wooden deck and Femi takes his hand, pleased to be guided but also to feel his touch again. His skin is warm but to her dismay she has massive fingers compared to his long slender ones and she snatches her hand quickly away. He flinches but says nothing and he stands aside to let her look inside.

'It's quite bare, but I was thinking I might put a small shelf on the left for a kettle and small fridge over there, and then a sofa so that I can use it in the winter, what do you think?'

'Have you rented it?' she asks.

'I bought it.'

Femi stares at him.

'Look,' he says, pointing at the sea and the setting sun. 'Isn't it amazing? Isn't it the most perfect view. The pink one down below was for sale too but it doesn't have this view. You need the height and then the sunset is even more spectacular.'

Femi turns to look at the view and she covers her mouth with her hand. The descending sun is still bright and although there are some clouds the setting sun is breathtaking with its myriad of colour.

'Do you like it?' he asks. 'Sit here, Femi, please. I brought a bottle of Prosecco down earlier so it would be nice and chilled for us.'

Femi sits in a camping chair unable to speak and simply gazes at the view across the sea. The sun is sinking, as the sky turns misty oranges and purples she's distracted by couples and lovers taking photographs of each other with the scenic backdrop.

'Here, take this. Cheers, Femi.'

Automatically Femi takes the glass. Lawrence taps hers with his but she doesn't notice. He sits beside her in the other camping chair and stretches out his legs and a small happy sigh escapes his lips.

It takes Femi a while to assess everything and inside she begins panicking. She'd said it as a joke. A throw-away comment. She'd enjoyed Lawrence's company but she never expected this. This isn't what she wanted him to do. He's bought a beach hut! Why has he done this?

'Well?' he asks. 'Is Madame impressed?'

Is that why he bought it?

'Femi?'

Femi sips her Prosecco and the bubbles are perfect on her tongue. Everything is perfect. Lawrence. This beach hut. The Prosecco. Everything is simply perfect.

'Femi, are you alright?'

She places her glass on the small table, stands up and stops at the steps. 'I—I forgot. I have to get back. I have to— Sorry, I have to—' She begins running, down the steps and then she's running really fast, weaving in between the beach huts and sobbing hard. Eventually, when she's run out of breath, she stops and leans with her back against another beach hut and coughs hard. She isn't used to such physical exertion but it isn't just that. It is much worse than she could possibly have imagined. She wipes her eyes with the back of her hand and stands resolutely, shoulders back with her heart thumping erratically. She needs to be at home with her boys. She can't cope with all this. Nothing is perfect. Nothing lasts. Everyone dies or moves away. She doesn't want any more heartbreak. She can't cope with any more loss.

Why can't Lawrence just stay away?

* * *

Femi and Sandra are sitting in the corner of the The Ship. It isn't busy and it's also a night that Ricky isn't working so Sandra orders them another double gin.

'So, you haven't seen him since you ran off?'

'No.'

'You have to apologise,' Sandra says with conviction.

'I didn't know he was going to do that.'

'For goodness sake, Femi. Everyone could see it at the party. Lawrence likes you.'

'I didn't know—'

'You didn't guess that Ahmed invited Lawrence because he wants you two to be together?'

'No, how could I know that?'

Sandra shakes her head with exasperation. 'Femi, how dense are you?'

'Lawrence can't be a father figure for him.'

'Why not?'

'Because, because we're not— How did you know and I didn't?'

'Can you not see that Ahmed is crying out for love and that you both give it to him in different ways? He's a romantic at heart. He sees you and Lawrence in his future.'

'No.' Femi shakes her head sadly. 'I had no idea. That's even worse than—'

'What's worse?'

'Well, Ricky put it into my head a while ago that Lawrence and Ahmed, you know—'

'No.'

'He insinuated that Ahmed had a crush on Lawrence.'

'And you believed him?' Sandra's voice is raised. 'You believed, Ricky?'

'No, but Lawrence was, is and has been very attentive toward Ahmed. Unusually so—'

'But you never said anything?'

'No, I didn't want to because Lawrence seems so nice and his credentials checked out but I kept my eye on them and, I asked Lawrence if he was gay—'

'For goodness sake, Femi—' Sandra runs her hand through her purple hair.

'I know but, I had to be sure.'

'Lawrence is a decent guy,' Sandra says. 'He's encouraged Ahmed to go to the refugee centre.'

'Ahmed's spending a lot of time there with Faisal and he's more his age.'

'Look Ahmed, said to me at the party, wouldn't it be nice if Auntie and Lawrence became more than just friends?'

'He did?'

'Don't sound so surprised.'

'I wanted to be friends with Lawrence so that I could keep an eye on him. It's important that Ahmed has a friend who can teach him about nature and things, but I never dreamed that Lawrence might be interested in me. How could he—?'

'Do you find him attractive?'

'Yes, of course but—' Femi giggles and covers her mouth with her hand.

'Then how could you be so silly?'

Femi shakes her head. 'I guess I've been busy trying to keep everyone on track, you know, Ahmed at the refugee centre, Albert and his father, and then the missing money, and then Ricky and Ashley — I want them all to be okay.'

'And they are. Everyone is okay, except you. How do you feel about Lawrence, now?'

'Terrified.'

'Why?'

'Because, you know why, Sandra. People don't stick around. That's the problem, isn't it? It's hard enough coping with the fact that I could lose the boys with one wrong move but—'

'Look,' Sandra says, 'Your Dad died. That was tragic. You lost him at a very young age and your Mum couldn't cope. You lost them both in a short space of time. But you have to live, Femi. You have to move on. It's alright to fall in love. Lawrence won't go anywhere. He lives right beside you, for heaven's sake. You have to speak to him. Go home tonight. Go next door. Tell Lawrence how you feel and once you share that vulnerability with him, he will understand. Everything will be alright, trust me.'

* * *

Femi knocks tentatively on Lawrence's front door. There's no bell, so she knocks again and she waits. There's no answer so she heads down the side passage to the gate but it's locked.

She sighs and turns away. She'd try again tomorrow.

Back in her house, everything is quiet and there's a parcel on the doorstep. Albert's new trainers. He will be delighted.

She kicks off her shoes and sees a pretty pair of pink sneakers belonging to Ashley under the coat stand. Hanging on the hook is the jacket that Faisal wore last weekend at the party. She'd felt so sorry for him. He was a nice lad and she was horrified at the place where he was living. She was under no illusion. Refugees had it hard and she knew the dangers of their rat-infested accommodation and how many unstable adults prey on young boys. Criminal exploitation from gangs and grooming is a real threat. Most boys his age and with his background have invariably been enticed into a world of escapism; drugs and petty crime. It always starts small but very soon these boys find it increasingly hard to keep clean clothes for their jobs, maintain a healthy body and regime that's needed for interviews and work, and often they're not equipped for the subtleties of addicts, thieves and conmen. Secretly, Femi marvelled that Faisal was doing so well, even holding down a job.

Femi fills the kettle and reaches for a tea cup, happy that Faisal can shower upstairs at least it might be one night that he stays over and can feel safe and he can sleep without fear.

She sits at the table, feeling suddenly weary, and thinks about the boxes in the lounge. Her memory boxes have been moved from the kitchen and stacked in the corner for months. Now she knows she must open them. Perhaps by sharing her past and opening up, it might encourage her boys to feel safe too. It might also help her come to terms with her own traumas and prepare her for a future — a future that she could only ever imagine but never once dreamed that it might turn into reality.

Sandra was her social worker four years ago, and she knows her better than anyone. She's a good friend and Femi knows that Sandra would think carefully before giving her advice so freely and sincerely.

Femi takes her tea up to bed and just as she goes into her room, Ahmed's face appears around the door.

'Auntie?'

'Yes.'

'Are you alright?'

'I'm tired,' she replies truthfully.

'Have you been crying?' He frowns.

'No.'

Ahmed pauses and then asks, 'Can Faisal stay tonight?'

'Yes. There's a spare duvet and pillow in the cupboard and he can sleep in the lounge on the sofa.'

'Thank you, Auntie. Goodnight.'

'Goodnight, Ahmed. Sleep well.' She opens the door to her bedroom and pauses when he speaks.

'I thought you might be crying because you heard about Lawrence.'

Femi turns quickly. 'Lawrence?'

'He's gone.'

Femi can't speak. Her throat has seized up and her mouth hangs open and she finally asks, 'Gone where?'

Ahmed continues, 'I don't know but all his bird boxes have gone too.'

20

Chapter 20

The following morning there's an envelope through the front door with her name on it.

Dear Femi,

I'm really sorry if I upset you. That was never my intention. I have to go away for a while but I've spoken to Ben Taylor. He's very keen to exhibit some of Ahmed's work. He's taking some great photographs and it would be a shame if no one saw them. I took the liberty of saying you'd call him to discuss it.

Take care,

Lawrence.

Femi shows Ahmed the note and although he tries to hide it, Ahmed is upset.

'What happened?' he asks.

'Nothing.'

'Did he upset you?'

'No, he didn't upset me. Sometimes people need space and you need time to sort out your emotions.'

'But he never said goodbye,' he whispers.

'People can't always do that,' Femi explains. 'I imagine it was something business related.'

'Is he coming back?'

'I don't know,' she answers truthfully. Ahmed glares at her as if he knows she's hiding a great secret.

But taking guidance from Lawrence's note, the next Saturday morning she walks with Ahmed into town. They walk along the promenade and past the beach huts and Femi stares up at the pretty lavender and white one where she last saw Lawrence.

It's all closed up now and although it's only been a week, it's beginning to seem like she saw him a long time ago. She knows the feeling of loss; the distance with familiarity, that endless feeling of grief but she's determined to push it to one side and carry on with her life.

'Don't be silly,' she chides herself, 'I hardly know the man.'

'Pardon?'

'I hardly know Ben Taylor,' she says and Ahmed frowns.

When they arrive at the art gallery, Ben Taylor greets them both with enthusiasm. 'I'm very excited about your photographs,' he says, to Ahmed. 'Lawrence speaks very highly of you. Come on, let's go next door.'

To their surprise, Ben leads them out of the art gallery and into the Harbour Bistro next door. It's still early and it isn't yet open to the public but there are two waiters setting up the tables and polishing glasses and Femi spies a chef, dressed immaculately in white, in the kitchen.

'Have you been in here before?' he asks.

They both shake their heads.

'Amber manages this, and the Harbour Cafe and I spoke to

her about having your photos on the walls in here.'

Ahmed's jaw falls open. 'You mean, on display in here?'

Ben smiles. 'She's sorry she missed you but she had to pop up to London today. You can meet her next time.'

Femi looks at the small intimate booths and the romantic tables. She notices the details; red candles, gold table decorations and the way the glasses shine like they've been polished for hours. It is simply beautiful and the smell of the curry, garlic, cinnamon and cumin are already heady and making her stomach gurgle.

Ben shows them around and indicates where he would like Ahmed's pictures to go and Femi suggests Ahmed takes notes.

'What thoughts do you have? asks Ben. 'What do you think would be suitable, Ahmed?'

Ahmed appears speechless and when he does speak his voice is a croak. 'Portraits, scenes of Westbay or wildlife?'

'Okay, why don't you get a few things together and I'll send Femi an email to confirm it all and when Amber is back we can all hook up and make a decision, does that sound good?'

Ahmed nods.

'We can put a price on them, and then the diners can see them and if they like them, they can pay us here and we can credit your bank account.'

'Do you take a commission?' Femi asks.

Ben laughs. 'No, not at all. Amber said she'll be happy to have the pictures on the wall for three months, that will include Christmas and the New Year, so you may even sell a few as gifts.'

Ahmed blinks quickly.

'That's kind of her,' Femi says.

'Amber wants to help, and so do I.'

'Thank you.' Ahmed's eyes are bright and excited and that, thinks Femi is priceless.

After Femi and Ahmed leave and they're walking down Harbour Street, Ahmed begins laughing. He's laughing so loudly and so hard that Femi joins in and people turn to stare at them. Ahmed clutches his stomach, still laughing and Femi feels pains in her stomach from the laughter too. She has never seen him this happy. They can hardly speak, and as they walk back along the promenade, Ahmed looks up at the beach huts.

'Will I tell you something, Auntie?'

'What's that?'

'When I get rich, I'm going to buy one of these beach huts.'

Femi follows his gaze and it settles on the beach hut where she sat with Lawrence. Two painters are stripped to the waist, painting the woodwork carefully, and that's when Femi realises that Lawrence has already sold it and, she wonders if he will ever come back.

* * *

Freddie hands Femi a cup of coffee. They're on a break at work and it's been the first opportunity he's had to speak to her since the party.

'Lawrence has gone then?'

Femi stares out of the windows into the busy street. The clinic overlooks the back of the harbour car park and although it's mid-morning and it's for trade only, it's already filled with vans and lorries.

'When is he coming back?' Freddie stands beside her, dipping custard creams into his coffee.

Femi sighs. 'He hasn't said.'

'Have you messaged him?'

Femi shakes her head.

'So, you think he bought this beach hut to seduce you and then, when you ran off without an explanation, he ran off too and now he's sold it?'

Femi shrugs.

'What a fine pair you both are.' Freddie shakes his head. 'It seemed like a perfect match. At least if you had a proper relationship and argued, you could both run away and never have any confrontation of any kind.'

'It's not about confrontation.'

'Do you think I don't know that? It's all about commitment, Femi. You're frightened to commit to anyone because you lost your father when you were thirteen.'

Femi stares at him.

'What? Don't look so surprised. I'm your friend and I've watched you. I've seen you dating the odd guy here and there and you've never given any of them a chance.'

'There haven't been that many—'

'Maybe not, but that's also because you're too frightened to look.'

'I'm not—'

'I'm telling the truth, Femi. It's not rocket science. You can't hide it. It's who you are. It's not hard to know what you're like, it happens every time. You pretend you want to meet someone but the reality is — you hide.'

'I don't—'

'You've lost all this weight and for what? For who — or for whom?'

Femi strokes her dress over her hips. She hadn't noticed

she'd lost weight. What was Freddie talking about?

'I don't hide.'

'No, you're right. You run. Wasn't there a film where the leading lady kept running? She was frightened of commitment — a Julia Roberts film? You're like her only you never even get as far as the wedding.' Freddie turns away. 'You should contact Lawrence.'

'I don't have his number.'

'Ahmed does.'

'It would cost a fortune to call him, if he's gone back to Malaysia, besides, what do I say? Anyway, maybe he has gone because he's had an emergency. How do I know? Maybe he is telling the truth.'

'So, what will you do?'

'Nothing. I'm not making a fuss.'

'Has Ahmed heard from him?'

'No.'

Freddie shakes his head. 'You can't teach your boys these lessons, Femi. You can't let them develop your hang ups. You can't put all your insecurities on them. You're teaching them not to have commitment.'

'I don't— I'm not—'

'You have to open up. You have to open that Pandora's Box of unhappy memories and share them. Get them all off your chest. Then, that way, you can begin to heal so that when Mr Right comes knocking on the door you will be ready and waiting like a proper Princess, instead of a sad old soul who's terrified of their own feelings.'

'I'm not terrified.'

'You're frightened of falling in love.'

'I love my boys.'

'That's different. They're different. I know you love them. But I'm talking about a grown-up love. A mature love with a man, where you even get to *make love*,' he whispers dramatically.

'Stop being sarcastic.'

'Well, if your best friend can't tell you, Femi, then who can? You need to sort yourself out. You have this one perfect opportunity of falling for that lovely man next door, so get your house in order before he gets back, so that you can love him how he needs to be loved.'

'Wow.' Femi's mouth opens in surprise.

'He's a decent guy. We all like him and I chatted with him for ages. It's a confident man who can chat with two gays like us and not feel intimidated.'

'You don't think he's gay?'

Freddie laughs. 'Not in the slightest. Don't be silly.'

Femi sighs.

'Now, if you thought that, then that just goes to show how off kilter you are with everyone. Lawrence is sensitive, kind, funny and intelligent. He's also comfortable with who he is.'

Femi sighs. 'I've messed up, haven't I?'

'Big time, my darling but you can still be a Princess if you try hard enough. You just need to sort yourself out and hurry up, because you're pushing on a bit if you want children of your own.'

* * *

It takes Femi another week to find the courage to face her past. It's the beginning of October and early on Sunday morning when Femi lifts the first box and places it reverently on the kitchen table. She stares at it for a second and then, with a sudden decisive gesture, she lifts the lid.

Inside, is her old school memorabilia; school photographs, writing books and badges and certificates. She spends a while sifting through them, allowing the memories to infiltrate, each one triggering a recollection of a fragmented scene of her past like in an old movie. She searches for clues as to who she was when she was a child when she had a family and how she felt later when she packed everything away.

Femi spies a familiar book and she gasps. She picks up a worn turquoise copy of AA Milne, *When We Were Very Young*. It's a small book of poetry, the pages have turned yellow, and she holds it to her nose and inhales, smelling the acrid smell of tobacco, that she associated with her father. She hasn't read any of AA Milne for years. She'd stopped reading poetry. Daddy had been so proud of being in England. He loved the Queen and Buckingham Palace and, as she flicks open the pages her eyes rest on the worn page of *Christopher Robin* and then *Buckingham Palace*.

Her eyes are misty with tears and in her memory, she can hear her Daddy's proud Jamaican voice. She turns to the back and reads the last poem *Vespers*, remembering his soft voice; *'Oh, God bless Daddy— I quite forgot.'*

Another memory quickly invades her thoughts and his quiet voice whispers, 'I'm so proud of you, my darling. You're a beautiful young girl. You are going to do so well. I just know it. You'll be successful and happy.'

How had she forgotten?

She closes the book, remembering his unique smell, and the spicy cologne he wore on his cheeks and she's filled with a sadness so deep and painful that she fears it might break her into pieces. She places the book to one side.

The second box is bigger, it contains more books; books she'd forgotten she'd read. She'd loved Enid Blyton and there was also a series of Jamaican books and one with the cover torn at the edges. Femi holds it in her hands and remembers her sister. It's the first time she's thought about her for years, but now her sister's presence appears and it's like the kitchen shrinks to the size of their old shared bedroom and her sister's is looming over her.

'It's mine. Give it to me,' she'd demanded.

'It's not yours, Daddy gave it to me.'

'It is mine.' She'd reached out and made a grab for it but Femi had been quick and she'd pulled away but not before her sister had grabbed the corner and it had torn off in her hand.

Femi was horrified. 'Look what you've done!' she'd cried.

Her sister smiled. 'I've got a corner of it,' she cried triumphantly.

Femi shakes her head to get rid of the memory. Her older brother and sister were both white children from her mother's first husband who used to beat her regularly. Her sister had always been jealous and it had come out in different ways. It had been subtle at first, but then as they all grew older and their mother was numbed with drugs, they had become bolder.

When Femi's father was working night-shifts at the hospital, her mother was often drunk and she'd tell them awful stories about her first husband; how he had pulled out her hair and once how he'd head butted her and that's why her nose was crooked. They all hated it when she told them stories of her past especially when she cried, and on the nights she passed out, her brother and sister would bully Femi. But they behaved impeccably in front of her father. He was a good man and he was kind to them. He encouraged them with sport and their studies and they often vied for his attention and Femi became the butt of their anger when he wasn't around.

Rain is hammering against the kitchen window and suddenly realising where she is, Femi looks up. She tries to remember the good times, especially about her mother and how she had been so in love with her Daddy. They had often kissed in front of her. Once her sister had poked out her tongue.

'Yuk! He's a black man.'

Although he'd been kind to her, her sister had never disguised her hatred for Femi's father behind his back.

Femi remembers the last time when he returned from holiday. He'd bought Femi back the traditional dolls but he'd also brought a pretty Caribbean doll for her sister. She'd smiled sweetly at him and mummy had been happy, but then in their shared bedroom, she'd tossed it in the wardrobe.

'I'm not playing with that black thing.'

They'd gone to the same school and her sister had been one of the bullies in the playground, encouraging other girls to laugh and make fun of her skin colour and Afro hair.

Femi stands up, and she blocks out the memories while making fresh tea, another of her Daddy's customs. He'd often said, 'If you can drink tea properly then, when you go to Buckingham Palace, you'll fit right in — like a Princess.'

Mummy had laughed at that and she'd scorned him. 'Don't fill the girl's head with silly dreams, Fitzroy, like you did with me.'

'You have to dream, Paula,' he'd replied. 'You have to dream big. Dream of a kingdom and if you fall slightly below the bar, you'll still have a happy, wealthy life.'

'Is that what's important?' Mummy had replied.

'No, sweetness, your health is important. Please stop drinking for the sake of the children and you don't need no drugs, either.'

She'd pushed him away. 'You weren't thrown out of the nest like me.'

'You weren't thrown out, Paula. You chose me, remember?' He had stood proudly then and Femi has such a strong memory of him with his shoulders back and his chest thrust out, he could almost be sitting with her at the kitchen table. 'You chose me, because I wasn't like *him*.'

Femi looks at the rain lashing at the windows. Her father must have been referring to her first husband, the father of Femi's siblings. She'd never met him, but so often Paula had said to her son, 'Don't turn out like your father.'

Why did she remember her saying that?

Femi lifts a few more books that mean nothing to her but perhaps Albert or Ahmed might like to read them one day. She puts them back into the box and then goes into the lounge to collect the third box.

It's smaller. It's an old chocolate box that might once have had a big ribbon around the sides and a pretty red bow on top. When she opens it, she realises these are not her memories — these are all her mother's personal items.

21

Chapter 21

Later that afternoon, Femi, Albert and Ahmed are sitting round the kitchen table looking at Femi's old photographs when Ricky comes home from football practice.

'What's going on?' he asks.

'We're looking at Auntie's memory boxes but this one belongs to Auntie's mother, Paula,' Albert replies.

He has been particularly interested in the Jamaican connection of Femi's father and he loves listening to Femi's recollections. He listens attentively as she relates the stories which he in turn, relates to Delroy. Although Albert doesn't yet realise it, he's merging the two men, their past and their history together so Femi's father and Delroy become one and the same; honest, kind, funny and loving.

Ricky glances at the table where the old school photographs are laid out — photos of Femi in a school uniform. She's very young and in one of them she's missing her front teeth but she's still smiling happily. There are also some hazy polaroids. There's one picture of Femi cuddling a giant teddy bear, she remembers the threadbare bear but can't remember its name.

There's a memory associated with the teddy but she can't think what it is. It's niggling her. Is it related to her mother –Paula?

'This is Auntie's dad.' Albert pushes a photograph across the table and Ricky picks it up.

Ricky knows that Femi's father died in an accident in Jamaica and that she went into foster care but he's curious and he stares at the image looking for a likeness of Femi. She looks more like her father than her white mother who, to his surprise looks like his own mother used to look with glazed, hollow eyes, a sallow complexion and a lacklustre smile.

He looks at some more of the scattered images and he picks one up of Femi sitting on her mother's knee. She's probably about four years old, then another of Femi's mother; who is clearly pregnant and her father on their wedding day.

It's an official photograph outside a London Registry office.

'Paula and Fitzroy,' he reads the names on the back of it.

'She was having a baby,' says Albert.

'That was me,' whispers Femi.

'Not many people at the wedding,' Ricky says.

'Mum said it was just the two of them and a couple of witnesses.'

Ahmed asks, 'No uncles or aunties?'

'No grandparents?' asks Albert.

He stares at the photos of Femi's father on his wedding day looking to see if Delroy looks the same but he decides they don't look similar because Delroy is thin and wiry and Femi's father is big and broad and always smiling like his daughter.

'Who are they?' Ricky points at a different school photo-graph of Femi with two older children.

'That's my half-sister and half-brother. My mother was

married to a white man before she met my father and then they had me,' she explains.

'Do you see them?' Ahmed asks.

'No.'

'That's sad.'

'Not really. We weren't close.'

Ahmed flicks his fringe.

Femi begins to gather up the photographs.

'What's this?' Ricky pulls out a worn envelope from the box, it's been hidden with tissue paper, and Femi frowns, she hasn't seen it before. She feels the eyes of her three boys watching her as she slides out the sheet of paper and as she does so, a photograph drops onto the table. It's an old snapshot of a couple smiling and squinting into the sun and they appear dressed for a special occasion.

The letter has an address she's never heard of, a place in Devon, dated the month Femi was born. She puzzles over the name, dragging memories from the past.

'Who's Davidson?' asks Ahmed, reading the name quickly.

'I'm not sure.' Femi scan reads the letter.

Dear Paula,

I don't know what you think you're doing with your life. You're not the daughter we hoped for.

When you married Graham, we thought that you were made for each other. You can see how happy we were on your wedding day. You have ruined our lives. You are selfish, ungrateful and you have no regard for us at all. You have driven him away to Canada and he's heartbroken.

We did everything for you. We couldn't have done more and we don't know why you've now married a Jamaican.

It is beyond our comprehension that our daughter, who we have loved and tried to bring up in a traditional Christian family, could behave so badly.

We heard your excuses about Graham but he is your husband and I will remind you of your marriage vows – your FIRST marriage – that should be for life.

You have let us down, upset us and embarrassed us.

You are no longer our daughter.

We want nothing more to do with you.

Your behaviour is beyond reproach.

Never contact us again.

From your disgusted and angry father.

* * *

Femi tries to shield the letter from the boys but it's impossible. They gather around her and when Ricky pulls a seat closer, she feels his arm protectively across her shoulder.

'Who's Paula?' asks Albert.

'My mother,' Femi whispers.

'So your grandfather wrote this?'

'Yes, it looks like it.'

'You had no idea?' asks Ricky.

'No, Mum never mentioned her parents, I just assumed they were dead.'

'Well, they were, sort of,' Ricky says, 'He's clearly pissed off with her.'

Ahmed picks up the photograph of Femi's grandparents. 'They do look happy here. This must have been taken at Paula's first wedding. Do they know about you?' he asks.

Femi shrugs. 'I have no idea.' Her head is spinning, too

many questions and not enough answers.

'Why don't they like black people?' asks Albert.

'Because they're not very nice,' replies Ahmed.

Ricky says, 'How could they not love you? You didn't do anything to them.'

'Well, it looks as if my mum left Graham—'

'But that wasn't your fault,' argues Albert.

'What do you remember?' Ricky asks.

Femi shakes her head. 'I know that mum's first husband, Graham, used to beat her up and was very unkind. She left him. She moved out into social housing and that's when she met my Dad — in hospital. He was a porter.'

'Was she in hospital?'

Femi frowns. 'Yes, I think so but I can't remember, they didn't speak about it.'

'Did she go and live with him?'

'Yes, Dad had a small house and mum moved in with her kids and then she got pregnant with me—'

'That's when they got married,' chips in Albert.

Ricky pats Albert's head. 'You'll make a great detective.'

'I don't think they're kind people,' Ahmed says, still studying their photograph.

'I agree,' Ricky says. 'You can't force people to stay together when one is violent.'

Femi suddenly collects the letter and the photograph together. All these boys have so many more pressing emotional issues and she doesn't want to affect them with her past traumas.

'Come on, now you're all home, let's get some dinner organised. Wash your hands. Ahmed you're on pasta duty, Albert can clean the mushrooms and Ricky can dice the chicken, come on, chop chop!'

They move reluctantly as Femi packs up the box and then Ricky asks, 'What are you going to do?'

'About what?'

'The letter.'

'Nothing.'

'But if they know you exist, then they will want to meet you. You're their granddaughter.'

Femi shakes her head. 'No, I'm nothing to them. That's how they wanted it and that's how it will stay.'

'But what about the grandmother,' asks Ahmed. 'She didn't sign it.'

'She probably didn't get a choice,' says Ricky.

* * *

His hand taps my leg.

'Come on, it's your turn,' my brother whispers.

My eyes are glued together in sleep.

'Come on,' he insists.

I groan and roll away onto my side. I'm tired and I try to make sense of things. My Daddy is at work. Mummy is probably fuzzy with sleep.

He taps me harder.

When I open my eyes, the room is dark except for the yellow lights from the cars on the main road that travel across the ceiling. The lights are both reassuring but also unsettling.

He smiles. 'Come with me.' His tone is cajoling.

I'm not sure where he wants me to go.

'What do you want?' I mumble.

My sister's voice echoes in the small bedroom. We have

single beds in a narrow room.

'Don't bother with her, she's too young.' She sounds bossy. It's her haughty voice.

But he laughs and slaps my legs. 'Come on.'

My sister throws back her sheet. 'I'll come,' she says. Her skin, unlike mine, is pale and white and her blond hair is tied back with a navy ribbon. We are opposites in every way.

His laugh is low and excited. 'Hurry up, then,' he hisses.

I close my eyes tightly. Darkness envelops me wrapping me in the security of its rich blackness. I'm drifting off but my heart is racing and my stomach curls in familiar knots until bile rises in my throat. I feel sick.

I'm eight – my sister thirteen – my brother fifteen.

The bedroom is quiet. Even though it's the middle of the night, traffic outside hums past on the main road. I watch the car lights travel across the ceiling, wishing my father was home.

Burning with a sense of fear and anger, I push back the bed covers. Something isn't right.

It's cold and I shiver. The floorboards are bare and I stub my toe on the iron bed frame. On the landing there's a lingering smell of bolognese, last night's dinner, wafting up from the kitchen.

I hammer on the bathroom door with my small fist.

What am I too young for?

What are they doing?

My sister never speaks to me. At school she stands with the white kids while I hide in a corner with my friend Connie, one of the other dual heritage kids.

She ignores me. Sometimes she smirks. Other times, if her friends acknowledge me or say hello, she pulls them quickly away.

We don't talk. We're not at all close. My sister is so jealous. I'm the youngest child with mummy's second husband. A black man. My lovely Daddy.

I am his favourite.

I love my daddy more than anyone.

I bang loudly on the bathroom door again and again, it opens suddenly.

'You ruin everything,' she hisses and pushes past me. 'You always do.'

He saunters out behind her. He's smiling down at me.

Mummy's voice comes from behind me, from her bedroom doorway. 'What's going on?' But she doesn't wait for an answer. 'Go to bed, now!'

He leans down and whispers, 'You'll be next.'

'You have to know what's going on,' I shout. My voice wails in the darkness. 'It's not right, Mummy.'

'I don't want to know. I'm tired. You should be in bed. All of you. Get to BED!' she shouts.

I turn around but my brother and sister have already disappeared. It's me alone who faces the wrath of my mother's drug addiction that we call tiredness.

'Go to bed,' she hisses, shaking her head, as if she's already forgotten where she is, who I am and, why she's there.

I lay in bed. Daddy will be tired when he comes home from work in the early morning. He often crashes out, too exhausted to get to bed, sometimes on the sofa.

The headlights cross the bedroom ceiling like search lights but there's no one here, only me lying in the dark. I'm crestfallen. I wanted to do something kind for her.

I wanted to save her.

Was I the saviour or was I saved?

Or, do I just want my sister to like me?

When I open my eyes, the room is dark except for the yellow lights from the cars on the main road that travel across the ceiling. The lights are both reassuring but also unsettling.

He smiles. 'Come with me.' His tone is cajoling.

I'm not sure where he wants me to go.

'What do you want?' I mumble.

22

Chapter 22

'Auntie!' Ahmed cries. 'Auntie.' He shakes her shoulder. 'Wake up.'

Startled Femi bolts upright in bed expecting to see her step-brother's smile. She was eleven when he started to abuse her. It's been a reoccurring dream for five nights and Femi is exhausted. Her forehead is covered in perspiration and her heart is beating rapidly.

'I heard you screaming from my room.'

'I'm sorry.'

Ahmed flicks on the bedside lamp. 'Are you alright, Auntie?'

'It's.. it's … just a bad dream,' she stutters.

Ahmed looks wary and he goes into her bathroom and pours a glass of water. 'Here.'

'Thank you.'

'It's not the first night,' he says. 'I hear you for several nights.'

'Heard. You've heard me for several nights. I'm sorry, Ahmed.'

'What's wrong?'

'Nothing.'

'Is it from your family — memories?'

'Maybe.'

'It's scary, isn't it?' He sits beside her. 'I get frightened too.'

'Are you frightened here?' Femi sips her water and offers the glass to Ahmed but he shakes his head.

'No, not here but in here.' He points to his temple.

'Do you speak to Lily?'

'Sometimes.'

'What about your therapist?'

Ahmed shrugs. 'It's difficult to relive it all and I want to forget.'

'I can understand that.'

'They tell me, and I think it's true, that I must focus on the positive and that I must make a new life and... new friends.'

'That's true.'

'You must do the same, Auntie. You are very lonely and you need someone special.'

'I have you and Albert and Ricky.'

'I mean someone very special. Someone to love.'

'You sound very wise tonight.' Femi nudges him and smiles.

'It is because I have met someone special.'

'Faisal?'

He looks up surprised. 'You know?'

Femi is pleased that Ahmed has Faisal as a close friend but she's also aware of the difference in their ages. In the eyes of the law, Ahmed is still regarded a boy. She knows that her duty of care must be a priority and that's why, when Faisal stays overnight, he must sleep on the sofa in the lounge.

She replies, 'I'm pleased you've told me.'

'I don't want to be sent away again.'

'You won't be.'

'I'm sixteen and Faisal is eighteen.'

'I know.'

'I like him a lot.'

'He seems a very nice person.'

'You, you don't…. You're not angry with me?'

'No, I was hoping you would tell me, when you were ready. You can trust me.'

'He understands me.'

'I think he's probably been through a similar nightmare to you.' Femi rubs her eyes. She's very tired and she covers her mouth as she yawns.

'We have all been hurt, Auntie.'

'I know,' she replies softly.

'But we must block it from our minds and focus on love and kindness.'

Femi is suddenly uncomfortable with these wise words from her young foster boy.

'Thank you, Ahmed. Now it's time you went back to bed. Come on, or you'll be tired in the morning.'

He stands up reluctantly. 'I think Lawrence is a good and kind man.'

'I'm sure he is.'

'Goodnight, Auntie.'

'Good night, Ahmed.'

* * *

'You have to tell Emma,' Sandra says over the phone the next day. 'She has to know about your nightmares.'

'You know what it's like Sandra, there's so much to talk about and so little time.'

'Did you tell her that you'd opened your mother's Pandora Box.'

'Yes, because I was with the boys and I didn't want my traumas reflected on them.'

'So, you've written it in your journal and told the boys' CSWs?'

'Of course.'

'But you haven't mentioned your childhood trauma?'

'No, not in detail.'

'You have to tell her about the recent nightmares and your past.'

'She probably hasn't even had time to read my case file yet, I know Peter never read it. He just relied on me to tell him the bits that bothered me as and when they cropped up.'

'For heaven's sake, that's not the point. Listen, you haven't had a break for months, Femi, and I don't think you should be volunteering at the RNLI either—'

'Why not?'

'Because, you know full well, that you need to have your wits about you, and if you're not sleeping and you're exhausted most of the day then you won't be much help to anyone if there's an emergency.'

'Alright.'

'Look, Femi. You've made the time to tell me, so for heaven's sake pick up the phone and talk to your social worker. You owe it to your boys.'

After the call is finished, Femi picks up the traditional dolls her father gave her. She lifts the skirt of the girl and there's a scar on the wood, near her thigh, beside her vagina. Femi remembers using a knife to score the doll, she was determined not to forget. How could she forget? It was scored into her memory.

* * *

Femi is about to dial Emma's number when Albert wanders in and Peanut follows him. They've been out for a walk and Albert tosses the dog lead on the table. He has been quiet for the past few days and she wonders if it's because of the photographs and memories that she shared with him. Although she's tired, she makes an effort to sound upbeat and cheerful.

'You haven't lost your new trainers yet, then?' She nods at his feet.

He manages a smile and shakes his head.

She sits at the kitchen table and indicates for Albert to sit with her.

'You're very quiet,' she says. 'How was your walk?'

'Fine.' He slides onto the chair and fiddles with Peanut's lead while Peanut takes long gulps of water and settles himself onto his bed.

'Did the photographs of my family upset you?' Femi asks.

Albert nods.

'Why?'

'I-I-I-—'

'Take your time, there's no need to stutter, you're safe and you haven't done anything wrong.'

Tears well-up in Albert's eyes and Femi reaches across the table to hold his fingers but he pulls away.

'Your father is different to mine,' he says.

'Do you mean the photos?'

'Yes, your dad looks happy and he–he- he's kind.'

'He was very kind, but like everyone, I guess he made mistakes, I think the secret is that we don't just keep making the same mistake but we learn from it, don't you?'

Albert nods. 'I thought because he was like you and me, and we're all from Jamaica that he was good.'

Femi waits patiently and when Albert looks up and she doesn't reply, he continues.

'I thought he was different and that he wouldn't be bad to me anymore.'

Femi sits a little straighter. 'Do you mean your father?'

Albert nods.

As far as she is concerned there's been no sign that Delroy has been in touch with Albert. 'Has he hurt you — by not visiting?'

Albert shrugs. 'It's about the money.'

Femi stares at him before replying, 'The missing money?'

Albert nods. 'And my trainers.'

'Trainers?'

'I sold them. Delroy told me he needed the money to visit me.'

Femi regards Albert thoughtfully. She guessed it was Albert who was stealing the money but she trusted him with the trainers and she feels a pang of disappointment. She also notes that Albert has switched to calling him Delroy.

'Did you give Delroy money?'

Albert nods.

'How much?'

'All of it?'

'All the money you stole from me, and Ricky?'

'Yes, and from kids at school.'

Femi stares at him, thinking of the enormous fallout that this could have on her and Albert, and what Jamie might say. 'Stealing is a crime,' she whispers.

'Will I go to prison?'

Femi shakes her head, her mind racing. She needed to speak to Jamie urgently, she had to do some damage limitation and she would need Emma on board too or they could take Albert away and place him somewhere else, with another family in a different county. Albert was family. She had to fight for him. Femi takes a deep breath. There is no way social services would want to move Albert from his stability, family membership and network of support. She must keep calm.

Albert reaches into his pocket and lays an unfamiliar phone on the table.

'Delroy gave me this.'

'When?'

'In April – when Ahmed arrived.'

Femi picks up the phone and quickly scrolls though all the messages from Delroy and Albert's plaintive, heartfelt responses and, she wants to cry. She's sad for them all. Albert was so desperate to be with his father and in return Delroy had made him steal money from the people he loved and trusted.

There was enough evidence on the phone for coercion that would have Delroy in trouble for years. He wouldn't be allowed near Albert for a very long time but what about this poor young boy who she'd grown to love?

'Why have you only just told me now?'

'Because I saw how upset you were over your family photos and that your grandparents didn't want you. That blood family aren't important and I realised that you're my family, Auntie.

You've been kinder to me than anyone in my whole life and I love you.'

* * *

Femi is thinking of having an early night but at nine o'clock her bleeper goes off then she calls Sandra.

'Ricky,' she calls up the stairs. 'I've got a shout. Sandra's on her way here.'

'OK,' he calls downstairs.

'Tell Albert and Ahmed if they ask.'

'OK.'

She grabs her car keys and by the time she's arrived at the station and struggled into her gear and the lifeboat is launched, Femi is conscious that she's extremely tired. Although she's told Emma about her recurring nightmares and she has been referred to a counsellor, she's yet to have the first appointment.

It's very dark. The moon is tucked in behind the clouds and she squints into the sea mist, the engines roaring loudly as the salty water splashes against her cheek. They head toward the English Channel looking for a kite-surfer who disappeared hours ago. The coastguard had been alerted and the RNLI called out.

Max, the Helm, is steering. Femi is on radar and Nitesh is beside her looking at the chart. There are only three of them tonight and the tide is high and the wind is churning the waves. They spot the board and a person who is hanging onto the side. It takes them a while to haul him onboard. Femi checks him for hypothermia and dehydration and Nitesh pulls the kite board onto the boat. They can't cut it loose as it would be a shipping hazard.

Max guns the engines and as fast as possible they head back to the station and dry land. It's only then they can radio a call for an ambulance. By the time they've taken the man off the boat and the ambulance crew have stabilised his condition, Femi is exhausted. She can barely stand up and she's hungry and tired.

She remembers the night Ahmed arrived at her home and what he must have suffered crossing the Channel.

The crew has changed and they're drinking hot chocolate in the station when Nitesh frowns at her. 'You look exhausted, Femi.'

She rubs her eyes with her sleeve.

'Have you lost a lot of weight?' he asks.

'I'm just a bit tired. It's been a gruelling week.' And, in the quiet of the room, she tells him about her mother's box of memories and, in particular the letter, how Ahmed found her having a nightmare and that Albert has confessed to stealing money.

Nitesh sits silently beside her listening before he asks, 'What will you do?'

'I know what I should do, but what I want to do is a different matter.'

'I guess you'll have to go to his social worker.'

'I suppose so but they may take him away from me and then what?'

Nitesh puts his arm around her shoulders and she leans against him, grateful for his strength and friendship.

'I don't know what to say to you, Femi. Sometimes there are no words,' he whispers. 'Whenever you're supposed to do the right thing, it's not always right for the people involved.

Sometimes, life seems very unfair.'

23

Chapter 23

Ahmed is pleased with his exhibition in the Harbour Bistro and he's been down a few times to speak to Amber but she tells him it's early days yet for a sale, although she has purchased one that she liked for herself. It's a photograph of the beach huts taken at sunset, that she says will look nice in their home.

Ahmed is thrilled. For the first time he's earned some money using his own skill and hard work and he puts the fifty pounds carefully in his pocket. Beside him, Faisal watches proudly. Ahmed had wanted to show him where his work was being shown and just as they're leaving Ben comes into the restaurant.

'I thought I saw you guys,' he says by way of greeting, clasping Ahmed's hand and smiling broadly at Faisal. 'How's it going? Do you want to see some bird boxes?'

Ahmed blinks. 'Bird boxes?'

'Not here,' Ben laughs. 'I have them next door in the studio. You see, I teach a group of lads how to do carpentry, and Lawrence thought bird boxes might sell — especially at Christmas time, do you want to take a look?'

Ahmed and Faisal follow Ben out of Harbour Bistro and into the gallery and Faisal looks around in awe. He's been working for two weeks without a break and he's asked Ahmed to get a burger later, as he can't bear the thought of going back to his sheltered housing. His favourite days are when Femi asks him to stay over for dinner or sometimes she takes it for granted that he will stay the night on the sofa in the lounge, but he doesn't want to abuse her friendship. He's determined not to break any rules.

Ben takes them into the back where there's a big workshop.

'It's like Santa's grotto, in here.' Ben laughs but then realises his joke has fallen a little flat as these boys have never experienced an English Christmas.

Ahmed recognises the bird boxes. 'Are these Lawrence's?'

'He left them here before he went away, so that we could copy them. I've some lads in London, who like to make things from wood and then we sell them so they can learn the craft and make a bit of money.'

'Who are they?' asks Faisal.

Ben straightens up. 'They're very often young lads who've got into a spot of trouble with the police or with their families and they haven't had a chance in life, so I try and help them.'

Ahmed looks impressed and Faisal turns away.

'Look at this.' Ben uncovers a wooden cart. 'We used this last year for the Christmas lights switch on.'

The boys stare at the cart in awe and Faisal runs his hands long the length of one of the handles. 'I would like to make one,' he says.

Ben replies, 'Come here any Saturday morning and I'll show you, then. Amber's usually working in the mornings anyway.'

Faisal shakes his head. 'I work twelve hour shifts and

sometimes no day off. I have no time.'

'Where do you work?'

'Stacking boxes, in a warehouse.'

'Where do you live?' asks Ben and when Faisal tells him, Ben's face hardens.

'That's a terrible place,' he says.

'It's all the government can give me.'

Ahmed says, 'There's rarely hot water, there's rats and there's a man who lives next door who threatens to rape him most nights. He has to wedge the door shut with a chair but this man is violent,' Ahmed says. 'I'm frightened for Faisal.'

Faisal places his hand on Ahmed's shoulder and whispers quickly in Arabic. 'Please, don't embarrass me. No one will do that again. I will kill them first.'

* * *

When Femi arrives home from her shift at the clinic, the grass has been cut. She stares out of the window scarcely able to believe it. All summer it's been too long, and now the season is over and it's turning damp, someone has actually got out the lawn mower. But as she leans forward to look harder, there's some grass in the middle that's still uncut. Femi takes the stairs two at a time and from the landing window, she can look down into the garden. She laughs aloud for the first time that day. Whoever cut the grass has left a big green heart in the middle of the garden.

She puts on the kettle wondering what she will make them all for dinner when the back door bangs open and Ricky is standing there with Ahmed. They're both smiling.

'Did you see the grass?' asks Ricky.

'Did you do that?' She claps her hands with delight.

'We thought it might cheer you up,' he says.

'I'm not sad,' she replies holding back tears.

Ahmed holds out a plastic bag with neatly wrapped packages inside. 'I bought us all fish and chips for supper.'

'How can you afford that?' Femi cries.

'Because Amber bought a photograph and I get paid for the first time ever.'

Femi moves forward and the boys accept a clumsy hug from her, as they busy themselves getting the salt, tomato ketchup and vinegar.

'Where's Albert?' she asks.

'He wanted to help, so he's cleaning the shed and the lawn mower,' says Ahmed. He opens the door and calls into the garden, just as Faisal appears.

'Hello, Auntie,' he says. 'Ahmed said I may join you all for dinner.'

'Of course.'

Femi stands aside and watches her boys get organised around the kitchen table. Albert bursts in and washes his hands, and very guiltily, Femi realises she's said nothing yet to any of the social workers about Delroy, the phone, and the missing money. She sighs. She will tackle that problem tomorrow. In the meantime, this was very close to perfect. All her boys around the table, happy in each other's company and pleased to be at home with her.

She smiles happily and, for some very strange reason, she wishes that Lawrence were with her to see them all and to share her joy.

'Auntie?' Faisal asks seriously. 'Do you celebrate Christmas?'

She laughs happily. 'It's probably my favourite time of year,' she replies.

'Could you tell me about it and what happens here?'

All the boys turn to look at her. She's spent several Christmas's with Ricky and he smiles back at her knowingly, and when she meets Albert's eye, he grins back at her too. His rich dark eyes are filled with happy memories of their last Christmas. This year Femi wants the perfect Christmas.

Femi removes the batter from her cod and chews the fish slowly before replying, 'Well, it's a time of joy, love and laughter and, above all, it's about sharing it with family and friends...'

* * *

Emma has checked her watch three times and each time her phone pings she glances at it to see if it's more important than her conversation with Femi.

'Sorry,' she says after the third ping.

Femi smiles patiently.

'So, these nightmares are still ongoing?'

'Well, they're not as bad as they were. But last week it was every night.'

Emma has straight dark hair, a plain face and wears no make-up. She also wears a baggy sweater over a long skirt that makes her look willowy, like she might bend and sway in the wind.

'And this week?'

'It's happened twice.'

Emma makes notes on her computer. 'And you're reliving your past experiences.'

'Yes.'

Emma's phone pings and she's momentarily distracted.

'Look, Femi says, taking charge. 'I thought you ought to know, in case it affected Ahmed because he woke me up, nothing more, I'm fine now.'

Emma stares at her with a patient expression on her face. 'Well, I've noted it down. Do you feel as though you would benefit from some more counselling?'

'I've had three sessions,' Femi replies.

'I can request more, if you like?'

'I think I'll be fine.'

The phone pings.

'Is there anything else?'

Femi opens her mouth to speak. She's exhausted and she can't think straight. She must tell her about Albert but the words catch in her throat, and she thinks how Albert gave her the phone that Delroy had given him. By telling Emma now, it would be a sure way to stop Albert from going to live with Delroy but worse, could they take Albert away from her? She knows Albert needs protecting from his father's emotional abuse and exploitation – this may have set him back considerably. Having seen his face last night when they talked about Christmas, Femi knew she wasn't ready to do this. She just needed a little more time to decide what to do, and in the meantime, she would hope it would all work out for the best. She is too tired to think properly.

* * *

It's Friday evening and the end of October, Femi is preparing burgers and sausages for a Halloween dinner. Ahmed is scraping out a pumpkin and, at Albert's insistence, he's placed the seeds and pith strategically to look like vomit. Both boys are shaking and giggling with laughter. Albert has picked some long grass from the garden and has stuck it on his pumpkin's head making it look funny and grotesque. Ricky's pumpkin lies untouched.

Femi is happy. She likes to hear them laughing and she joins in with their banter, she checks her watch, disappointed that Ricky is working at the pub tonight. She would have liked him to be at home with them all.

Freddie and Nitesh arrive promptly at seven and Sandra a little after.

'Nice hair,' Albert says. 'Jet black - you're like an African Princess.'

Freddie laughs. 'More like Morticia Addams.'

'Who?' asks Ahmed, and Freddie pulls up a photo on his phone and they begin giggling.

Nitesh is dressed in his voluntary RNLI uniform of navy jeans and thick sweater, they're both on duty this evening, so he's nursing a sparkling water, as they sit around the kitchen table, eating jacket potatoes and meat, followed by home-made toffee apples — the fruit from the trees in the garden that Ricky collected last week.

Femi says to Sandra, 'Ahmed is very worried about the man in the room beside Faisal, he's become increasingly aggressive and Faisal has contacted the authorities, I've bought him a security lock.'

'There's no guarantee that he will stay safe,' she replies.

'It's dreadful accommodation.'

'It should be pulled down but the Council need every room they can get with the influx of refugees coming over on the boats from France and also now, because the amnesty of help provided for the Ukrainians is coming to a close, they too need shelter,' Sandra says.

'Ahmed is laughing as he speaks, toffee is stuck between his teeth and he crunches the apple delicately. 'I love Halloween,' he says.

'Christmas is better,' replies Albert.

Femi can't help but smile. She's seen such a difference in him, and she's sorry that Faisal is working this evening and can't come over to be with them.

Femi checks her watch. It's almost half past ten and Ricky isn't home yet, so as the conversation, banter and laughter continues around the table, she stands for a few minutes at the window to check the street but there's no sign of him on his bicycle.

When she calls Ricky's number it goes straight to voicemail. By eleven o'clock she's very worried and she phones Paul.

'Hi Femi, no Ricky didn't turn up tonight. He said he wanted the night off so I assumed that as it was Halloween he would be at home with you.'

'He hasn't been working at all tonight?'

'No, I'm sorry.'

Without wanting to alarm Ahmed and Albert, she suggests it's late and they go to their bedrooms.

'I want to wait up for Ricky,' Albert wails.

'You can read you book in bed,' she replies, pushing him upstairs.

After the two boys have gone, Femi sits at the table with her head in her hands. 'Now what?' she asks.

'Where could he have gone?' asks Freddie. 'The girlfriend?'

'Do you know where she lives?' asks Sandra.

'Somewhere near the big supermarket. He never goes there much, she tends to come here.'

'Has everything been alright with him?' Sandra asks. 'He hasn't been upset or anything?'

'No, the opposite. He's seemed very happy. He even mowed the grass and left a heart -which was a lovely thing to do. And he's happy with Ashley.'

'What about social media?' asks Freddie. 'Could we find Ashley that way?'

'Great idea,' replies Femi, already reaching for her phone.

After going to Ricky's Facebook page she finds Ashley. 'I'll send her a message.'

She types quickly.

Hi Ashley, have you seen Ricky? Is he with you?

'Do you want to go for a drive around?' asks Nitesh.

'What for?' asks Freddie.

Nitesh shrugs, 'Just in case he's hanging around the town?'

'At this time?' says Freddie.

Nitesh replies, 'It's just another option.'

Femi's phone pings. 'It's Ashley,' she says and reads the message aloud. '*I've been calling Ricky all day. Thought he was sick.*'

Femi types quickly. 'Didn't he go to school?'

'No.'

Femi bites her thumbnail. Then she dials Ashley's number.

'Sorry Ashley, I know it's late but I guessed he was at school and that I missed him between coming home and going to the pub. But he wasn't at the pub tonight either.'

'Oh?' replies Ashley. 'Where is he then?'

'We have no idea. Has he been alright with you recently?'

'Yes.'

'No arguments?'

'No.'

'And he didn't tell you where he was going or what he's doing?'

'No. Do you think he's alright?'

'I don't know what to think. I saw him leave this morning for school.' Femi stands up and heads to the utility room. 'He had his sports bag with him so I guessed he was playing rugby today.' She scans the room but Ricky's boots are on the shelf. 'He didn't take his gear,' she says. 'Look, sorry Ashley—'

'Do you want me to ask around? You know, ask any of the others if they know anything? Jordan, his mate, they play football together, he might know something.'

'Yes, please.'

'I'll text you.

'Thank you.' Femi comes off the phone and stares at her three guests. 'He took his bag but not his rugby gear. I'm going to check his bedroom.'

Femi goes quickly up the stairs trying to be silent so as not to disturb the boys and she switches on Ricky's light half expecting him to be curled up and asleep in his bed but his duvet is crumpled up and pillows have been discarded on the floor. The room is a mess but also empty. She glances around, she doesn't want to invade his privacy and she doesn't know what she's looking for either but she lifts papers, magazines, clothes and hair products and moves them all to one side. Sandra joins her and stands in the door watching.

Femi looks up. 'I don't want to call the police. Ricky must have planned it if he's taken his rucksack. I don't want this on his record.'

'Nitesh is calling the hospitals — A&E,' Sandra says.

Femi pulls open his drawers and wardrobe. 'I think his good jeans and grey hoodie are missing.'

'Could he have gone to meet someone?' asks Sandra. 'Do you know if his family have been in touch?'

'That's the obvious answer but what if he's got into trouble?'

'Don't start thinking of the worst, Femi. If his bicycle is missing, he must be somewhere near here. He can't have gone far, and his family are all from the north.'

'So, he must have stayed local,' Femi agrees.

She sits on the edge of the bed and moves her hair off her face. She's hot and tired. 'Where could he have gone?' She moves her fingers under the mattress and feels a plastic box, and she pulls it out.

'Money?' asks Sandra.

'It looks like he's been saving,' Femi replies looking at the notes. 'He wants to take Ashley to Harbour Bistro at Christmas.'

'Well, that tells us that he hasn't taken his money and he's coming back.'

'So why didn't he tell us where he's going?' Femi's heart sinks. 'I hope he hasn't been knocked off his bike?'

When they go back downstairs, Nitesh says, 'There's no one matching Ricky's description in any of the hospitals.'

'Look, we're going to make a move. I'm working tomorrow and it's gone midnight.' Freddie stands up. 'But we will take a drive around the town and see if there's any sign of him.'

Sandra says, 'Do you want me to stay the night?'

Femi's phone pings and she reaches quickly for it, her heart racing, thinking it might be Ricky.

Ashley's text reads:

I've checked with everyone and no one has seen him since

Thursday after rugby practice.

Femi texts back:

Thanks Ashley.

Ashley replies:

Text me when you get some news. It doesn't matter what time it is. I told Mum and we're both worried. Xx

Femi writes:

Thank you. Will do.

Femi stands looking at her friends feeling very sick. What if he's got into trouble and lost his temper and something awful has happened to him?

24

Chapter 24

They are saying good night when Femi and Nitesh's bleepers ping simultaneously.

'Oh, not a shout, not at this time!' moans Femi, cursing herself for not taking her name off the duty roster on the availability app.

Then Nitesh's phone rings and he speaks quickly while looking at Femi. 'She's with me. We'll be right there.' He hangs up. 'Emergency. They need a crew now. Dave reckons they need a paramedic. I'll drive.'

Femi frowns. 'What about Ricky? What if he turns up?'

'I'll stay here,' Freddie says, 'Just in case he comes home.'

'I'm here, too,' Sandra is resolute. 'Go on, you two. Get going. There's an emergency.'

Nitesh drives fast and skilfully through the deserted streets and Femi stares out of the window craning her neck at every turning, every alleyway, looking for Ricky. There's a group of people sauntering home, but they're too old. A driver crosses them at a junction on a scooter and then Femi sees someone on a bicycle in the dark, passing under a street lamp.

'There!' she squeals. 'That's him.'

Nitesh floors the accelerator and the bike disappears down a pathway. 'We can catch up at the other end of the street. It's on our way.' He drives expertly and when the cyclist reappears, it's an old man in a cloth cap. Nitesh veers the car in the direction of the harbour.

'I suppose that was too much to ask,' she says quietly in the darkness.

'He'll come back. I know he will.' Nitesh swings the car into the parking space beside the station and they jump out.

Dave is already dressed.

'You the Helm?' Nitesh asks.

'Yes, Bill's in the tractor, and Jessie is coming with us.'

Femi's heart is thumping as she pulls on her woolly bear and winter thermals. She pushes her body into the dry suit and it seems easier tonight. She has less bulk. She throws her arms through the life jacket and secures it between her legs and within minutes she's inside the lifeboat with the rest of the crew who are hauling the basket stretcher onboard while Dead Fred, the resident dummy, lies discarded on the floor.

'Femi, you drive!' Dave shouts.

Behind her, Nitesh is on radar and Jessie is on charts. Dave is at the rear phoning the coastguards registering their RNLI numbers in case of an accident.

Bill the tractor driver pushes the trailer with the lifeboat toward the sea edge. It's a shallow water launch and the tractor is more likely to get stuck in the mud but the Shore Team are there to guide them and help Bill navigate the best route. It takes longer than a high tide launch and Femi can feel the rising frustration in the team.

Femi's spent years launch training and practising drills and she knows from experience that calmness is the best option but tonight she's anxious, she's focused on Ricky.

'Come on, Femi. What you waiting for? Let's go!' shouts Dave and Femi is propelled into action as she launches the Atlantic 85, inshore lifeboat. It picks up speed in the darkness, top speed is 35 knots, but before she can reach this, she realises the swell of the sea is stirring and the crew are tossed aside against a freak wave she didn't see coming. She's learnt how to right the boat after capsizing but tonight isn't the night to have to put that training into action. She swallows hard following the instructions from behind her, listening to the voices on the radio, guided by their directions.

'We're looking for a pleasure boat,' shouts Dave, 'It's on fire.'

Femi's already forgotten her friends in her house celebrating Halloween. It seems a long time ago that they were relaxing without a worry and now Ricky is missing and there's an incident.

'Fireworks set off from a pleasure boat, ten miles, north.' Dave's voice rings in her earpiece.

The waves gain height and the choppy swells become deeper. They travel at maybe 10-15 knots and then there's a flat patch of sea so Femi floors it. Suddenly the lifeboat rises up onto the crest of a wave before slamming violently on the other side.

She hears a shout from Jessie who's a novice. This is only her second shout and Femi shudders thinking it will be a steep learning curve. It's colder than Femi anticipated and she shivers with a premonition of disaster. Now, she isn't just worried about Ricky coming home and she begins to think of her own mortality wondering where her boys would go if anything happened to her.

* * *

Femi can see wreckage in the sea. The stern is still on fire and she circles the boat before deciding on the best approach.

Then Dave is beside her. 'It looks bad, Femi. You'll have to go over.'

A woman is waving frantically and through the sea mist and smoke, Femi sees other people and bodies lying on the deck. At the stern a man is frantically trying to douse out the flames, pulling a bucket from over the side and throwing it into the air but most of the sea water is whipped away by the wind. It appears to be a futile exercise.

Femi suspects they'd set off fireworks from the stern of the boat and one had turned rogue or maybe a spark hit the boat and now not only is it burning there's a danger that it may sink too.

Femi moves aside for Dave to take the helm. She knows she's the only paramedic and the only one who is casualty-care trained. She grabs the First Aid kit and heads to the side of the boat where Nitesh is already grabbing the rail of the burning boat.

'It looks like there are few of them,' he says through the mic in her helmet, and he thrusts a hand radio at her. 'Use this, you might not get much signal. Let me know if you need the basket. Jessie can go with you.'

Femi is already swinging her leg over the side of the boat and when she slips Nitesh grabs her arm. She pulls the clips from her pocket to secure herself safely to the other boat and then leans forward waiting for the swell to work in her favour.

A woman on the boat is shouting out, calling out above the wind but Femi can't hear her. When she leaps forward the woman pulls on her arm, points and shouts, 'My daughter needs help and my father is injured.'

Nitesh throws the First Aid kit after her and Jessie lands with a small thud beside her. Femi's paramedic training kicks in and she assess the chaotic situation quickly: man at the stern attempting to put out the fire, middle-aged woman, three children and a man leaning with his back against the cabin. His eyes are closed.

Femi kneels beside the older child who is lying on her back. On first inspection there are no signs of burns but the child is unconscious.

The woman shouts, 'She's diabetic and my Dad has hurt his leg.'

'When did she last eat?' Femi has already opened her medical bag.

'I'm not sure. We've been out here for hours.'

'What happened?'

'The fireworks went off, there were sparks and the boat caught fire.'

Femi shouts to Jessie, 'Check the children for burns.' She nods at the two young boys sitting huddled on the deck then pulls out a glucose gel. She opens the girls mouth and rubs it on the inside of her cheek. When she turns to check on Jessie, she's leaning over the two boys and she has her casualty check cards in her hand.

'Who else?' Femi shouts.

'My Dad.' She points to the man lying on his side. 'I think he's broken his leg.'

Femi moves quickly and she crouches over the man. He's lying in a pool of blood and it covers her gloves. His leg is contorted. It's certainly broken. She checks the wound for blood loss and fearing the man may die, she reaches for her radio. 'We'll need air rescue - asap. Man - probably mid-seventies. Broken femur and serious bleeding.' She pulls a bandage from the box to use as a tourniquet.

'I'm on it.' Nitesh voice crackles in her ear.

'And, we need the basket for an approximate thirteen-year-old girl, diabetic,' she adds.

'It's ready with the ropes,' Nitesh replies.

The two boats are bobbing beside each other. Dave is careful to keep the lifeboat close enough but not too close that they will collide or that the flames will cause danger to the lifeboat. There's a sudden swell and the boats crash after the wave, the four-year-old screams as he's pulled from the arms of his brother. He falls forward and Femi catches him. He clings to her, terrified and sobbing. Femi pushes him to his mother who pulls him against her chest. Tears fall down her cheeks.

'There's skin loss and blisters - probably second degree,' Femi shouts.

Jessie looks up from her casualty cards and nods. She pockets the cards before opening her First Aid Kit.

Nitesh's voice comes over the radio, 'We need to get them all off the boat. The fire's spreading and if it gets much nearer the engine you'll all go up. Chopper is on its way.'

Femi pulls on Jessie's arm. 'We're evacuating,' she shouts. A wave crashes over the side of the boat, but the flames at the back are untouched, she turns to the woman.

'A helicopter is coming to pick up your Dad and take him to hospital. Your daughter is coming with us in the basket and we'll get her checked out. But we're getting you all off now. Quickly, take your boy.' Femi leads them to the rail, pulls the boy from the woman's grip and although he's crying and screaming, she passes him across to Nitesh. The older boy is next. He manages to scramble across and Dave grabs him by the jacket and pulls him into the lifeboat.

Nitesh is swinging the basket between the boats to Femi and she catches it and guides it onto the burning boat.

'Come on,' Jessie shouts at the woman. 'Your turn.'

'I can't leave my—'

'NOW! Hurry up.' Femi propels her toward the rail and Nitesh and Dave are pulling on her arms to help her across.

Femi pulls on the basket and manoeuvres it into place with Jessie at her side. The young girl is on her back, her eyes flutter open and appears she's disoriented.

Femi leans over her. 'We're going to get you into the basket. We have to get you off this boat. OK?' Femi and Jessie lift her into the basket and strap her in. Once she's in the stretcher and the ropes are set up, Femi leaves Jessie to guide the basket across the rails. 'Go with her,' Femi orders. 'Give her a snack bar to eat.'

Nitesh has helped the boys into the lifeboat and leaving Jessie to help the mother, Femi makes her way to the stern.

The father is still scooping up and throwing buckets of water at the flames, but his energy is failing him and he's leaning exhausted against the rail watching the evacuation. The sea appears to have calmed and Femi can feel the heat growing from the flames.

'We've got to go,' she shouts at the man. 'Is there anyone else on board?'

He can barely raise his head but he shakes it as exhaustion takes over. 'No.'

Now she's there to help him, he appears to give up and he sinks to the ground. Femi hooks her arms under his shoulders and pulls him backwards, his heels dragging on the deck. The flames are gaining ground and they're licking at the wheel house. Her strength is ebbing and she cries with frustration as his foot gets caught on the wheel house door. She kicks it away and gasping for breath, drags the man to the railing. Looking up, she sees Jessie is back in the lifeboat with the basket.

Behind her, the flames at the stern gain height. Femi uses all her strength to physically lift the exhausted man up and on to the rails. Nitesh leans forward and grabs the man's jacket collar, and tries to haul him across and Femi grabs his legs, pushing and shoving the dead weight, from one boat to the next, then there's a sudden explosion.

Femi is propelled backwards and hits her head against the cabin door but Nitesh quickly grabs the man and hauls him forward.

'It's a firework!' shouts Nitesh, 'There must be more on board.'

Femi regains her footing, as another explosion propels her forward and she's thrust against the rails. She screams and the radio flies out of her hand. The pain in her ribs is intense and she curses loudly while her breath is carried away on the wind. She crawls on her knees to the old man, panting hard while checking his breathing and then she hears the helicopter above her; it's blades whirling as it circles with a light illuminating them against the black sea. Femi knows that the coastguard, the pilot and Dave will all be talking to each other.

She's relieved as the paramedic winches down. They work together and quickly secure the old man. When the paramedic gives the thumbs up, Femi helps guide the unconscious body into the air and off the boat before turning back to the lifeboat.

'It's not safe, Femi. Hurry up!' Nitesh shouts in the

darkness.

The flames are licking at the cabin, eating the wood greedily like a hungry monster. Femi reaches out and touches Nitesh's hand but the pain in her ribs is excruciating. The boat shudders from a small explosion inside the cabin and she's propelled sideways and she misses his grip. Her feet are suddenly covered in water and the boat begins sinking quickly.

'Femi!' Nitesh shouts, reaching as far forward as he can, he grabs her sleeve and pulls hard. Using her last remaining strength, Femi hurls herself forward and they tumble back into the lifeboat together. Femi's face hits the deck and she lies gasping, spitting out sea water, conscious of the pain in her ribs and blood oozing from her head.

'GO!' shouts Nitesh.

Dave at the helm, spins the boat away as the fireworks explode into the sky. Sitting on the deck, holding her ribs with blood pouring from her head, Femi watches in disbelief as the most spectacular firework display lights up the night-sky. Colour after colour, rockets spiralling, zooming, exploding into the most incredible light show.

Exhausted. She closes her eyes but that's when there's an almighty, reverberating bang across the water. Femi sees the pleasure craft make a final tilt, and then suddenly it's gone. It's as if it never existed.

* * *

The lifeboat is secured on the tractor and Bill pulls them ashore. By the time they're on dry land, the family have climbed down from the lifeboat and the shore crew have secured the girl in the basket, the two ambulance crews arrive.

The father is sobbing and crying, apologising to anyone who will listen and his wife is placating him. The first ambulance crew takes the girl to the hospital and her mother climbs in beside her. The second crew checks the two boys and their father who looks haggard and beaten.

A paramedic comes over to examine the blood from the back of Femi's head. 'You'll need to get this checked out.'

'I'll be fine. I'll keep an eye on it,' she replies.

'And your ribs?'

Femi grins at her. 'We both know there's nothing anyone can do for that so I'll take paracetamol.'

They both smile and look up as two cars pull into the harbour.

Nitesh comes over to her. 'Let's get out of here, unless you want to be interviewed by the press?'

Femi stands up with difficulty and in the changing room Jessie helps her out of her dry suit and then her woolly bear.

'Thanks for helping me tonight, Femi,' Jessie whispers. 'I'm really sorry, I just froze when I saw their burns so I was checking the casualty cards.'

'That's what you have them for.'

'You saved me a lot of time.'

'You're doing well, Jessie. You're still new but you were a great asset. Well done.'

'Can I be on your team when we do the Eight Float?'

Femi grins. Jessie is referring to the fun training day when they compete against each other on various boat exercises. 'Of course.'

'And me?' asks Nitesh hopefully, from across the changing room.

'Without you tonight, Nitesh. I wouldn't be here.' Femi

smiles suddenly feeling very vulnerable and extremely tired. She checks her phone but there's no word from Ricky.

* * *

Femi is still shaking as Nitesh drives her home. They are both physically and mentally exhausted. Femi can still feel the lifeboat rocking from side to side and she hugs her arms close to her chest taking comfort in the blanket still around her shoulders.

'We logged the forty-fifth shout of the year tonight,' Nitesh says quietly.

'Can we go via the train station?' she asks.

Nitesh looks sideways at her. 'It's five o clock,' he says, 'it's still closed at this time of the morning.' But he turns the car toward the darkness of the station, illuminated only by yellowy greenish lamps. It's deserted and won't open for another hour. He pulls up at the front and Femi climbs out. She walks around the back to where anyone might leave a bike and there, under the glow of the lamplights, Ricky's bike is chained to the fence.

She climbs back into the warmth of the car.

'Alright?' Nitesh asks.

'His bike is there.'

'Really?'

She stares ahead. 'I think he's gone to find his family.'

'Why now?'

'I think, when I shared photographs of my past life it may have triggered memories for him. I was worried about Ahmed and Albert, it never crossed my mind that Ricky might still be curious but I guess...'

'Guess what?' Nitesh asks softly.

'I guess now that he may have fallen in love with Ashley, he's thinking about relationships, family and children. He'll be wondering who he is and where he's come from. He'll be questioning his own parents. Who they are and who he is now.'

'It's a difficult time, Femi. Try not to think of it tonight. You've been through too much already and you need to rest.'

At home Femi shares her train of thoughts with Sandra and Freddie. They sit around the table drinking hot chocolate until the sun rises.

'I know he's not thinking about marriage but he must be questioning where he came from and who he is.'

'You have to tell the police,' insists Sandra.

'No. Not yet.' Femi is adamant. 'His bike is at the station. He will come home. I know he will.'

'You'll have to speak to Jenny about this in the morning. She'll know the details about his family.'

'It's his Dad. I think he'll want to contact him. He doesn't want to turn out like him and he's always been so desperate to stay away from him.'

'Don't jump to any conclusions, Femi. You're too exhausted and you need to go to bed. I'll stay up and wait and if there's any news I'll call you,' Sandra says.

'Wake me at eight o'clock. I'll call all the hospitals again and if there's no news I'll have to report him missing to the police and Kent County Council.' Femi brushes away a tear. 'I don't know how he could do this — he could be taken away from here and sent to another foster home, what is he thinking?'

'Let's give him the benefit of the doubt,' replies Freddie.

'I just want him to be safe,' Femi says.

'He'll be fine.' Sandra rubs her friend's shoulder. 'He's a survivor.'

'He needs me,' Femi says, 'They all do.'

'Come on, let's get you to bed.' Sandra hooks her hand under Femi's arm and she's too tired to resist. When she gets into bed she's asleep instantly, dreaming, tossing and turning as if she's on a wild and ferocious ocean that has no horizon. The waves are so giant in size, she feels small and helpless and she's shivering so hard that she thinks her body will never, ever, be still again.

25

Chapter 25

Sandra wakes her.

'Good news,' she says.

'What time is it?'

'Ten.'

'What?' Femi throws back the covers and winces at the pain across her ribs. Her head is thumping.

'Ricky's been in touch with Ashley,' Sandra says quickly. 'She's just phoned.'

'What?' Femi sits up and fights off the dizzy feeling that's floating around her head. 'Where is he?'

'On his way home.'

'I'll kill him.'

Sandra laughs. 'You won't.'

'I will. What is he playing at? Where has he been?'

'You'll have to be careful with him, Femi. He might have had a terrible time and it might take a while for it to manifest itself, especially if he hasn't got the answers he went looking for.'

Femi leans forward and rubs her head. She feels sick but

she's overcome with joyful relief that he's safe and on his way home.

'What about Ahmed and Albert?'

'Albert and Freddie have taken Peanut for a walk and Ahmed left early. I think he's worried about Faisal and he's gone to meet him at the refugee centre.'

'He went on the bus?'

'Yes, just after eight o'clock.'

'That's early.' Femi frowns. 'I'll text him.'

'Have a shower first and I've got breakfast ready for you downstairs.'

'You're a star - perhaps you can tell me what I should say to Jenny?'

Sandra looks thoughtful. 'We'll have to devise a plan but let's hear what Ricky says first.'

They agree that it's best if Femi is at home alone when Ricky arrives so that they can talk together without interruptions and without worrying Albert.

Femi is sitting at the kitchen table nursing a coffee when she hears Ricky opening the shed door for his bike and then he walks in through the back door. He looks exhausted and sheepish.

'Hello, Auntie.'

'Hello, Ricky. Would you please sit down?'

He looks dishevelled and tired as if he's spent the night sleeping rough on the streets. He pulls out a chair.

'Where have you been?'

He pauses and won't look at her. 'I'd prefer not to say.'

'You're not the President. You don't have the right to the Fifth Amendment.' Femi's tone is serious.

He remains silent so she continues.

'What you have done, is to place us both in a very serious situation. You disappeared without a word, your phone went to answer machine and you didn't respond to my messages or texts. Ashley tells me, and I've checked, that you didn't go to school on Friday. That means you've been missing for almost twenty-eight hours,' she pauses. He doesn't look up. 'I have a responsibility as your foster carer to call the police immediately—'

His head jerks up.

'You didn't, did you?'

'I'm also obliged to tell Jenny because, as you know full-well, I have no control over your life. All I can do is to provide you with a home and care for you and, perhaps sometimes, even love you.'

He stares at her.

Her voice softens, 'I've been sick with worry, Ricky.'

'I'm sorry.'

'Why couldn't you tell me?'

He shakes his head. 'I messed up.'

'Where did you go?'

He shakes his head and remains resolutely silent.

'Are you alright?' she asks in a quieter tone.

'Yes.'

'Are you hurt?'

'No.'

'Have you sorted out what you wanted to?'

He pauses. 'No.'

'I didn't call the police.'

His shoulders visibly slump and she can see how tired he is. 'But, I will have to tell Jenny. You can't go AWOL and not tell me. Do you want to know why?'

'Why?' he asks sullenly.

She leans across the table and flinches when her ribs hurt. 'It's called respect, Ricky. You know that's how we work in this house. We have respect for each other, we communicate, we talk and we let everyone know where we are all the time so that no one has to get worried. Nitesh was calling all the hospitals, Freddie and Sandra stayed the night. You have very selfishly upset many, many people.'

'I'm sorry.'

'Sorry doesn't cut it. I'm furious with you.'

He meets her angry stare.

'There are no more words. You look terrible. Go upstairs and take a shower and think very carefully what you'd like to tell me when you come downstairs. You can't disappear like this. I don't know what Jenny will say. You have to set an example to Ahmed and Albert. When you go AWOL, everyone is upset, and it rocks their foundations too. This is a home, Ricky. Not a hostel.'

'Yes.'

'Go, now and please, please when you come down, make it good.'

'Yes, Auntie.'

* * *

Ricky has just gone upstairs when Ahmed comes in the door with Faisal.

'I was just going to text you.' She smiles but then she sees Faisal's bruised eye and cut chin.

'What happened to you?' She stands up and winces in pain.

'What's wrong, Auntie?' Ahmed is beside her in an instant.

He holds her arm as she regains her balance.

'I have a couple of broken ribs,' she replies. 'We had a problem on the boat last night and I fell.'

'But you're OK?'

'Yes, stop worrying and pop the kettle on. Let's look at Faisal. What happened to you?'

Faisal shakes his head and looks embarrassed.

'Ahmed insisted I come back here,' he replies.

'Auntie, he can't stay there. That man broke his door in last night. He kicked it down. He attacked him.'

'Have you reported it?'

'Of course.'

'And what did they say?'

Ahmed interrupts, 'They've given him another room but the place is worse. We went to look at it and it's full of prostitutes and drug addicts and there's no hot water. The mattress was damp, and there's mould on the ceilings and it's disgusting, Auntie.' He pulls out tea cups and fills the teapot.

'Make toast for yourselves boys and I'll give it some thought.' Femi's head is spinning and she's tired and dizzy.

Ahmed looks at her intently. 'I think you should lie down.'

'Ricky is back,' she says to him.

He nods and smiles. 'I knew he would come back.'

'Do you know where he went?'

Ahmed shakes his head solemnly.

Femi sighs and accepts tea gratefully and over the cup she sees Faisal close his eyes. He looks exhausted and there are dark circles around his eyes. He's so young and he's done well to get by in a foreign country where he has no relatives or friends. He works hard and she can see his hands are calloused and strong.

'Could you speak to Ben?' Ahmed asks.

'Ben?' Femi says.

'I think he helps out boys off the street in London and if Faisal didn't live in this council housing then he would be on the streets anyway. Maybe Ben could help him before it happens?'

'Not everyone has a bottomless pit of reserves to help people,' Femi replies, she places her head in her hands and closes her eyes. She feels dreadful for telling Ahmed the truth. The world is changing; everything is going up, all the prices in the supermarkets, petrol, bills and the cost of living crisis will affect everyone and when this happens people will draw in their purse strings. They will be very wary how and what they spend their money on and there probably won't be very much left over to help the homeless, refugees or anyone else on the poverty line.

'It's not a problem, Auntie. I have no wish to cause you trouble.' Faisal's voice is calm and quiet and it's only when he gives her a reassuring smile that she sees his split lip and missing tooth.

'I hope you hit him back?' she says.

'I defend myself,' he replies.

Ahmed slides the toast in front of Faisal who looks like he hasn't eaten in days. He reaches for the marmalade immediately and begins to eat the toast without bothering to cut the slice in half.

Ahmed says, quietly, 'I think the police might want to speak to Faisal, again.'

* * *

It's the end of November and there are already signs of Christmas in Harbour Street. The annual parade, organised by Amber and the Christmas committee last year was a great success and this year, once again, the atmosphere is exciting and fun. It's earlier this year, the beginning of the celebrations with the Christmas lights switched on by a local celebrity, a friend of Amber's, so that the local shops can benefit.

Femi stands beside Faisal and Ahmed who join in with childish enthusiasm as they eat hot dogs, standing in the street as a carnival of marching bands, entertainers and local clubs and societies file past - all waving happily, throwing sweets and clapping to the Christmas music.

Santa is on a big wooden sleigh built by Ben's students and Femi recognises one of the shop owners who wears the red suit and white beard. She waves back.

Ahmed wipes his mouth with the back of his hand and folds the tissue paper delicately. Femi has noticed he's become more delicate and gentle in recent weeks and she believes that's because of his desire to care for and nurture Faisal.

By comparison Faisal eats three hot dogs and laughs with his mouth full at the crazy driving of Ozan and Yusef who weave their motorbikes between the crowd. Yusef, wearing dark sunglasses, looks like a movie star and he singles Albert out and stops the bike to let him climb up. Albert beams and waves wildly back at the crowds then as the bike moves his face freezes and he suddenly flings his arms around Yusef's waist.

'Hang on,' Yusef calls. 'We're going to Santa's Grotto.'

Albert looks reassured and manages to laugh.

This year, the church has been converted into Santa's Grotto. Frances, the vicar, has already told Femi that it's God's house and if baby Jesus can be born in one corner of it, then it's only right that children can come and collect presents from Santa in the other. Already there have been more visitors to the church than Frances can remember and she is happy to welcome all visitors of any denomination. She waves to Femi across the street.

It's a busy afternoon and she thinks of Ricky working an extra shift in the pub. Since returning from his trip away he's been very silent. He's seen Ashley a few times who seems to have accepted that he needed to take himself off somewhere without telling her where, and Femi is also learning to live with it.

After the parade has passed, they walk past the art gallery where Ben and Amber are talking to Eva from the flower shop.

Ahmed stops to talk to Ben and Femi smiles at his new-found confidence. Gone is the little boy who used to hide in the garage at the bottom of the garden. Now she sees this young man who is alive and vibrant, filled with energy and enthusiasm and she's warmed by the kindness of the local people in town who respect her boys and treat them as equals.

'Femi?'

She turns at the sound of her name.

'We haven't met properly, I'm Amber.' She is looking directly at her smiling.

'Thank you for exhibiting Ahmed's photos in the Bistro,' Femi says.

'It's a pleasure,' Amber replies.

'And, thank you for purchasing his first sale.' Femi smiles.

'He deserves success.' She takes Femi's elbow and leads her toward Eva's colourful display of flowers.

'I saw the news on TV, are you alright?'

There had been a lot of cover on TV about the rescue of the people on the pleasure boat. Femi hadn't realised the woman was a well-known fashion designer from London and she'd never imagined the fuss they'd make about her rescue. Femi hadn't spoken to the press. But the RNLI had instead issued a statement which pleased Femi. She is embarrassed at having broken ribs and a cut on her head.

'It looks like you've both been in the wars,' Amber says. 'What happened to Faisal's face?'

Femi turns back to look at Faisal who has joined the conversation with Ben and Ahmed.

'He is living in terrible accommodation; rat infested, with junkies and addicts and last night one of them broke down his door.'

Amber looks horrified. 'That's not right. What will he do?'

'I've said he can stay with us and sleep on the sofa for a few nights but I'm not allowed to do that permanently. I can get away with an odd night but I just don't have the extra room.'

'I might be able to help out.'

'Really?'

'Well, you know Karl, my manager in the cafe? He used to rent a caravan, but since I moved in with Ben last year, Karl and Molly now live in my flat above the cafe. Would Faisal like the caravan?'

Femi can't speak. She's overwhelmed with Amber's kindness and she squeezes her hand.

'I do understand,' Amber whispers. 'You're not on your own.'

'I'm sure he would love it. It would be luxury compared to where he's been staying. That would be amazing, Amber — if it's not too expensive.'

'Ben says he works all hours at a warehouse stacking shelves, is that right?'

'Yes, and he hates it.'

'Perhaps he'd like some training in the hospitality industry. Karl is excellent at what he does and he could train him in café. That might give him the waiting experience he needs and then if he wants to stay on or perhaps work in Harbour Bistro and, if not, he might find a more sociable job. What do you think?'

'I think that's an amazing idea.' Femi smiles. She wants to hug Amber but knows the pain would be unbearable.

'Good.' Amber grins.

'That's very kind of you.'

Amber shakes her head. 'We've all got a past, Femi. Ben's had a really rough time and he recognises someone who wants to better themselves and who is prepared to work hard to be successful.'

'I think Faisal would like some carpentry lessons too.' Femi laughs. 'If that's not asking for too much?'

'Not at all. Ben loves showing off his skills and he loves to seek out new apprentices. Do you want to ask Faisal about this proposal or shall I?'

'I think it would be lovely coming from you. It's a Christmas miracle for him.'

Amber smiles. 'Ah, so you believe in Christmas miracles too. I thought I was the only one.'

26

Chapter 26

After the Christmas lights switch on — by a local soap star — they stand in the street watching Ahmed and Faisal with younger children marvelling at the snow pumped out from the machine. Couples, families and shop owners walk across the street to congratulate Amber on another successful Christmas parade. Femi is content to nurse her glass of mulled wine and watch the crowds. She's thinking of her Christmas list and what to buy the boys when Ben suddenly appears at her side.

'That whole idea of training in the cafe and living in the caravan seems to have raised his spirits.' Ben nods at Faisal.

'I don't think he can believe it, and it means that he can still spend time with Ahmed.'

'You're an incredible foster mum,' he says.

'Thank you.'

They stand in silence for a while watching people walk past in the cold, content to occasionally stop and linger over the stalls and barrows and then Ben says, 'Have you heard from Lawrence?'

Femi frowns but she won't meet his gaze. 'No.'

'Are you upset with him?'

She shrugs.

'Did he tell you where he's gone?'

Femi shakes her head. 'He left a note saying he had to go away.'

'Did he tell you about his brother?'

She turns quickly. 'He never mentioned a brother.'

'That's what I suspected.'

'What brother?'

Ben barely pauses before answering, 'Lawrence had a twin brother, Martin. I met him when I was travelling in Malaysia over eighteen months ago—'

'You met his brother?' Femi repeats.

'He was staying with Lawrence at the time.'

'Are they alike?'

Ben smiles. 'They had a similar sense of humour, and neither of them got on with their parents, but that's about it.'

'Lawrence said he didn't get on with them.'

'Martin was gay. They were against homosexuality and their father was a bigot. He'd call Martin names and bully him growing up. Lawrence always tried to stick up for Martin but they had a tough life.'

'He said he had a sister.'

'Yes, presumably she's as bad as the father. Martin had a tough time. He was in and out of counselling and therapy for years. He began taking drugs which also became an issue for the family and Lawrence blamed them for not supporting Martin whilst they blamed him for indulging him.'

'How awful.'

'Yes.'

'When Martin tried to take his own life, the first time, they didn't care.'

Femi gasps. 'How dreadful.'

'He was recovering from another attempt when I met him,' Ben's voice trails off and he chooses his words carefully. 'He'd tried to take his own life in his flat in London. His boyfriend found him and after a stint in rehab so Lawrence invited him to stay with him in Malaysia. He thought that if he got Martin out of his normal city life and routine, that he would enjoy nature and find some sort of spirituality out there but sadly, Martin didn't make it.'

Femi looks around the busy street but sees nothing. She's absorbing Ben's words.

He continues, 'Martin struggled to lead a normal life anywhere and he was very damaged. When Martin attempted suicide again, he was successful. He died a few weeks after I left Malaysia.'

Femi's mouth opens in shock. 'Lawrence never told me.'

'It was a big shock. Lawrence found Martin.'

'Oh, no.'

Ben nods. 'Lawrence was a wreck afterwards. He went travelling for a few months and he didn't want to stay in Malaysia and I persuaded him to come over here. I told him it would be a fresh start, away from those bad memories in Malaysia.'

'That's when he moved in beside me?'

'Yes.'

Femi thinks back to last spring when she first saw Lawrence in his garden. He wasn't an ageing hippy. He was a man grieving for his twin brother. How quickly she had judged him.

'I'm so sorry.'

'I thought he might not have told you, but I think you need to know.'

'Why?' She frowns.

'Because he really likes you.'

'Then why did he disappear so quickly?'

'It was the anniversary of Martin's death and Martin's boyfriend wanted closure. He begged Lawrence to take him back to Malaysia to show him where he'd lived in the last months.'

'So, he's gone back?'

'Yes, he too has to find closure – he felt responsible.'

'But no one is responsible for other people's happiness.'

'Ah, that's true.' Ben smiles. 'But don't we always keep trying to make other people's lives that little bit better? Isn't it kindness that makes us all thrive and our hearts grow?'

* * *

'You promised you'd tell me.' Ahmed is upstairs, on the top floor, which he's never been to before. It's where Ricky and Albert have their bedrooms and it seems strange up here. He looks around Ricky's room. It's bigger than his and he has posters of footballers, cricketers and rugby players on the walls.

'I'm tired.' Ricky throws himself on the bed.

'You must keep your word, as I did.'

Ricky puts his hands behind his head and regards Ahmed, thinking how much he's changed in the seven months he's lived with them. He seems taller and, even though he's skinny and delicate, there's a strength and resolve about him. Ricky can feel his determination. At first, he's amused but under

Ahmed's dark eyes and fierce gaze he wavers. He has respect for Ahmed. Ahmed has earned it. He's helped Auntie lose weight and now she looks amazing. He's helped Albert develop confidence with his looks by taking photographs of him and boosting his ego and, he's kept Ricky's secret.

It would still have been a secret had Ahmed not caught him going through Auntie's mother's memory box. The Pandora's Box of terrible secrets. He had the grandfather's letter in one hand and photograph of the couple in the other hand when Ahmed had spied him though the living room window. He was in the garden and it didn't take Ahmed long to corner Ricky in the kitchen a few minutes later.

'What are you doing with that?' He asks.

'It's none of your business.'

'I'll tell Auntie you've taken the letter and the photo.'

'I haven't,' Ricky lies.

'You have, I checked the box and it's gone. What are you doing with it?'

'I'll put it back.' Ricky is wondering if he could shut Ahmed up. Could he threaten him or boss him or bully him?

'Tell me what you're doing with it.' Ahmed insists visibly distressed. 'Auntie, trusts us.'

Ricky sighs visibly annoyed. 'I know, she does.' He meant to bluster his way out of it but he felt guilty. His last intention was to betray Auntie. 'If I tell you, you'll have to keep it a secret. Can you do that?'

'Depends.'

Ricky tilts his head to one side. 'If you can't keep a secret, I can't tell you.'

'Does it hurt, Auntie?'

'Of course not, you dope. Who do you think I am? It's the

opposite. I want to help her.'

'How?'

'I'm going to speak to her grandparents.'

'Why?'

'Did you see her face? Did you see how sad she was knowing she had grandparents who had thrown her mother out of their home? It wasn't her fault. I want them to know they have a loving granddaughter who looks after all of us. If they know that, then they will love her and want her in their lives.'

'They didn't want Femi's mother in their lives.'

'That was Paula. This is Femi. Why should she be punished?'

Ahmed doesn't have the answer so he asks, 'Have you got their phone number?'

'Don't be silly, I'm going to visit them in person and then I can come home and tell her the good news—'

'They're a long way away.'

'Devon. But there are trains and I have money for a ticket.'

Ahmed doesn't look too sure.

'They might even drive me back home.' Ricky smiles. 'All will be well, Ahmed. It's about time we did something lovely for Auntie, she always does so much for us.'

'But they'll know you've gone missing.'

'I'll take Friday off school and cancel my shift in the pub and I'll be there and back in no time at all. No one will even know I've gone.'

'But what if Auntie finds out? What will I say?'

'You must promise me, you'll say nothing because if it does go wrong and they want nothing to do with her, then it will be double the rejection. It's all very well them throwing Paula out of the house, but if they want nothing to do with Auntie either, that would be doubly tragic.' Ricky puts his finger to his lips. 'Mum's the word.'

Although he doesn't know why he's doing it, Ahmed copies him and places his index finger across his closed lips and all he can think about is that his fingers smell of chlorine from developing photos in the studio. Then, for some strange reason, he wonders what his mother would look like now. Was his memory of her fading?

* * *

Ahmed sits on the edge of Ricky's bed, beside him, with his hands in his lap listening to Ricky and imagining the scene he describes.

'I caught the train first thing which was the easy part, but when I got there and checked Google maps it was further to walk than I'd thought—'

'Is it a nice house?'

'It's a bungalow on the outskirts of a town, suburbia,' he replies.

Ahmed thinks he understands. 'What time was that?'

'Well by the time I'd got the train to London and then a connecting one, I arrived at their house a little after two o'clock in the afternoon.'

'Did he answer the door?'

'No, the grandmother opened the door.'

'What's she like?'

'Grey. Grey hair, grey eyes and grey complexion.'

'What did she say?'

'I said, hello I'm Ricky. I'm Femi's son.'

Ahmed looks up. 'You told her you were Femi's son?'

Ricky straightens his shoulders. 'Of course, but stop interrupting or this will take all night and I'm tired.'

Ahmed nods seriously. 'Carry on.'

'Well, she looked at me like I was a second-hand car sales-man, like I'd been let out of prison or something, and she tried to close the door on me but I put my foot inside to stop her. I pulled out the letter and the photograph and thrust them at her. She recognised the picture immediately and took it. She looked at me, you know, really looked. She studied my eyes, my ears and I swear she'd know every hair on my head.

''Femi, is your granddaughter,' I said.'

Ricky looks at Ahmed but he's studying his socks so he continues, 'It took her a few minutes to read the letter but then a voice shouted out from inside.' He imitates a man's deep voice.

''Close the bloody door, woman. There's a draft.''

'She looked up shocked. She pushed the letter and the photograph back in my hands. "You must go," she said. ''But this is your granddaughter'', I said and I showed her a picture. One that you took of her sitting on the beach hut steps in the summer. The pretty one where she's wearing the green and yellow turban.'

Ahmed smiles. 'I like that one.'

Ricky continues, 'But she shook her head in denial and closed the door.'

'So, what did you do?'

'I sat on the pavement outside in the road.'

'How long for?'

'I waited. I waited and at five o'clock, she came out with a shopping trolley and she seemed surprised to see me and I walked with her to the local shop. I waited outside while she went inside.'

'And what did she say then?'

'She didn't want to speak to me. It was like she was scared but then I walked alongside her on the way home so she didn't have a choice. I told her that Femi, her granddaughter, is a paramedic and she fosters children. I told her she'd been placed in care before being fostered at thirteen and the old lady looked horrified — as if she hadn't known. So I walked back with her to the bungalow and she said, ''Don't let him see you.''

Ricky sighs. 'I stood at the door, but she kept me at arm's length. I think she was frightened I would push my way inside but I wouldn't have done that. So, I looked through the gap in the front door, where the hinges are and he's in the lounge, lying in this hospital bed connected up to a mask and wires. It was awful. She saw me looking and she told me that he wouldn't go into a hospital or a home, and that he insisted that she must care for him at home.'

'What's wrong with him?'

'He had a stroke several years ago.'

'Did she ask you inside?'

'No.'

'Did she know how far you'd come?'

'I told her we live in Westbay.'

Ahmed is silent for a while and Ricky remembers standing in the doorway shivering. He'd only taken his bomber jacket and it was so much cooler down there and it was getting late. She'd seemed confused and then she'd said to him. 'You'd better go now.'

'Did she give you any food?'

'No.'

Ahmed squeezes his hands tightly together. 'She doesn't

sound very nice.'

'I think she was frightened. She said, 'the shock of hearing about Femi would kill him' and so I said, 'What about Femi?''

'Did she care?' asks Ahmed.

'She said she knew nothing about the letter. She didn't know her husband had written it. She'd assumed that her daughter didn't want anything to do with her and they'd lost touch over the years.'

'Was she lying?'

Ricky shrugs. 'I don't think so.'

'So, Auntie's grandfather wrote the letter and he never told her?'

'Maybe.'

Ahmed sounds more optimistic. 'So, that's a good surprise, right? I mean, she does want to see Auntie, doesn't she?'

'No. That's the problem. That's why I couldn't tell Auntie where I'd been. The grandmother didn't want to know anything. She couldn't wait to get rid of me and she kept trying to close the door in my face and then I ran out of things to say and she just stared at me until eventually she said, ''Go, home.''

Ahmed shakes his head. 'Auntie will be very upset.'

'We won't tell her. It will have to be our secret.'

'She's not a nice grandma, is she?'

'She did keep the photo of Auntie, I hope that's okay?'

'I can print another,' Ahmed says. 'So, why did it take you so long to get home?'

'By the time I'd walked back to the train station, it was late and I'd missed the last train to London and so I had to wait until the next morning. I slept on the bench on the station platform.'

'Couldn't you have gone to a hotel?'

'I didn't have any more money. I never expected to stay the night. I thought they'd be so happy to see me, and that we might all call Auntie together, you know a video call so that they would meet her but—'

'Why didn't you phone Ashley?'

'Because if she didn't know where I was, then she couldn't lie to anyone. I didn't want to put her in an awkward position.'

'Was she mad at you.'

'Not when I told her the truth.'

'It must have been cold sleeping outside at the station?'

'It was freezing but the train came quite early in the morning which was good. I just had a long wait in London. I knew everyone would be looking for me and I half expected the police to find me and haul me off to a foster home somewhere else.'

'But we can never tell Auntie, can we?'

'No,' Ricky says quietly. 'I think she would be very upset if she realised I'd actually spoken to her grandma and she wanted nothing to do with her. It wouldn't be fair. Auntie has enough to worry about with all of us.'

'She didn't tell Jenny, did she?'

'No, not yet but I think she might tomorrow. It's been a busy weekend with everything that happened with Faisal too, and then the Christmas parade. She seems exhausted.'

'She's more than exhausted. On Friday night while she was waiting for a call from you, Nitesh and Auntie had a shout. It was very dangerous.'

'What?' Ricky looks horrified. 'She never told me.'

'She's got broken ribs and she's in a lot of pain.'

'I had no idea.' Ricky shakes his head.

'Auntie almost died. It's been on all the news.'

27

Chapter 27

The first week of December flies past. Freddie spends most evenings with Femi, and she helps him with his costume. He's one of the ugly sisters in the local Panto.

'Which sister?' asks Femi.

'The ugliest one,' replies Nitesh, laughing.

Femi helps Freddie rehearse his lines and the boys soon become familiar with his high-pitched voice, stilettos and jaunty, colourful dress that Femi has made from one of her Caribbean dresses.

Some evenings, Faisal sits with them. He enjoys the company and the fun of the spectacle and on Friday evening Amber and Femi help him move into the caravan.

It has one bedroom, a bathroom and a spacious lounge, kitchen and diner. Faisal is surprised by the comfort and warmth and he's touched when Amber makes up his double bed with a clean duvet. 'There's a second one in the wardrobe,' she says, 'So you can wash your bedding without worrying.'

'You can bring your washing to mine, until you get sorted out,' says Femi. She has brought extra tea towels, food and cleaning products and they help Faisal, with Ahmed's advice, to make it look warm and cosy.

'It looks very homely,' Ahmed grins.

'It's a safe site, and there's a manager if you have any problems but it's out of season and reasonably quiet.'

'I love it.' Faisal laughs, and Femi thinks she should pay for him to get a crown on his tooth. She would save up for him.

Amber, Femi and Ahmed leave Faisal in the caravan with him promising to start his training with Karl in The Harbour Cafe, on Monday.

'That's so kind of you, Amber,' she says walking to the car.

'He's doing me a favour, Femi. We're short staffed coming up to Christmas but he's a fast learner and when I introduced him to Karl, they really got on well together. We can only give people opportunities. It's up to them what they do with them.'

Femi nods in agreement and fumbles for her car keys in the dark.

Ahmed climbs in the car.

'Have you seen Lawrence?' Amber asks.

Because it's dark, Amber can't see the look on her face.

'N— no,' Femi stammers.

'Ben said he was coming home and I wondered if he was back yet.'

'I haven't seen him,' Femi's heart begins to thump more quickly.

'Well perhaps you will later.' Amber kisses Femi quickly on the cheek. 'Ben reckons you're a perfect match and for him to say that — it means a lot.' She laughs. 'I hope you feel the same.'

Femi shrugs. 'I don't know—'

'Let nature take its course,' Amber says. 'That's what I did and I'm very happy.'

* * *

'Jamie has been complaining to me that he thinks you're not telling the whole truth,' Emma says.

'Truth about what?' replies Femi vaguely.

It's Monday afternoon and it's been a long and busy weekend. She wants to be on her own. She has made a list of the jobs she wants to do to prepare for Christmas and she wants to check she hasn't forgotten anything.

'Well, this phone that Albert had been using, Jamie thinks you knew all about it.'

'Why would I have kept that a secret?'

Emma looks at her, then her iPhone pings and she's distracted momentarily. She checks her screen and then looks back at Femi and continues writing. 'But you read the messages between Albert and Delroy and you know that Albert was stealing for him?'

'I do now, but I didn't then. When money went missing I spoke to all the boys.'

Emma sighs. 'And Albert only gave you the phone yesterday?'

'Yes — the same day that Jamie called me to say the police had read Delroy's messages on his phone.'

'Isn't that a coincidence?'

Femi holds her ribs. 'There's been a lot going on.'

'I know I saw the rescue on TV.'

Femi looks away and Emma continues, 'We have to be on top things like this. Did Jamie tell you that Delroy is back in prison and the chances of Albert living with him are now very thin — he's taken advantage of him. Especially as he got him to steal for him.'

'I've never made any secret of the fact that I think it's best for children to be reunited with their parents, but in this case, and now that Delroy will be in prison for a few years, it's best Albert stays with me. Albert's very happy here and all the boys get on together and so I don't think there's any reason for him to be moved.'

Emma taps her pen against her teeth and smiles. 'I don't think we would have wanted to move Albert. He's clearly happy and settled here.'

Femi shrugs. 'You never know in this life what's going to happen.'

'Clearly.' Emma's tone is firm. 'But you must tell us what's going on, Femi. We all want what's best for Albert and I want to help you.'

'Sometimes life gets in the way,' Femi adds lamely.

Emma says, 'There's also this incident of Ricky. The teacher at school thinks he went missing, is that true?'

'Why would he think that?'

'There were rumours and he wasn't at school, on the—' She checks the date. 'Friday?'

'He had food poisoning, I think,' Femi replies. 'I'm really sorry to be so vague but the incident with the RNLI at sea has really knocked me for six—'

'I read that in your journal. It says here you have cracked ribs and possibly concussion.' Emma had read the papers and seen the TV. Femi was a hero. And it appears that everything seems to be sorted out so it isn't worth investigating anything further. That might only cause more distress and more trouble for everyone.

Femi says, 'I think it's affected my memory, not everything of course, but sometimes I'm confused and I'm very tired, finding it hard to remember all the details around that time ...'

'Do you need a break, some respite?'

'No. Sandra has been here helping me out.'

Emma frowns. 'So, you've noted Ricky down as off school that day, but you didn't call anyone.'

'It's just been a crazy time.'

'And what about Ahmed?'

'You'll see from the journal that he's doing well. He's attending the Syrian Refugee Centre each week and he's making new friends.'

'He's mentioned Faisal.'

'That's his friend, they met at the centre.'

'He's older than Ahmed.'

'Just a couple of years but Faisal knows friends of friends of Ahmed's family, so there's a real connection there for Ahmed.'

'Does he talk about going back to Aleppo?'

'No, and besides, that's for Lily to discuss with him.' Femi skilfully nudges Emma away from where the conversation is heading.

'And if he were to leave?'

Femi shrugs. 'I just want him to be happy and so long as he is here, I will help him. He wants to look at universities.'

Ashley makes notes. 'Do you have any other concerns?'

Femi shakes her head.

'No concerns about Christmas? You don't think Ricky will want to find his family?'

Femi shrugs. 'He's been with me for over four years and I'm helping him to get to Uni but the choice is his.'

This is something that is bothering Femi. She still hasn't got to the bottom of his disappearance and probably never will but his behaviour seems normal. In fact, he and Ahmed were enjoying a joke over the weekend in the kitchen and she'd been delighted to see them laughing as they'd gone into the lounge with Albert to play football on the Wii. But it doesn't take away that niggling sensation that the boys lie to her. Albert kept a secret relationship with his father on an iPhone that she knew nothing about, and Ricky has refused to tell her where he's been. Although she doesn't tell Emma, this has rocked her confidence because for her, trust was at the centre of their relationships. She provides a safe, caring and trusting environment for them all and her one condition has only ever been that they tell her the truth.

'I think they'll all be just fine.' Femi reaches for the paracetamol.

'I've almost finished,' Emma says. 'You'll be getting a new social worker in the new year.'

'I'll be sorry to see you move on,' Femi says.

'So, plans for Christmas?'

Femi's about to say, 'I'm going to lie on the sofa in my knickers and get horribly drunk for a fortnight but instead she says, 'The Panto, Christmas dinner and lots of walks with Peanut.' Femi smiles charmingly. 'And you, Emma, what are your plans?'

'It's a family time. It's always about the children and my parents,' Emma replies quickly, and when her phone pings, she says, 'Sorry, I have to get this, Femi.'

* * *

After Emma leaves, Femi checks her watch and that's when the doorbell rings.

'Oh, what's she forgotten now,' Femi curses.

Lawrence is standing on the step. His hair has grown longer, his new beard is trimmed and his eyes are a little darker but he smiles.

'Hello, Femi.' He's holding a pretty red poinsettia.

'Is that for me?'

'Of course.'

'I suppose you want to borrow a cup of sugar?'

He shakes his head. 'I want to apologise. This is a peace offering.'

She stands aside to let him indoors and she takes the plant. 'I'm letting you in, because it's my favourite Christmas plant. You have five minutes Lawrence, because I'm a busy woman,' she says, placing the plant on the table, wishing her heart wasn't hammering quite as hard.

He stands in the kitchen, with his hands in his jeans pockets, looking around as if seeing it all for the first time.

Peanut stretches and leaves his basket to greet Lawrence, wagging his tail and jumping up with excitement. Femi wishes Peanut wasn't so free with his emotions but she feels her heart softening and her mood brightening. Lawrence looks tired but more relaxed. The stress has gone from his eyes.

'Does five minutes include coffee?' he asks hopefully.

She shakes her head. 'I've a list of jobs to get done.'

Lawrence nods and looks embarrassed. 'I just wanted to apologise for leaving like I did. I was—'

'There's no need.'

He looks up suddenly and Femi continues, 'But you can make up for it. Are you busy?'

'Now?'

'Yes.'

'Not really—'

'Then come and help me. It's about time you came back. How do you expect me to manage all the Christmas preparations in my state?'

'Ben told me about your accident. Are you alright?'

'A few cracked ribs.'

He winces. 'Ouch.'

'Exactly.'

'What can I do?'

She reaches for her car keys. 'Come on, we haven't got long. We have a busy evening ahead of us and I have a lot to get done before the boys come home.'

She'd meant to buy the Christmas tree at the weekend but she hadn't had time. Now, with Lawrence's help, they drive to the garden centre, choose a Christmas tree together and tie it onto the top of her car. When they get it home, Lawrence manages to carry it inside.

'Do I get a reward for helping?' he asks.

'Yes, I'll get it for you — milk and sugar?'

She heads for the kitchen and reaches for the kettle. 'When you've done that, I need you to go up into the loft for me and get down all the decorations. I was going to ask Ricky to do it when he gets home, but now you're here it will be a lovely surprise for them all. We can decorate it this evening after dinner.'

He follows her into the kitchen. 'What are you cooking tonight?'

'Bolognese.'

'My favourite.' He grins at her.

'I'm not sure you've done enough to qualify for an invitation to dinner.'

'Ah, so what's a man to do?' he asks, sitting at the kitchen table and rubbing his eyes.

'You must be jet lagged?'

'I am.'

It's the first quiet moment they have so Femi says, 'Ben told me about your twin brother. I'm really sorry, Lawrence.'

'Thank you.'

'Did it go alright over there?'

Lawrence's eyes darken. 'Yes, under the circumstances. It was tough, it was bound to be, but life goes on and Martin was always a very troubled soul. He never made it easy for me or for any of us. He felt it was his destiny to suffer and my parents allowed him to think like that. He was a victim of their small-minded mentality.'

She places the tea on the table.

'Thank you.' He sips the hot liquid. 'You see, even now they are very right wing. They don't like foreigners, gays or anyone else that threatens their status quo. It's as though they're stuck in a time-warp and to be honest, I couldn't wait to get away. I had to leave, Femi. They poisoned my mind to the attitude of people in this country and I began to think that everyone was bigoted like them.'

'Is that why you went abroad?'

'I couldn't wait to get out. I didn't have any contact with them for years. I saw the damage they'd done to Martin; years of their bullying, controlling and snide comments had made them stronger. They enlisted my sister to support their attitude.' He rubs his beard. 'I was ashamed, Femi. I didn't want to introduce them to any friends. I'm so totally unlike them but for a while I felt I was tainted by their attitude, and I—,' he pauses, 'I didn't even want a relationship because I thought if anyone knew what my parents were like, then they'd stop loving me. That's why I'm...I'm romantically inept.'

Femi shakes her head. She can see the tired despair in his eyes.

He says softly, 'I just wanted to be on my own. I had to move abroad. I had to move away; away from this life and the bad vibes from my family. So, I immersed myself in my work over there and I found I could lose myself, keeping busy and having friends but I didn't allow anyone to get close to me. After Martin tried to kill himself the first time, I felt my own weakness. I felt helpless and frightened but I was also angry. I was angry with my family and I phoned them up and I told them it was all their fault.'

'Were they upset?'

'They denied doing anything wrong. It was Martin, they said, who led a despicable life. It was all rubbish. Neither of us was good enough for them. We hadn't given them grandchildren like normal sons and Martin couldn't even look after himself.'

'But you looked after him.'

'I paid for a plane ticket to get him out of London. He came over to me but he was very anxious and depressed. I thought the different lifestyle would suit him.' He shakes his head. 'But he was too far gone. I couldn't reach him. I tried to get him help but he didn't want it. He was so used to being—'

'—a victim?' finishes Femi.

'I felt so responsible. I should have booked him into rehab.'

'You weren't to know. That might not have helped either.'

'I think Martin was beyond my help and had been for years, but I've only realised that now. Going back there allowed me to look at the events differently, with a different perspective and I can live with that.'

'I'm pleased it's helped you.'

Lawrence nods. 'Martin always had this distant look in his eyes; this vacant stare of terror and I guess that was why I could identify so quickly with Ahmed. When I used to see him in the garden and then when he was in the garage—'

'Luxurious photographic studio.' She smiles.

'Luxurious photographic studio,' he repeats and smiles back. 'There was something about Ahmed that reminded me of Martin. He was delicate, introverted, insecure and when he was Ahmed's age, he was bullied by our father, so when the kids bullied him at school too, he became used to it. Martin was repressed, gay and depressed and accepted it all.'

'No one should get used to bullying.'

'That's why I think I probably felt protective toward Ahmed.'

'I'm sorry.'

He holds up his hand. 'Don't be. I understand your concern. You have every right to protect your boys and you have your own crosses to bear with these kids. Besides, we all have to live with our past and that's what I was doing. I was bringing my past into my present.'

'I prefer to live in the present.' Femi refills their mugs.

'Any biscuits?'

'No, I don't buy them any more.'

'That's why you've lost so much weight?'

Femi laughs and reaches for the tin of biscuits. 'Can you imagine me not buying biscuits? I'd have a mutiny on my hands with the boys.'

'That's what I love about you, Femi. You're always so upbeat.'

Femi smiles. It wasn't always true but she'd take the compliment. 'Where are you for Christmas?'

'Well, I'm not going to my parents, that's for sure. As well as being atheists, and my sister is just like them, I really enjoy Christmas and it's been a long time since I've celebrated one in England. Ben said I'm welcome to join them in Harbour Bistro, if I don't get a better offer.'

'Goodness, you'll never get a better offer than that. You can't turn that down.'

The back door opens and Albert stands in his school uniform with his hand on the doorknob, looking at the man sitting at the kitchen table.

'Lawrence?' he exclaims. 'Oh my, goodness. Ahmed is going to be so pleased when he sees you — Oh, my... ' He looks beyond the kitchen and into the lounge, and he moves forward. 'Is that what I think it is? A Christmas tree, Auntie?'

Femi smiles. 'We're going to have to show Ahmed and Faisal a typical English Christmas, starting tonight, I thought that we'd start by decorating the tree together.'

'I'd love that. Do you remember we bought a tree decoration last year?'

Femi puts her arm around his shoulders. 'That was your first Christmas with us but we will do that every year, Albert. We'll buy one for each of my boys.'

'Ricky has four decorations. I remember counting them last year.'

'This will be your second one,' Femi says.

'I might get an angel,' Albert replies.

'We can shop tomorrow if you like?'

Albert grins. 'What about Lawrence? Is he having one too?'

'If he'd like one,' Femi replies.

'I've never had a personal Christmas decoration before either.' Lawrence is happier than when he was in Malaysia. It's a mystery now, how he could ever have thought of that place as home when this is all he's ever really wanted.

'You'd better stay for dinner tonight or you'll disappoint Ahmed.' Lawrence meets her smile. 'And you'll have to come shopping for a Christmas decoration.'

Lawrence reaches across the table to take Femi's hand but Albert doesn't see any of this because he bends down to stroke Peanut who is under the table at Lawrence's feet. Albert sits on the floor and he clambers onto Albert's lap and tilts his head for an ear rub.

Albert whispers, very softly in his ear, 'I never really wanted to move to London, this is home, Peanut and I'll never leave you.'

Peanut has no idea what any of them are saying but he knows he's happy and he snorts contentedly before rolling over onto his back for a tummy rub.

28

Chapter 28

'The weeks leading up to Christmas are my favourite time,' Femi confesses to Lawrence. 'It's quite magical and I think the anticipation is sometimes better than the actual day.'

They're walking back from Harbour Street, arm in arm, with Ahmed and Albert at their side. They have all chosen their new Christmas decorations and Albert carries them in his rucksack; he's chosen an angel and Ahmed a snowman because, apart from the fake snow at the parade, he's never seen real snow. To Femi's delight, Lawrence has chosen a Christmas robin.

'I can't remember many Christmases that I've enjoyed and certainly not traditional ones like this,' he says.

'I like to see the town decorated and all the pretty, colourful gifts in the windows. I tell the boys there's a maximum limit we spend, so Christmas doesn't cost them a fortune and besides it makes them look harder to find something special that's cheaper.'

'My parents never celebrated, they said it was ridiculous to spend so much money for one day.'

'They have a point. Some people do go crazy and get into

debt and money is wasted on unwanted gifts. That's why I think it's important to have some fun leading up to it.'

'I'm certainly enjoying this time,' Lawrence says. 'It's very special.'

'I managed to get a ticket for you for tomorrow.'

'Thanks, Femi, I haven't been to a pantomime since I was a child.'

'Oh yes you have,' Albert cries with delight.

Ahmed joins in with the lines he's learnt. 'He's behind you.'

Albert laughs. 'No, you have to wait, until he's actually right there.'

'Where?' Ahmed frowns.

'Behind you!' Femi and Albert say together, and they all burst out laughing.

Ahmed says, 'Faisal is so excited to spend Christmas with us, Auntie. Karl told him that last year, they all had a meal in Harbour Cafe, because Amber didn't own the Bistro then and on Christmas morning Ben had arrived with two baby kittens and she called one Cheesecake and the other Pudding.'

'Can we get a kitten?' asks Albert?

'Maybe.' Femi replies, happy to enjoy their banter as they walk home together.

'Are we having eggnog tonight?' asks Albert.

'The adults are and I'm making you guys some cocktails.'

'With alcohol?' Albert asks happily.

Ahmed nudges him. 'I looked up some recipes with Auntie and they don't have alcohol, silly.'

'Wicked,' replies Albert.

'We also bought lots of shopping for the party, didn't we?'

'Well, it's not really a party, just a few friends.'

'They're like family though, aren't they?' Ahmed says.

'They are,' Femi agrees and she sees Ahmed staring up at Lawrence with a huge grin on his face.

Ahmed is much happier now that Lawrence is back and that Faisal has moved into the caravan and started his new job in Harbour Cafe. If that wasn't an early Christmas present, then Femi couldn't think of anything else more perfect.

Once they get home, Femi gives them all a job. Albert prepares the kitchen table for the buffet. Ahmed reads out heating instructions and with Lawrence's help they put pigs in blankets, short ribs, chicken and sausage rolls in the oven.

'I'm cheating,' she says apologetically to Lawrence. 'It would take too long to make all this from scratch.'

He smiles. 'I don't blame you, Femi.'

The back door opens and Freddie waltzes in. 'Disaster, my darling, I have such a disaster happening. It's a nightmare. I need help.'

They all stop what they're doing to look at Freddie who's holding his hand above his head. 'It's broken. It's a disaster. I can't go on stage.'

'What's happened?' asks Femi.

'I fell and its broken.'

'Your hand? It's not in plaster?'

'It hasn't even been X-rayed, yet. I came here to tell you, first. I can't go on stage tomorrow. I'll never be able to manage now.'

'Let me look,' Femi says, reaching for his hand.

'Careful, careful, it hurts.'

'I'll be very gentle. Now, sit at the table and tell me what happened.'

Freddie does as he's told and Femi takes his hand and feels his wrist. 'Does this hurt.'

'Ouch!'

'And this?'

'A little.'

'Can you move this finger?'

'Just about,' Freddie replies. 'It's not good, darling. They'll have to send on the understudy. I'll call the theatre now.'

Nitesh comes through the back door, smiling. 'Sorry, I had to find parking. How's the English patient?' He winks at Femi.

Femi returns his smile. 'It looks very bad. I'd say he'll have to have it in a plaster cast all over Christmas and New Year - at least seven weeks.'

'Seven weeks?' repeats Albert.

'But my ankle was in plaster less, Auntie.' Ahmed stares at Freddie's wrist. 'And it doesn't even look swollen.'

Lawrence looks over his shoulder at Freddie's hand, which looks perfectly normal, and then catches the knowing glance between Femi and Nitesh.

'How did you fall, Freddie?'

'I–I–I stumbled.'

'And it hurts a lot?' Femi says.

Freddie nods.

'How about a glass of eggnog before you go to the hospital?'

Freddie nods. 'I think that might help.'

Lawrence gets the hints and pours a glass for them just as Ricky comes home. Ricky looks at Auntie for approval to see if he's allowed an eggnog.

'Just the one,' she says as he turns his attention to Freddie.

'Not this old chestnut.' Ricky laughs. 'What is it this year?'

'It's his wrist,' replies Femi.

'Ah, wasn't it your knee, last year?' Ricky slaps Freddie on the back.

'No.' Freddie is indignant.

'That was the year before,' Femi says. 'Last year it was his toe and he couldn't stand.'

'Have another eggnog,' Nitesh says to his husband and you'll be fine.

Ahmed pulls food from the oven and begins placing it on the table with Femi's help. 'I think you should eat something, Freddie,' she says.

'I don't think I'm well enough.'

'But if it's your wrist, you can still eat,' insists Albert. 'You've got another hand.'

'No, I'm shaking and I think I will upchuck the whole lot.'

'Upchuck?' asks Ahmed.'

'Puke, vomit, sick.' Albert giggles.

Lawrence frowns and shakes his head. He's clearly bemused by Freddie's whole performance until Femi whispers in his ear, 'Stage fright.'

'I think my dress will be too tight and I'll look ridiculous.' Freddie tips his head back and finishes his drink. 'I think it's best to cancel. I'll look silly with a plaster cast.'

'I'm so looking forward to it, Freddie.' Lawrence refills his glass. 'It's been a long time since I've looked forward to anything like this.'

'It's going to be great fun,' Albert adds.

'I've never seen a panto and Faisal is coming too,' Ahmed says. 'We've learnt all our lines.'

'Your lines?' Freddie frowns.

'He's behind you,' sings Ahmed. 'Oh no, he's not.'

'Oh, yes, he is,' cries Albert, Femi and Lawrence together.

Freddie pauses momentarily and then he laughs. There's barely a pause before he dramatically holds his glass out for a refill.

'I think my wrist is feeling a bit better, Femi. I always say you have magic fingers. I always feel better when you check me out. So, you don't think it's actually broken, just perhaps, twisted?'

'Maybe it's a little sore but that will wear off.' Femi smiles.

'Do you think the show can go on?' asks Nitesh seriously. 'For the sake of these lovely people?'

'I'll do my very best.' Freddie smiles, raising his shoulder and sticking out his chest. 'I couldn't possibly let down all these panto virgins, now could I?'

* * *

The afternoon after the panto, the boys are still excited as they walk down into Harbour Street. Ahmed is reliving it. He remembers most of the scenes and some of the lines, which he randomly blurts out and Albert is still humming along to the chorus. Even Lawrence, is still praising Freddie's performance when Femi says, 'Did you sell the beach hut easily?'

Ahmed and Albert walk on ahead, but Femi and Lawrence pause on the promenade.

'Sell?'

'Well, after you left, I saw them painting it.' She points to the beach hut where she'd sat with Lawrence, in the summer, about to watch the sunset before she'd run off. 'I guessed you'd sold it?'

He shakes his head. 'No, I hired the painters before I left.'

'So, it's still yours?'

Lawrence smiles. 'I'll only tell you if you promise not to run off.'

'I'm sorry about that, I panicked.' They walk on more slowly, behind the boys. 'You were so kind and I didn't know what to do.'

Lawrence nods. 'Well, I was shocked but then I did work it out. I spoke to Ben and also to Amber and they just got it. They understood you.'

Femi frowns. 'But they hardly know me.'

'Presumably Ahmed has filled them in on a few details.'

'Ah, so that's how you've been so understanding.' Femi looks at Ahmed walking along with Albert, such different boys but both with traumatic pasts, and to hear them laughing and chatting together, Femi cannot be upset.

'Ahmed insisted I met him in Harbour Cafe and he told me that you needed someone special.' He laughs.

'Oh, no.'

'He hinted that it should be me and when it didn't work out, he spoke to Ben. Ahmed trusts Ben,' he says.

'It's good for him to have a male role model or two.'

Lawrence links his arm though Femi's.

'I think you were the first though,' she says

'The first are always the best.'

Femi smiles and she wonders about the warm happy feeling, growing deep down in her stomach, but there's also a familiar niggling sensation that tells her it won't last.

29

Chapter 29

Faisal is wearing the long French-style apron and white polo shirt; the uniform of Harbour Cafe. His smile is as broad and welcoming as Karl's, the manager. He finishes cleaning a table and, under Karl's watchful eye from where he's standing behind the counter, Faisal appears with a notebook to take their orders.

'You look gorgeous,' Femi says.

'Very professional, Faisal. It's like you've been here for years.' Lawrence nods at him.

Ahmed beams and blushes, while Albert grins and then concentrates on the menu.

'I bet you'll want fruit cake?' Faisal says to Ahmed and he beams back at him happy that he's remembered his favourite cake.

As they finish their order, Femi is content to sit in the window looking out at Harbour Street's Christmas lights and colourful windows. She's finished her Christmas shopping: a new rucksack for Albert, an old Polaroid camera for Ahmed to pull apart and, a new sports hoodie for Ricky. And as she watches the shoppers stopping to admire the Christmas window displays, her mind turns to Ricky. Although he's been working a lot of evening shifts at the pub, he's been avoiding her and tonight, he's taking Ashley to Harbour Bistro for dinner.

Across the road, Ben's Art Gallery is still open and Eva's flower shop is busy. People hurry past laden with shopping bags and Femi wonders what she could buy for Lawrence.

'Auntie?'

Femi turns at the sound of her name and she's surprised that Faisal has returned already with their order. She was so lost in thought.

'What are we doing on Christmas Eve?' Ahmed looks serious. 'Is that more special?'

'For some people it is. If you're a believer then that's the night baby Jesus arrived.'

Ahmed nods. 'Do you go to church?'

'I thought I might go to the Carol Service at the church this year but if you don't want to join me then you can stay at home.'

'Can I come with you?' Albert asks. 'We went last year, didn't we?'

'I'll tag along too, if you don't mind.' Lawrence sips his coffee.

'The more the merrier.' Femi's heart could burst.

This is far more than she could have hoped for. At one stage she thought she'd lost Lawrence and she ran the risk of losing all of her boys but today, everything seems absolutely perfect. As if it should always be like this.

Lawrence smiles at her and she pokes out her tongue.

She can't afford to be complacent. Experience has taught her that at her happiest times, come the shocks, and the downfall. She wishes she could shake off this growing premonition that something is about to come crashing down on them all and shatter her perfect Christmas.

* * *

Femi heads into the lounge where she begins hanging up the Christmas stockings for the boys. Lawrence has stayed in town to meet Ben for a drink in The Ship. Ahmed has gone upstairs and is now on his computer waiting for Faisal to finish work and Albert has announced, as if it was a big secret, that he was going upstairs to wrap his Christmas presents.

Now, she puts her feet up, and with only the Christmas tree lights on and the fire glowing in the hearth, she's happily deciding what to watch on TV.

She misses Sandra who, for the first time, has gone away for Christmas with her husband, cruising around the Caribbean for two weeks. Freddie and Nitesh will go to Freddie's parents in the New Forest as they normally do for Christmas Day, and Femi is relaxed and feeling far better than she has in a long time. She's searching though the TV guide when her phone rings. It's Amber.

'Hi, Femi, look I'm sorry to bother you but I've had an idea. If it doesn't suit you, then please tell me.'

'Of course.'

'You don't have to answer, right now. Give it some thought, if you'd like. But Ben and I would love to have our Christmas lunch with you guys—'

'Fantastic, come over to us,' Femi says, delighted at the thought of having adult company.

'Well, I was thinking, perhaps you guys would all like to come to Harbour Bistro. We've invited Karl and Molly too, and it could be great fun.'

'I think the boys would love that.' Femi is thinking how much Ahmed would enjoy it, and Ricky really likes Ben, and Albert will be happy if they can take Peanut.'

'Well, it's Christmas and we'd love to share a big table with our friends.'

'Thank you, Amber. What can I bring?'

'Absolutely nothing.'

'I'll give it some thought and we can talk tomorrow, we can't come empty handed,' Femi insists.

'OK, I'll tell Ben and Lawrence. They'll be thrilled.'

After she hangs up Femi is lost in thought. She'd be spending Christmas this year with adults for the first time in a long time and she feels a shiver of excitement. Can this possibly be happening to her?

Ricky pops his head around the door. 'I'm off,' he says.

'Let me look at you?' She smiles.

He stands formally at the door, self-consciously, tugging at the hem of the navy jacket he's borrowed from Lawrence. He looks very handsome in a white shirt and maroon tie and he looks older than his seventeen years. Femi suddenly feels very proud and emotional.

'You look lovely,' she whispers.

Seeing her alone. He ventures into the room and sits beside her feet on the sofa.

'Thank you, Auntie.'

'For what?'

'You know, for everything.'

'I hope you have a lovely evening with Ashley.'

'I'm a bit nervous.'

'You're not going to propose, are you?' Femi laughs.

Ricky smiles. 'No, I'm not leaving you.'

'You will one day.'

'I'll always be here for you,' he whispers. 'Just as you have for me.'

'Are you being mushy?'

He grins. 'Well, I'll be honest, you know I didn't like Ahmed at first, but I've seen what you've done for him, and Albert and how they've changed and grown and developed. You're just an incredible person.'

'Thank you.'

'Look.' He grips his hands together. 'I wanted to tell you where I went but I was frightened.'

'I only ever ask for the truth.'

'I know but I think you'll be upset.'

'You evading me and not telling me where you are or levelling with me, upsets me more than anything you could have done.'

'I went to Devon.'

Femi frowns. 'What for? What's in Devon?'

'Who is in Devon?'

Femi shrugs.

'You're maternal grandparents.'

It takes a while for Femi to adjust her mind and realise what he's saying and then it dawns on her. 'My mum's parents? What did you go there for?'

'I thought I could speak to them and tell them how lovely you are and that magically they would want to meet you.' Femi waits and Ricky continues slowly, 'But they didn't. They weren't interested.'

'You actually spoke to them?'

Ricky nods. 'I spoke to your grandmother. He was ill in bed. She didn't let me inside the house. She didn't want to know.'

Femi reaches forward and wraps him in a big hug while trying to protect her ribs. He allows her to squeeze him hard. 'I'm so sorry, Ricky. That must have been awful for you.'

He pulls away. 'I felt awful for you. I didn't know how to tell you so I stayed quiet. I didn't want to make you sad.'

'I'm not sad, Ricky. You boys are my life. You're all I need.'

'I know but I thought it would have been nice for you, especially as Lawrence wasn't here and you were so upset—'

'I wasn't upset.'

'Ahmed said you were having nightmares.'

'That was from something else but they've gone now.'

'Really?'

'Of course.'

'Good.'

'That was a very kind thing you did, Ricky. I'm sorry that things didn't work out as you wanted them to but sometimes that's life.'

'We've still got each other.'

'That's the most important thing.' She smiles.

He checks his watch and stands up. 'I'd better go or Ashley will be left waiting.'

'Have a fabulous time and give her my love.'

'Thank you, Auntie. What are you going to do?'

'I'm going to read an old book that my dad used to read to me, especially at Christmas time. It's a wonderful poem, *Vespers*.'

'Perhaps you'll share that with us all over Christmas?'

'Maybe I will. Go on, get out of here or you'll be late and

she'll dump you.'

***

Christmas Eve is Femi's favourite day in the whole year. She's up early and she tidies the house while she waits for Ricky to get showered and dressed. They leave early for the supermarket to buy the last bits and pieces to take to Amber and Ben's tomorrow. She needs Ricky's help to carry the shopping bags, as her ribs are still sore, before he heads to The Ship for a washing-up shift at lunchtime.

'I'm going to the Carol Service in the church at four o'clock,' she reminds him.

'I should be finished by then so I'll join you.' He gives her a peck on the cheek as he leaves and she hums happily to the music on the radio in the background.

Albert has gone to Harbour Street. He wants to finish his Christmas shopping in town and he's taken Peanut which leads Femi to think he's probably gone for a walk on the beach and will end up buying a toy for Peanut in the pet shop.

She checks her watch before going upstairs. It's unusual for Ahmed not to be downstairs and pottering around with a camera or reading at the kitchen table while having breakfast.

'Ahmed?' she calls.

There's no answer.

'Ahmed?' She taps on the door and when he doesn't answer, she thinks he may have gone out and she puts her head around the door. He's sitting up in bed, as if in a trance, unmoving and unblinking.

'Ahmed? Are you alright?'

He turns his head slowly as if registering her presence for

the first time.

'Ahmed? Is something wrong?' As she moves closer there are tears trickling down his cheeks, so she sits on the edge of the bed and when he finally looks at her, she can see the pain and misery in the depths of his eyes. They are swollen and sore as if he's been crying all night.

She reaches for his hand and whispers, 'What's happened?'

He shakes his head unable to speak.

'Is it Faisal?'

He shakes his head.

'Has anyone upset you?'

He shakes his head.

'I can't play guessing games, you have to tell me and then I can help you.'

He wipes his eyes with the back of his pyjama sleeve and nods in acknowledgement.

'Do you need some time? I can wait here or you can come downstairs, which do you prefer?'

'Here.' His voice is a croak, barely a whisper.

Femi wiggles further onto the bed to get comfortable. 'Okay, so what is it?'

'I've had a message from Mama.'

'Your mother?'

'She's contacted me through the refugee centre.'

'That's great news then, isn't it?' Femi's tone is upbeat yet she feels her heart sinking. The thought of losing Ahmed would be unbearable.

'I'm frightened,' he whispers.

Femi nods. So is she. 'Why?' she asks gently.

'What if she wants me to go back?'

'Can you speak to her?'

Ahmed nods. 'I have this number to call.' There's a scrunched-up piece of paper on his bedside table.

'In Syria?'

'She's in Turkey now.'

'Is she a refugee?'

He shrugs.

'You must speak to her, Ahmed. You must find out what is happening. Why are you frightened?'

'I like it here, with you.'

Femi pats his hand. 'You'll always have me, but you must speak to her. Everything will be alright.'

Ahmed reaches for the number and Femi stands up but he holds onto her hand. 'Stay with me?'

Femi sits down again and she waits while Ahmed dials the number on his phone. There's static when it's answered and Femi can't tell if the voice is male or female.

Ahmed speaks seriously in Arabic and Femi sits beside him in the bedroom. She notices the dust collecting on the skirting board behind his bedside table and she makes a mental note to organise a deep clean for his room in the new year. Around the room there are photographic magazines, discarded bits of cameras but his clothes are neat and tidy.

Suddenly he squeezes her hand and she looks up. He looks fearful and he's shaking, so she soothes his hand as he speaks. He sounds angry and his voice goes up in volume. Femi frowns. He lets go of her hand and he's waving his arms, speaking quickly, then he listens, says a few words and is monosyllabic before he looks at Femi. His brown eyes are tired and he's stressed. Then he hangs up and tosses the phone onto the duvet beside him.

'Well?' asks Femi. 'Did it go well?'

'She's remarried,' he replies flatly. 'She's married a friend's cousin.'

'Did you speak to her?'

He nods. 'She wants me to go to Turkey and meet her.'

'Are you happy to do that?'

He doesn't answer at first and then he says,' My sister is in Syria. She is married now to an old man and I am angry with my mother. That shouldn't happen any more.'

'What did she say?'

'She said it was to keep her safe.'

'She might have a point.' Femi crosses her legs. 'It probably isn't easy for women and children over there.'

'I would have helped them but *he* didn't want me to do that.'

'He?'

'My uncle.'

'Why?'

'He told her, I wouldn't survive.'

Femi smiles. 'Well, look at you. You have survived and you're very happy.'

He turns and looks at her. 'Auntie, can I stay here? I can't go back, Auntie.'

'I know.'

'I don't want to go to Turkey, either.'

'You don't have to go anywhere, Ahmed. I told you the night you arrived, this is your home and you're safe here.' Femi knows they're processing his asylum application and despite her reassurances he could get sent home. But, she also knows she will fight to keep him with her.

He throws himself forward and into her arms and she can feel his wet cheeks against her own. His wiry body is fuller now and he's changed from the child with a broken ankle eight months ago into a maturing young man. Even his tears have changed. These are tears of relief and happiness. He pulls away from her and Femi stands up.

'Right. I'm going to the Carol Service in the church at four o'clock if you want to come with me.'

'I have to buy Lawrence a present,' he replies, throwing back the bed covers, suddenly energised. 'Auntie?'

She pauses at the door and looks back to where he's sanding and smiling happily.

'You were right, they do come true.'

'What's that?'

'Birthday wishes.'

Femi frowns and he continues.

'When you gave me my birthday cake and told me I could make a wish and I blew out the candles — I wished to stay here.'

Femi throws her head back and laughs. 'Well, that's just perfect then, I've wished for the same thing.'

30

Chapter 30

The church is packed and Femi has never known it so busy. Her ribs still hurt and she's walking gingerly with Lawrence at her side. They've walked arm-in-arm, companionably with Albert along the sea front, past the beach huts, through the harbour and along Harbour Street where Ahmed, in his new winter duffel coat, is waiting outside the church.

Inside, the pews are filling up and they slide in beside Ben, Amber, Karl and Molly, greeting each other happily. Amber has invited them all to Harbour Bistro for Christmas Day lunch and Femi can't believe that she'll finally eat in that lovely restaurant.

As they sit down, Femi notices Faisal has joined them. He's sitting in the row behind with Ahmed and just in front of them are Freddie and Nitesh. Femi waves at her friends and is relieved when Ricky appears and slides in to sit beside her.

This is perfect, thinks Femi. I have my family and friends all around me, apart from Sandra who is probably in the Caribbean on the ship drinking cocktails.

Frances, the vicar, tells the story of Jesus's birth with the help of a few readers, the choir and an enthusiastic organist and the congregation stand to sing the first carol. Femi's heart is filled with joy and she remembers happier Christmases from the past, looking up at her father, and hearing his baritone voice above everyone else's. Her heart is filled with joy, knowing that he's probably looking down on her and saying: 'You've done well, Femi. Considering all the cards were stacked against you, you've done very well. You're my girl, I knew you'd make a difference in life.'

Beside her, Albert stares up at the ceiling, Ricky is fidgeting while trying to sing in tune and over her shoulder she catches Ahmed, filled with the Christmas spirit, smiling at Faisal.

Femi loves the Christmas story and although the boys pretend they're not interested, it has a magical capacity that she's sure captures their hearts and imagination. It's a happy story, she'd told them.

'Remember, it doesn't matter where you've come from, even Jesus was a refugee and he was born in a barn. What matters is how kind you are, and how you treat other people. You,' she has told them all individually, 'can make a difference.'

Life is transient, she realises.

Ricky will have to stay out of trouble and keep on track to get to university, Albert must continue to do well at school and not be tempted to steal for or from anyone else again and he must also monitor his hopes of moving back in with his father. As for Ahmed, well, after speaking to his mother today, the lines of communication are open again. She's happy for him but under no illusion that she or their life together will continue to be a strong link that binds them together. He will want to see his mother, and that's perfectly normal, and just what power she will have over Ahmed in the future, remains to be seen.

She feels Lawrence's gaze on her and she turns to smile at him. His eyes are twinkling behind his glasses and she knows how important this church service is to him. He's been denied this by his parents. It's not as if they took him and let him make up his own mind, it's like they decided for him, as a baby, that he wouldn't be a Christian. Femi understands that Christianity and the Church are two different identities, and that spirituality is all about being a good or better person. She smiles back at Lawrence. She's under no illusion that he might find another woman, now he's home for good. He might meet another lecturer at the University, a woman who might put him first, a woman who will give him a family of his own but, in the meantime Femi can still call him her friend.

A man like Lawrence is a catch, intelligent, funny, kind and exciting — they don't come along often and they certainly don't move in next door, so she will keep him in her life for as long as he will stay and, when he says that he's met someone special, she won't be disappointed. He's her friend and, although it will make her sad, she will be very happy for him.

So, feeling a mixture of heady memories and emotions for her family and friends, Femi walks out of the church with an air of determination that everything will be well. This Christmas, with her boys and Lawrence and her friends together for Christmas lunch will be everything she ever dreamed of and, if she has the perfect Christmas for one year only, then it will be something she will always remember — forever.

* * *

After the Carol Service they head home with Amber and Ben. It's an impromptu suggestion from Lawrence and with Femi's consent they walk along the promenade to Femi's house, where Ahmed, Faisal and Albert begin playing Nintendo Wii in the lounge. Ricky has stayed behind to go and have a drink with Ashley and her mother.

The four adults huddle around the kitchen table. Lawrence opens a bottle of prosecco and they're all talking about Harbour Street and the colourful characters who own the shops.

Femi is contented to sit with her friends. She's never had a friend like Lawrence. They're not romantically linked unless you call a kiss on the cheek romantic, yet she feels happy and safe with him. Since he's come back from Malaysia, he's spent most of his time with her — or with her and one of the boys. They talk about everything. Their conversation is easy and he's understanding and non-judgemental. He's intelligent company and when she feels his shoulder touching hers, she doesn't move away.

To her complete happiness, Femi is also relaxed with Ben and Amber. They are kind people and she knows how much they have helped Ahmed and Faisal and for her, that's the kindest thing anyone could have done. Looking around the kitchen at them all, she realises how much easier it is to cope with everything when you have friends and support.

So, along with Sandra, Freddie and Nitesh, Femi is pleased that her friendship group is growing and she wonders where her friendship with Lawrence will take her. How would she feel if Lawrence were to introduce a woman into their circle of friends, more importantly, where would Femi fit in?

Amber tells them the story of how she was a lawyer in London and how she bought Harbour Cafe for her girlfriend who then returned to the theatre.

'I was left to sink or swim,' she said.

'It's the best thing you did for the town,' Ben adds. 'And, then you bought the old travel agents and turned it into Harbour Bistro.'

'Getting a second mortgage so quickly was hard—'

'But you got rid of the town's nastiest person.'

'Who was that?' asks Femi.

'A woman called JJ, who ran The Ship,' says Ben.

'That's a story for another time.' Amber nudges Ben and winks at him.

Femi can see that Lawrence feels the same way. They both want to know the entire story and as Lawrence refills their glasses Femi pulls out plates of sausage rolls, devils on horseback, mince pies and the boys wander in and out helping themselves, Femi thinks life couldn't be more perfect.

This will be a Christmas she will remember for the rest of her life.

The front doorbell rings, and surprised, Femi stands up and straightens her red dress. Before opening the front door, she checks on the boys in the lounge. There's no sign of Ricky and her stomach lurches. He'd had a lovely evening with Ashley at Harbour Bistro last night and today after the Carol Service they were spending an hour with Ashley's mother in Canterbury.

Now, for some awful reason, Femi's heart beings to thump with fear. Ricky would always use the back door.

She opens the door. It's not Ricky and it's not the police.

Femi finds herself staring at a small, round-shouldered old lady with a beige coat and navy hat.

'Hello?'
'Femi?'
'Yes.'
'I'm your grandmother.'

* * *

It's a crazy moment. Femi finds herself having an almost out of body experience. This couldn't be happening to her. And besides, how does she know if this woman is her grandmother? She's never seen her before. She looks more like a bag lady off the street than a cosy, warm, safe grandma. The woman's nose is long and her face is thin and pinched as if caught in a vice.

'Can I come in?'

Femi's instinct is to step back and allow her inside. But she stands with the door half closed wanting to slam it shut. She wasn't ready to open the wounds of her past, she's too happy. For the first time in her life, she's having the perfect Christmas and now this woman has tuned up.

'Hello,' Lawrence's warm voice is over Femi's shoulder. 'Is everything alright?'

'Who are you?' asks the old woman.

Lawrence looks at Femi with a questioning look and it's Femi who replies, 'She says, she's my grandmother.'

The old lady places her bag on the floor at her feet. She looks tired and worn.

'If I'm not welcome, I'll go.'

'No, you won't go!' Ricky suddenly appears out of the darkness on his bicycle. He leans it against the wall outside and joins the old woman on the step. 'It's Christmas, even the Innkeeper had a room, come inside. You can talk in the warm.' Instinctively, as Ricky picks up her bag and takes the old lady's elbow, Femi and Lawrence step aside.

As if realising there's something of importance happening, Amber and Ben make a quick escape promising to see them tomorrow - Christmas Day - and before she knows it Lawrence and Ricky have also left the kitchen.

Femi is alone with the first relative she's known in twenty-three years. She reaches for the kettle, teapot and teabags and the old lady sits wearily at the kitchen table.

'Why have you come here?' Femi asks.

'Your boy, Ricky came to ours and he left a photo of you. On the back was your address.'

Femi reaches for the mugs.

'What have you done to yourself?' the old lady asks. 'Broken ribs?'

'How do you know?'

'I see by the way you move. I was a nurse.'

'Really? I'm a trained paramedic.'

'You did better than your mother, then.'

The old lady takes off her hat to reveal thin grey hair, and Femi guesses her to be eighty or more. Her long fingers are gnarled with arthritis.

'You threw my mother out of your house.'

'Her Dad thought it would be best.'

'It was cruel.' Femi places the mugs on the table. She's surprised that the old lady's hand is shaking. 'Do you want to tell me what happened?' she asks.

The old lady sips her tea. She slurps loudly as if she's deaf and she seems to gather her thoughts. Her eyes are rheumy and her face wrinkled with age. 'There's not much to tell. It all seems such a long time ago, as if it happened to someone else.'

'My mum, Paula, died twenty-three years go.'

The old lady shakes her head. 'I had no idea.'

Femi sits opposite her and waits, studying the old lady for clues that might link her mother with this gnarled old lady.

'Let me tell you,' Femi says quietly. 'Paula was beaten by her first husband and she had two children who ended up in foster care. I have no idea to this day where they are, nor do I want to. They were horrible children, bullies and abusers.' She lets the words sink in until the old lady looks her in the eye and a level of understanding is accepted.

'When Paula met my Dad, he was working in the hospital as a porter. She came in the first time with a broken nose, the second time because she'd overdosed and was seriously depressed, and that's when he knew she needed looking after.' Femi isn't as scant with the details as she was with the boys. She remembers her mother telling the story of how she was saved over and over again.

'She and her two children moved in with him. It was a small flat but they managed and they had me. Dad gave us all a lot of love and he showed them a kindness that they'd never experienced before but he worked nights. That meant that Paula missed him. She would drink herself into a stupor. I was young and vulnerable and she didn't protect me.'

The old lady doesn't move.

Femi continues, 'My Dad died in a boating accident when I was thirteen and Paula fell apart. I find it hard to call her mother or mum now, because she wasn't one. I didn't know she'd been thrown out by you because she married a black man, even though he was kinder to her than anyone else she'd ever met.'

The old lady looks at her gnarled fingers. She doesn't wear any rings.

'After my dad died, she took another overdose but I was the only one there. She was in the bathroom but I was too late. This time no one saved her. I failed her. After that, my siblings and I were fostered separately. I was lucky. The couple who raised me looked after me, loved me, invested in me and trusted me. Do you understand what that was like as a thirteen-year-old — to have no one?'

She shakes her head and won't look up.

'So, forgive me, if I'm not forgiving of you. I'm having a tough time working out why the hell you've come here and why now after all these years you've decided to wreck my perfect Christmas.'

The old lady looks up. 'Your grandfather died last week and I have no where else to go. I have no one.'

Chapter 31

The old lady looks tired and malnourished. She also looks ashamed. Femi takes her time and controls her feelings before she stands up and pulls out some bread, ham and cheese.

'Have you eaten?' Femi asks.

'No.'

'I'm sorry about your husband.' She can't bring herself to say grandfather.

'I'm not,' the old lady whispers. 'He was a bully and a tyrant.'

Femi places the food on the table and when he old lady doesn't help herself, Femi makes her a sandwich.

'Why did you stay with him?'

'I had nowhere else to go. I'm from a different generation. We were told, if you make your bed you lie on it.' She bites into the sandwich and speaks with her mouthful. 'Six weeks after we married, I knew I'd made a mistake, but my mother told me I didn't have a choice and she slammed the door in my face. He laughed at me, he knew I had no one and he made sure it stayed that way. After Paula was born, probably even before, he was having affairs.'

'How did he control you?'

'Through money, it's often that way. He would let me work at the hospital and he knew every penny I had and where I went and who I spoke to.'

'Paula said you were pleased when she left home.' Femi regards the old woman carefully.

'I was. I wanted her to escape. I wanted her to do better than I had. But she was so stupid. She married a man just like her father. He made her life impossible. How she found the courage to leave him, I'll never know.'

'My Dad, gave her the courage, he put a roof over her head and kept her safe.'

'He was a good man then.'

'You blocked us out of your lives.'

'I didn't. Eric did. I didn't know about the letter until Ricky showed it to me. I was shocked. Eric always said it was Paula's decision and I abided by that. I respected her. I wanted her to get away from him but I never realised he'd sent that awful, racist letter to Paula.' She wipes her eyes. 'He was so cruel.'

'You didn't know until Ricky visited you?'

She shakes her head. 'He controlled everything.'

'Ricky says he was ill.'

'He'd had a stroke but he refused to go anywhere for care. He said that I should be his nurse. He insisted. I couldn't do anything but I wanted to come here as soon as I could to see you.'

'Why?'

'To say sorry. I am, so terribly, terribly sorry. All those years. I never knew I had you.'

'Me?'

'I knew about the other two children but Eric told me they'd been adopted or probably gone to Canada to be with their father. Now, I think he lied about that too.'

'You didn't know I existed, that Paula had me?'

She shakes her head. 'Paula was never allowed to contact me after she left her first husband.'

'She said she wrote,' Femi says.

'If she wrote, then Eric would never have shown me the letter. He wanted to punish us both.'

'What about your other grandchildren?'

'Since Eric's stroke, I've had access to the computer and I've been trying to find them but I'm not good with these sorts of things. I've had no practice or experience looking for people, but with Eric gone, I can do what I like now.'

Femi smiles. 'You've been liberated.'

The old lady smiles back. 'I'd like to think so, I just hope it's not too late.'

Femi can hear the boys in the living room playing and she guesses Lawrence is in there with them.

'Do you want to meet my family?' she asks.

'Your husband seems lovely.'

'Lawrence? He's not my husband, he's just a friend.'

The old lady smiles and Femi calls them all into the kitchen and introduces them one by one, and she says, 'This is your grandma.'

The old lady smiles and a light appears to come from behind her eyes. 'Call me, Gladly.'

'Gladly?' Femi repeats.

'It's what Paula called me when she was young. She didn't call me mum or mother, and she couldn't say Gladys.'

A long-forgotten memory suddenly resurfaces. 'Mummy

gave me a teddy bear called Gladly,' Femi's voice is filled with wonder. 'Daddy used to say, Gladly my cross I bear.'

* * *

Femi lies in bed in the darkness. She's finally on her own and she's going over the events of the day, wondering how her Christmas Eve went from being perfect into the most bizarre evening she could possibly have imagined.

Ricky has since left her bedroom, he'd been deliriously happy that his trip to Devon hadn't been wasted and that Gladly want to find Femi.

'I'm really pleased she felt she could come here,' he says. 'Didn't you always say that we all need some place to run to, Auntie?'

'I did.'

'Then isn't it nice that she ran here to you, to us.'

'Thank you, Ricky.'

'And she didn't mind too much that I wasn't your son. I didn't really lie, you see, I never got the chance to tell her —'

'That doesn't matter, Ricky, you're everything to me.'

He'd hugged her then before saying goodnight.

Now, she's thinking about her family and the whole evening.

Albert had been less interested because she was from the English side of Femi's heritage and he was thinking of Delroy in prison over Christmas anyway. Meanwhile, Ahmed was exhausted with family matters and he'd taken himself off to bed early. He was still processing his own family situation and dealing with Femi's past just wasn't on his agenda.

Lawrence had been incredibly kind and supportive, interested without being intrusive, and thoughtful without meddling. He'd managed to tidy the plates of food away and stack the dishwasher before producing a lovely bottle of Remy Martin, and for an hour the three of them had sat in the lounge companionably, in front of the fire, talking quietly about life.

Femi had sat on the sofa, looking at the pretty Christmas tree lights, in the glow of the burning embers, with the stockings hanging on the mantelpiece and where the two Caribbean dolls, given to her by her father, now had a permanent place.

It was good to see Gladly, relaxing, smiling and enjoying a conversation with Lawrence and even laughing. After a while, she'd said.

'I suppose I should leave you young people to have some time alone.'

Lawrence had gallantly sprung to his feet.

'Not at all, you've come a long way. You must be exhausted. I'll leave you both in peace. Where are you staying tonight?'

Femi replied, 'I can sleep here on the couch and Gladly can have my bedroom.'

Gladly holds up her hand. 'Nonsense. I won't let you do that on Christmas Eve.'

'Why don't I suggest something?' Lawrence smiles and looks directly at Femi and her heart skips a beat. She's never known a man more handsome or more appealing in her entire life.

'Why doesn't Gladly stay with me, next door? You know I have an en-suite guest room and then you can get some rest, Femi.'

Gladly beams with delight. 'How kind of you, Lawrence.'

And, although Femi smiles, her spirits drop to an unimaginable level.

Now, in the darkness and safety of her room and with the

brandy wearing off, Femi knows she must manage her expectations. She chides herself on having feelings for Lawrence. He's just being kind, he's a good friend, so don't get confused and don't get hurt.

* * *

Femi is woken by a tapping sound. At first, she thinks it's a part of her dream, but then she realises it's a steady, rhythmic tap, and she opens her eyes. It's still dark and not yet dawn. There's another tap, and it's not inside the house, its coming from the window.

She pushes back the covers and opens the blinds.

Lawrence is standing in the dark using his phone for a light. He waves at her and she opens the window.

'Get dressed and come down,' he whispers.

She throws on a pair of jeans, two sizes smaller than eight months ago, a thick jumper and downstairs she opens the door. Peanut yawns and stretches, then gives a mock shiver because of the cold and curls up in a ball.

'Come on,' Lawrence whispers.

'Where are we going?'

'You'll see, hurry.'

She pushes her feet into boots, grabs a warm jacket and when she gets outside Lawrence takes her hand.

'It's very dark,' she whispers.

'Yes.'

'It's like we're hiding a body — you haven't—?' She giggles.

His laughter breaks through the sea mist along the promenade.

'No, you've only just found her. Give it time and if you don't like her, just let me know.' He squeezes her hand and she laughs louder.

'I like her,' she says.

'Me too. I think she's had a tough time, you know, with a controlling husband. I saw it in my family and my brother. Afterwards you think, how did I let them get away with that? But at the time you're so caught up in it all—'

'And with nowhere to go.'

'Exactly. Look how long it took me, and even now, I can't forgive my parents. But Gladly knew nothing about you or Paula and, I believe her.'

'Ricky said that he watched her reading the letter and she was shocked. She must have been horrified to know Eric did that without telling her.'

'Absolutely.'

'What's this?' Femi stops and Lawrence pulls on her hand. 'Come on.'

They climb the stairs to his beach hut and to her surprise it's unlocked, open. There are two champagne flutes and a bottle in a silver ice bucket. The seats are side by side facing the sea.

'I thought we'd watch the sunrise on Christmas morning together.'

'How lovely.'

'Well, I thought after the last time—'

'You're taking a big risk.' Femi laughs. 'How do you know I won't run away?'

'Not many people get second chances in life and it's such a shame because they're the important ones. We learn from our mistakes, we mature and we grow, and if we're very lucky, we might eventually get what we want.'

'Really?'

'You sound surprised.' He fills their glasses and Femi turns to the horizon where the clouds are separating and the first rays of sun come filtering through onto the shimmering sea. 'Besides, this is such a beautiful place and it's the start of a brand new day and I thought, it might help you clear your head after last night.'

'Gladly looked exhausted.'

'It was emotional for both of you, but at least you seemed to clear the air.'

'I think we've made the base for a new beginning.'

'I love your positivity. You're an incredible woman, Femi.'

Feeling suddenly self-conscious, she asks, 'Was Gladly still asleep?'

He smiles. 'I assume so, unless she's stolen all my silver and disappeared into the night.'

Femi giggles.

'Look, I have to tell you something,' he's says.

Femi's body goes rigid. She looks at the steps and thinks how she might escape if it's bad news.

'I've met someone very special,' he says, hands her a glass. 'I hope it's not too early for you?'

She swallows hard. 'It's to be expected,' she whispers, holding back her tears.

'Happy Christmas, Femi.'

'Happy Christmas, Lawrence.'

Femi can't run away. Lawrence is her friend and so long as he stays living next door, that's all she could ask for and she grins. 'And, it's never too early. Just for the record, I can drink champagne at any time of the day.'

'I mean for this.'

He sets his glass aside and opens a small jewellery box and sinks to one knee.

'I want to do this properly. This is the best Christmas but I really want it to be perfect.' He smiles. 'Femi, my darling, my beautiful friend and lovely neighbour please would you do me the honour of marrying me and spending all of our days fostering fabulous children and making crazy memories together.'

She laughs loudly and tears stream down her cheeks, as the sun bursts through the clouds turning them silver and golden. 'Oh gosh, I will, Lawrence. I really will.'

32

Chapter 32

After the excitement, Femi sits holding Lawrence's hand watching the sunrise, making plans; dreaming of a future together, raising the boys, thinking of their reactions and also what their good friends Ben and Amber will think.

The ring is sparkling on her finger.

'My hands look so big, she complains.

'Nonsense. You're beautiful.'

'Are you sure you've thought all this through?'

'There's nothing to think about, I just know, Femi. What about you? Do you need more time?'

'No.'

'There's one more small gift I have for you.'

'Something else?' Femi says, surprised.

He holds out a small present wrapped in white paper with robins and a red velvet bow.

She laughs. 'It has to be a book.'

'Happy Christmas.'

She pulls the bow and reads the title and laughs. '*Now We Are Sixty*.'

'It's written by Christopher Matthew,' he says. 'It follows the same rhymes and rhythms of A.A. Milne —it's a parody and it's very funny. Perhaps we will still read it together when we're older.'

'How lovely. How did you know? A book is always the best present.'

Lawrence smiles. 'I think I've known you from the beginning, Femi when I asked you not to cut down the twisted willow.'

'Because of the robins.'

'Yes.'

Femi laughs. 'I thought you were lonely sitting in the restaurant on your own.'

'You'd been drinking wine,' Lawrence laughs. 'I thought you were going to fall over.'

'You must have thought I was a terrible foster parent.'

'Never, you're the best. And talking of parents, you'll probably have to meet mine,' he says.

'I'm sure they'll be delighted you're marrying a dual heritage woman.'

He grins. 'One visit. One chance is all they will get, I promise you.'

'I'll take you to meet my foster parents, I've promised them I'd visit in the new year. They'll love you.'

'The most important thing is that the boys like me.'

'No, honey, the most important thing is that I love you.' Femi laughs.

'I'm so excited, Femi. I never expected to meet someone like you. What do you think the boys will say when we tell them?'

* * *

Harbour Bistro is everything that Femi dreamed it might be. There's a glowing fire, a perfect Christmas tree decorated with beautiful lights, and the most incredible smell of food from the kitchen.

Lawrence fusses around everyone, helping Karl and Ben, pouring drinks but he's so excited he hardly wants to leave Femi's side. He'd prepared the beach hut the day before, hoping to propose on Christmas Eve, knowing it was Femi's favourite day in the whole year, but then Gladly had arrived and all of his plans went pear-shaped. Not that it mattered too much as Gladly is a delightful woman and he can see today that Femi is now pleased to have her grandmother in her life. But Lawrence had been unable to sleep. Knowing he had one last chance when they could be on their own at Christmas and he'd taken the risk of throwing stones up at her window. Lawrence knows he's met the most beautiful woman and he's determined to give her the best possible life. He moves closer to her and he whispers, 'Have you ever wondered what it might be like to have a little girl?'

Femi looks at him and a multitude of thoughts spin through her head. She'd never wanted a girl because she knew she'd have to protect her, as she had never been protected. She'd never want to fail a daughter. Her mother had failed to protect her and Femi had failed to save Paula. But now, with Lawrence at her side, her fears seem to evaporate.

She wasn't on her own any more. 'I'd love a little baby girl,' she replies.

Lawrence grins. It was what he had hoped she might say and as he kisses her, Ben passes them carrying a fresh bottle, topping up the drinks. He grins. 'Get a room, guys.' And, this sends Femi into peals of laughter.

Gladly watches Femi and Lawrence with a mixture of pride and regret. She's furious with Eric and she's angry with herself for having put up with him for so long. He was controlling and he sucked the life from her, but already, in the past few weeks since his death, she has felt stronger and happier. She took the risk of coming here and reaching out to Femi, hoping for forgiveness, never realising what a big and generous heart her granddaughter would have. It would take time to come to terms with Paula but she knew that she and Femi would help each other.

She's delighted that Lawrence has proposed although they had looked so natural together when she'd arrived last night, that she couldn't believe it hadn't happened before. One day she would hear their stories. There will be plenty of time to get to know them all properly. She'd been made so welcome. Femi's boys are delightful, and today, Gladly knows it's the best Christmas since Paula was tiny, but she wouldn't tell Femi that. Today is Christmas Day and that sort of truth could wait.

The small tables have been put together to create one long table in the middle of the restaurant and after they've shared the news of their engagement and toasts have been made, Femi is happy to sit back, relax and share this special day with her family.

For the first time, her grandmother who now looks rested and happy, sits at her side. She's been engaged in conversation this morning with all of her children and this makes Femi feel much happier. She's interested and interesting and she has a wry sense of humour. As they tuck into a feast of turkey, ham and roasted vegetables, Femi cannot help but wonder what all the boys are thinking.

Ricky looks around the table feeling pleased with himself. If he hadn't taken the risk and gone to Devon, none of this would have happened. He will never forget the lonely night on the station platform. He'd been so angry with himself, the grandparents and with the world and his initial reaction after missing the train had been anger. He'd wanted to wreck the station — do some serious damage. He'd wanted to rip up the bench, throw the bins around and tip the rubbish on the track. He'd wanted to smash his fist through the shutters covering the window but he'd managed to contain his temper. For the first time in his life, he'd managed to reason with his angry self and instead, he'd sat on the platform and cried. They were tears of frustration, anger and hurt but little by little he resigned himself to his situation and he knew that whatever happened he would always have Auntie. Even if they found out where he'd gone, he was hoping that Femi would work miracles. She would save him. But, as it turns out, it hadn't all been in vain.

Gladly is really very sweet. She's like a teddy bear, one of those threadbare ones that needs looking after. She's well-worn and experienced and he's delighted that she knows all about sport. She told him that her husband Eric had been ill for many years and sport on TV had been her only distraction. They chat easily comparing footballers, clubs, transfer fees and then he discovers she also knows about rugby and cricket. Secretly, he can't wait for Ashley to meet her and he's already thinking that one day, it might be nice for him to take them all somewhere special for tea.

Opposite him, Albert sits with Peanut tucked under his chair and when no one is looking he slides small pieces of turkey onto the floor, after all, it is Christmas for dogs too. Frances, the vicar, said we have to be kind all year and not just at Christmas and she's right. He looks at Auntie laughing with Lawrence and he can't think of kinder people he wants to be with. Delroy seems to be a distant figure now. In the past few months Albert has grown up. He's decided he's not going to pursue that avenue any more. He's going to be more like Ricky. He'll study hard and go to uni. He doesn't want to design computer games. That sort of thing would be alright if you wanted to sit in your bedroom all day but Albert doesn't want to do that anymore. He's changed. He likes going outside, talking to people and he loves animals, so he's decided he wants to become a Veterinary Nurse. He can't wait to tell Femi and Lawrence about the decision he's made but it won't be today as they are clearly in love and too busy being lovey dovey. Albert is happy to wait. He slides a small piece of ham onto the floor and is rewarded by a small lick on his ankle. He's got Peanut and they'll be plenty of time to talk to Auntie, because she always makes time for them all and looks after them in her own special way.

Ahmed is happy. In fact, he's never been this happy and, with Faisal by his side and his family and friends all around him, it's like he's never lived anywhere else. Somehow, these incredible people have managed to eradicate most of the hurt, sadness and heartache of the past. It hasn't completely gone and Ahmed is realistic enough to know that there will be triggers. But now, they aren't as overwhelming and they are manageable. He can't believe his match-making has worked. Ever since he met Lawrence in the garden and spoke to him, he realised he was a good man. He'd met so few good men, but when he met Lawrence, he knew everything would be alright. Lawrence seemed to understand that he was different, and when he told him about his brother, Martin, it all made sense. Lawrence isn't like his father, or his brother Mohamed or like his uncle who'd paid for him to leave Syria.

Now, Ahmed can be himself. He loves Lawrence and Femi more than he could ever tell them. He will never forget that she converted the garage for him and helped him develop his love of photography and when she suggested yesterday that he might like to study Art and Photography at University, he was overwhelmed. Auntie was far more than a foster mother. She worked miracles.

Ahmed is looking down at his plate. There's just one thing missing this Christmas, something he doesn't have and he has to pluck up the courage to get it. If he wants to get what he wants in life then he must take the risk. He waits until they've finished the main course and they turn the lights off and Amber carries in a burning Christmas pudding.

They all cheer and whoop as the blue flames flicker and die then there's a spontaneous round of applause. That's when Ahmed pulls out his camera.

'Auntie,' he asks politely. 'Can we please have a family photograph?'

This is the last photograph he needs to complete his collection. The one thing he was missing.

She smiles happily. 'Of course, Ahmed. Smile everyone.'

If only life was this simple everyday, Femi thinks. But life is full of risks; the things we do or don't do. The decisions we make or don't make. The most important thing is that we are brave and we never stop trying to achieve our dreams — because without dreams there is no hope.

THE END.

<h1 style="text-align:center">33</h1>

Someone Else's Dream - Chapter One

Our flat is above the café. When we saw it for the first time we fell in love with its bay window overlooking Harbour Street and the flat upstairs with its two double bedrooms; one with a patio door leading to a small deck at the back. The view from the rooftop to the sea on the horizon was a dream and I'd thought it all had potential. Cassie had said it was quaint.

Now I realise it is pokey, riddled with damp and there's far more work to do than either of us had anticipated.

'I can't find anyone to work in the kitchen.' Cassie is frying ribeye steaks. 'It's impossible to get staff.'

I am standing in the doorway watching her. The galley kitchen is the only area of our flat that isn't littered with packages. My gaze wanders over the lounge still filled with boxes, untouched from our move three months ago. We haven't had time to unpack or decorate and on days like today I wonder if we've even made the right move. Everything seems so chaotic, disorganised and there's so much work to do. It's overwhelming.

I wander into our bedroom and it's overflowing with

Cassie's clothes, hanging out of boxes and a chest of drawers and a wardrobe that refuses to close. The second bedroom is stacked with books, DVDs and music in labelled cardboard boxes. You can't even open the door to the deck at the back.

Scruff-bucket is curled up asleep and purring inside a box on top of my sweater. I stroke her neck and she stretches appreciatively. 'You could win the longest cat competition,' I whisper, then I wander back through to the kitchen.

The flat is less than half the size of my last apartment in London which was new and modern and immaculately painted and decorated. I miss the space and I have a sudden pang for the familiarity of my old city life; for order and cleanliness.

The sizzling ribeyes make my stomach rumble. They cover the persistent smell of damp from the musky walls and I crack open the sash window.

'Cheers, Amber!' Cassie hands me a wine glass without taking her other hand from the frying pan handle.

We clink our glasses together and our lips meet in a brief kiss.

'I thought your friend Marion knew someone who wanted a job?' I say.

'She's taken a job in one of the big supermarkets on the far side of town – more money, she said.' Cassie's Scottish accent is soft and warm.

She forks the meat onto the plate and takes chips from the oven.

I stand beside the bistro table in the window and look down into Harbour Street. The shopfronts are prettily decorated and have colourful awnings in blues, greens and pinks. The window displays are filled with seaside themed gifts; striped cushions, lighthouses, oyster shells and wooden signs saying;

Gone Fishing and At the Beach. A multitude of colourful lamps, wooden lanterns, carvings and seascape paintings adorn the art gallery, and in the boutique, trendy, expensive, casual beach wear, sandals and flip-flops are on display. Wedged between the shops directly opposite our café is a boarded-up travel agents that looks weathered and neglected.

A couple, walking hand in hand, huddle together against the cold wind and disappear into the Indian takeaway next door.

I refill our glasses and look appreciatively at our supper. It's been a long week.

'You look exhausted, Amber. You worry too much,' Cassie adds, sitting opposite me.

'This place is such a mess. I don't know where to begin sorting it out. There's never enough—'

'Oh, Amber, stop worrying! Look, I don't have time to keep house for you and open my business. There aren't enough hours in the day. Close your eyes and you won't notice it.' She grins. 'What does it matter if everything isn't organised and in the right place? Don't you think this is much more fun than everything being so perfectly tidy and organised?'

'You told me you liked tidy.' I cut the steak and relish its juices on my tongue. 'You said you didn't mind me being a neat-freak.'

'But this is more thrilling, isn't it?' She uses her fingers to eat a chip. 'It's like camping.'

'It's been over three months, Cassie. I would actually like to unpack and find a space for our clothes—'

'It's not the end of the world is it? You're not going to make a fuss, are you?'

'No, but—'

Cassie silences me by pushing a chip between my lips, and I

smile.

'Lighten up, Amber. You've become very serious and it doesn't suit you. Don't you remember the fun we used to have when we met? You'd meet me after a show and we'd go for dinner to that little Italian in Covent Garden?'

'Of course I do.'

Cassie had been a singer and dancer in the West End. She had never taken the lead part but she had been in the chorus of most of the musicals in London in the past four years; *Grease, Les Mis, Billy Elliot.*

'That was in the days when you loved me...'

'I still do.' I smile.

'You don't show it.'

'I'm sorry. It's all the work and commuting every day to London. I seem to spend more time on the train than anywhere else.'

'Give it all up. Come and work with me in the café, Amber,' she says excitedly. 'We'd be a real team.'

'I can't.' I pause with wine glass halfway to my lips. 'You know it would be my worst nightmare. I would hate to work in a café. It's the last thing in the world that I would want to do.'

I see her smile fade. I don't want to spoil our evening completely, so I don't add that unless she opens the café very soon and it starts earning some money, I won't be able to finance this venture for much longer.

* * *

It's taking shape. We've spent the weekend painting the café walls white, hanging bulbous orange lights from the ceiling and a chalk board above the counter.

'The cash machine has arrived.' Cassie puts a cardboard box on the counter and pushes curls of red hair from her eyes with the back of her hand. There's a frown across her face when she says, 'The guy from the printer's shop wants a logo.'

'Have you designed one?' I smother a yawn.

It's Sunday evening and I am exhausted. After working all week and decorating the café over the weekend there hasn't been much time to rest and now I have a headache that is creeping gradually down my neck.

'I thought you'd design it,' Cassie says. 'You're more creative than me and you know how to do logos and stuff. Besides I thought you would want to be involved.'

'Okay. We can look at it later if we have time. Right, what else needs to be done?'

'You mean down here or upstairs in our flat?'

I stare at her. What we saw as an adventure is fast turning into a nightmare but I'm determined to stay positive.

'Let's tackle one thing at a time. Let's make a list. Perhaps you can get some of these things done this week.'

I grab a notepad and pencil and leaning on the counter I begin to write.

'Electrician – ring for coffee maker, Plumber – dishwasher and leaking downstairs tap, phone company Wi-Fi installation...'

'Carpenter – shelves,' adds Cassie. 'Downstairs or do you want him to do upstairs in the flat so we can unpack all those boxes with your books?'

'Let's concentrate on down here then you can open the café and we can get some money in. At the moment it's all money going out.'

'I'll need money for advertising,' Cassie says. 'A couple of thousand.'

'What?'

'There's a glossy local magazine that all the wealthy people read—'

'We can't afford it,' I say firmly. 'Let's do a small ad in the local paper and try and get a free editorial. You know, the sort of thing, 'well-known actress opens local café'.'

'I'm not well-known!'

'You're an actress, Cassie. Tell them you appeared in *Les Mis* and *Grease* and *Matilda.* They'll love it. They will be queuing for your autograph.'

'I don't want fans – I want people who will buy coffee.'

'Cassie, we are in the middle of Harbour Street. This is the place you wanted – the one you chose – the one you said you dreamed of. We have footfall passing by everyday: locals, tourists and day trippers from London all heading to look at the pretty harbour. We won't need to advertise in expensive magazines if we provide good food and great coffee, we can build up a reputation, which is what we need.'

'But—'

'The best form of advertising is word of mouth,' I insist.

'Marion says that all the shops advertise. She puts an advert in every month for her boutique.'

'She can afford it but this is a café and we are on a budget. Now, what about someone to help in the kitchen? Have you thought any more about the menu?'

'Marion says we should do all-day breakfasts.'

'But what do you think?' I am smothering a yawn and tapping the pencil.

'Marion says—'

'Well it isn't Marion who is running the café – it's you!' I reply tersely.

'You really aren't interested in helping me, are you?' Cassie's eyes blaze fiercely. 'You really don't care.'

'Of course I am, I do—'

'All you think about is your work. You spend all week in London in your bloody lawyer's office and when you come down here, you're too tired to help. You have no idea what I go through—' Cassie's eyes well with tears and she adds angrily, 'Thank goodness I have Marion.'

'Of course I care, sweetie. I really do. I've just been under a lot of pressure. Martin's been acting strangely at work and talking to me about his clients and... Look, I'm sorry, Cassie.' I reach out and pull her into my arms. I can't face the thought of an evening arguing. 'Come on. Let's go for a walk and talk about this outside. We've done a lot today and the café looks much better. Let's shut up shop and go look at the sea. It's silly to live so close to it and not go out and enjoy some sea air. It will do us good.'

'It's spring in a couple of weeks.' Cassie seems mollified. 'It might get warmer in the flat.'

'Exactly. Let's see if we can catch the last of the sun. It might even be a beautiful sunset.'

'Can we have dinner out?'

I suppress a sigh and dry her tears. 'Of course.' Then I lock the door behind us and take her hand, squeezing her fingers. Eventually I manage to coax a smile from her tearstained face but as we cross the road and head toward the beach, breathing in the salty sea air, I can't help but wonder what she has done all week and how I can keep affording meals out.

* * *

A week later, Cassie announces she's fed up with the café. 'It's so exhausting,' she complains.

'But you haven't even opened yet.'

'That's the point, Amber. If it's like this now, imagine the stress when it's open and I'm working all those hours every day.'

'Come for a walk and let's talk about it,' I say.

But she groans, clutches the pillow under her neck and rolls over. 'I want to sleep until mid-day,' she mumbles, so I decide to leave her and go out for some fresh air.

I walk with determined strides with my hands tucked deep into my trench coat pockets and my chin wedged inside the collar. The wind whips at my hair and I relish the wild recklessness that it inspires in me. It matches my mood as do the churning waves crashing onto the pebbles beside me. My mind is a pattern of swirling complex thoughts, and my eyes stream with wind-made tears. I wipe them away angrily with the back of my hand.

A flock of geese fly in dart-like formation skimming the water before landing beyond the breakwater. They honk and flutter settling noisily, and a barking golden Labrador is held back by its owner.

My time is too precious to sleep. It's the beginning of April and there's still so much to do. I gaze at the sea and watch the families around me and I'm suddenly lonely – feeling very alone.

Back in Harbour Street the pretty shops are coming to life, opening shutters, lowering colourful awnings, and yawning into life.

The tall blond man from the souvenir shop is hanging up crab lines and children's buckets and spades and when he smiles, I wave back.

Our café is still closed and inside the air is cool and a faint tang of curry still lingers in the air. It had been warmer to eat down here last night.

The room is long and the orange lights hanging down from the ceiling are already festooned with cobwebs and the floor is littered with boxes; new tables and chairs.

I throw my coat onto a peg and begin cleaning, taking a broom to the cobwebs, wiping counters and sweeping the mess. Then I unpack boxes of china, cutlery, serving dishes and pans. I wipe down the coffee machine and organise cups, mugs, glasses and saucers. I throw empty boxes to one side and unpack the cash register that has lain for two weeks in its box.

Behind the wall of the café is a narrow toilet, the exit to a patio garden, and a small kitchen where the microwave is splashed with remnants of tinned tomato and crumbs spill from the toaster onto the tiled floor.

It is after one o'clock when Cassie appears, her eyes red with sleep and her hair tousled.

'I told you I would unpack everything this week.'

'We could open this week,' I say with cheerful optimism.

'I can't manage the café on my own, Amber. Toast?' Cassie heads toward the kitchen and pushes bread into the toaster. Crumbs scatter to the floor but she doesn't seem to notice. She flicks the kettle to boil.

'Coffee?'

'Why can't we open this week?' I insist.

'Don't pressure me, Amber. Why do you have to do that? Every time you come down here, you complain that I'm not doing anything.'

'I haven't complained.'

'You have by implication, look at you, you always want to make me feel bad.'

'I want to help.'

'It's my café. I'll do things when I am ready. I was going to lay out the cups there and stack the plates over there.' She points using her mug. 'But you come in and take over.'

'Cassie, there were cobwebs hanging from the lights. The place was a mess—'

'Here you go again…'

'I thought you wanted my help.'

'Not like this.'

'Then what do you want me to do? I can't just sit around at the weekend. Each day the café is closed we aren't earning any money and there are bills to pay.'

'Oh, here we go, it's all back to money.' She tosses her hair over her shoulder.

'It's not all about money. It's about business.'

'So you keep telling me.'

'No, you told me. How many times did I hear that you were fed up with auditioning and that you wanted a café near the sea? How many weekends did we go scouring the country for the ideal spot? How long did you spend each night persuading me to leave London? You told me this would make you happy. This is what would fulfil you.' I face her and add softly, 'You wanted this and I agreed to finance it. But I can't live like this. It's been nearly four months, Cassie, and the café is *still* not open. It's been painted and decorated, you've ordered all the stock, everything is here.' I cast my arms wide. 'What more do you need?'

'I can't run this place on my own.'

'You've been interviewing for weeks.'

'Everyone has let me down. Even Liz went to the supermarket—'

'There must be lots of people—'

'Well, Marion did mention someone she knew was looking for work – maybe I'll pop around and see her—'

'Can't you just phone her? Then you can help me put things where you want them.'

'I can do that next week when you are at work. It will give me something to do.'

'You could open this week, maybe on Wednesday. What else do you need? Come on, let's make a list together, Cassie.'

'Stop pushing me, Amber,' she shouts. 'Why can't you just let me do things at my own pace?'

'I just want to help.'

'Then do it all yourself. I'm going to see Marion. I can't put up with this all day.' Cassie heads for the stairs at the back of the café that lead up to our flat.

'Don't go, Cassie. Please stay and let's do this together. I only want to help you.'

'You don't, Amber. You take over and you have no regard for me at all. You don't know how hard this has all been and how much energy I've put into this. It really is stressful and when you come home, you swan around down here and make out I've done nothing all week. I need some air. I'm going out.'

'Cassie—' I plead.

But she is gone.

Janet Pywell's Books

The Westbay Romance Series:
Someone Else's Dream
Someone Else's Child
Someone Else's Truth

Ronda George Thrillers:
The Concealers
The Influencers
The Manipulators
The Ronda George Thriller Boxset - books 1-3

Mikky dos Santos Thrillers:
Golden Icon – *The Prequel*
Masterpiece
Book of Hours
Stolen Script
Faking Game
Truthful Lies
Broken Windows

Boxsets:
Volume 1 – Masterpiece, Book of Hours & Stolen Script
Volume 2 – Faking Game, Truthful Lies & Broken Windows

About the Author

Janet Pywell writes gripping international mystery and crime thriller novels that will keep you quickly turning the pages.

After the Covid pandemic Janet published the first book in the **Westbay Romance Series** — *Someone Else's Dream* — a feel-good novel about courage, integrity and friendship. The other novels in the series will also leave you tingling with emotion.

Janet has a background in travel and tourism and she writes using her knowledge of foreign places gained from living abroad and travelling extensively. She currently lives on the Kent coast.

In April 2022, Janet Pywell published her first non-fiction book: **Ten Simple Steps for Writing Your Book**.

You can connect with me on:
- https://janetpywellauthor.wordpress.com
- https://twitter.com/JanPywellAuthorTwitter:
- https://www.facebook.com/janet.pywell
- https://www.instagram.com/janetpywellauthor

Subscribe to my newsletter:

✉ https://www.subscribepage.com/janetpywell